MW01029010

"*Lucifer is everywhere! From* Du of Warcraft, *he plays you like a [through The Rolling Stones and to his words or shut our ears? Is he misunderstood and deserving of our sympathy or does he just want to watch the world burn? The Devil is in the details and thankfully we have Plato, Kant, and Robert Arp to help us work them out.*"

—WAYNE YUEN, editor of *The Walking Dead and Philosophy: Zombie Apocalypse Now*

"*Have you ever wondered why Satan is an asshole? Why metal about the Devil is awesome? How to get demonically re-possessed? The devilish details of the Joker, Loki, Luke Skywalker, Keanu Reeves, and others? Get the answers to these burning questions and more. Six out of nine demons give* The Devil and Philosophy *two enthusiastic horns up.*"

—BENJAMIN MCCRAW, University of South Carolina Upstate

"The Devil and Philosophy *is a Hell of a book for those curious about the nature of the Dark One. You don't even have to sell a little bit of your soul to indulge yourself in these fascinating chapters, covering everything from Satan's epistemic privileges to the devils in the details of C.S. Lewis and* Star Wars."

—RONDA BOWEN, consulting exorcist in private practice

"*Buying* The Satanic Bible *was a rite of passage in the small town where I grew up,* The Devil and Philosophy *will soon join its ranks. With a mixture of music, movies, theology, literature, one or two exorcisms, and even the Joker, his royal wickedness has never been so well-examined. It will have you singing, 'Unlock the door, let the Devil in!'*"

—COURTLAND LEWIS, co-editor of *Doctor Who and Philosophy: Bigger on the Inside*

"*Just who is the Devil? How do we know him? What's his story? Can he truly be responsible for the terrible things that we so often do to each other? These are just some of the questions tackled by the infernal experts responsible for* The Devil and Philosophy. *With clarity, poise, and a welcome dose of humor these authors take on some of the most perplexing philosophical questions concerning the Prince of Darkness himself.*"

> —DAN BURKETT, Rice University

"*Whether you view the Devil as real or as a metaphor to inform our lives,* The Devil and Philosophy *helps us frame the balance of good and evil from both a personal and a universal perspective. Written in an accessible and often devilishly playful manner, these well-written chapters employ the Devil as a focus for reflecting on issues such as the soul, knowledge, suffering, and, of course, the Devil's Adversary.*"

> —JACK BOWEN, author of *If You Can Read This: The Philosophy of Bumper Stickers*

"*Whether examining facets of history, popular culture, or religion,* The Devil and Philosophy *explains the fall and rise of the Devil with an irreverence true to this enigmatic subject. Dissected over centuries, the multi-disciplinary Fiend who emerges from this book dances both provocatively and profoundly—and we can't help but watch.*"

> —NANCY KANG, University of Baltimore

"*Humans have an undeniable fascination for the Dark Side. Whether you believe that the Devil is real or not, you'll find much food for reflection in these wide-ranging, diverse, and often irreverent chapters.*"

> —GREGORY BASSHAM, author of *Original Intent and the Constitution*

The Devil and Philosophy

Popular Culture and Philosophy® Series Editor: George A. Reisch

For full details of all Popular Culture and Philosophy® books, visit www.opencourtbooks.com.

Popular Culture and Philosophy®

The Devil and Philosophy

The Nature of His Game

Edited by

ROBERT ARP

OPEN COURT
Chicago

Volume 83 in the series, *Popular Culture and Philosophy*®, edited by George A. Reisch

To order books from Open Court, call toll-free 1-800-815-2280, or visit our website at www.opencourtbooks.com.

Open Court Publishing Company is a division of Carus Publishing Company, dba Cricket Media.

Copyright © 2014 by Carus Publishing Company, dba Cricket Media.

First printing 2014

All rights reserved. No part of this publication may be reproduced, stored in a retrieval system, or transmitted, in any form or by any means, electronic, mechanical, photocopying, recording, or otherwise, without the prior written permission of the publisher, Open Court Publishing Company, 70 East Lake Street, Suite 800, Chicago, Illinois 60601.

Printed and bound in the United States of America.

ISBN: 978-0-8126-9854-1

Library of Congress Cataloging-in-Publication Data

The devil and philosophy / edited by Robert Arp.
     pages cm. — (Popular culture and philosophy ; vol. 83)
     Includes bibliographical references and index.
     ISBN 978-0-8126-9854-1 (trade paper : alk. paper) 1. Devil. 2. Demonology.
   3. Popular culture—Religious aspects. I. Arp, Robert, editor of compilation.
     BL480.D47 2014
     202'.16—dc23
                                        2014007559

Contents

Warning and Disclaimer

Many different philosophical and cosmological points of view are represented in this book. Some writers do believe in the literal existence of Satan while others (like me) do not. And those writers who do, don't all see His Satanic Majesty in exactly the same way. So please don't expect all the writers to agree on a single consistent portrait of the Prince of Darkness. Expect something more like a *pandemonium* ('all the demons') of discordant and contradictory voices—though, if you pay careful attention, you'll find that a strange and chilling consensus somehow emerges from the apparent disorder. Read, ponder, pray, and choose!

The editor, contributors, and publisher take no responsibility for any possible misuse of this book, and we recommend strongly against reading passages backwards, or translating any passage into Latin and chanting it aloud. Of course, if you do anything like that, nothing will happen, in all probability, but just in case it does, you're on your own.

Please Allow Me to Introduce Myself

As I write this, Halloween approaches and there are Devil and demon masks to be found in the aisles of Walmart, Target, and virtually every drug store. It reminds me of this one lady I knew who was a fundamentalist Christian and told me that her kids never dressed up at Halloween or went trick-or-treating because, as she put it, "It's a celebration of the Devil, and He can creep into your life without you even knowing it. We have to be sober and vigilant."

I recall her remarks vividly because of her partial quote from scripture (1 Peter 5:8), and it sharply reminded me that there are so many people in this World who actually believe there's such a thing as devils, demons, and even gods, angels, and the like immaterial beings. Her crazy belief was preventing her children from enjoying parties at school and, of course, from going trick-or-treating on Halloween night. Despite its origins in the Christian observation of All Hallows' Eve the night before All Saints Day, or possibly even in the Celtic harvest festival of Samhain, the last time I checked Halloween in the US had become a commercialized holiday as a time for scary events, costumes, parties, and a whole lot of candy—not a time to worship the Devil.

Thousands of Catholic and other Christian schools all over the US celebrate Halloween *with* parties and dressing up and *without* even a mention of the Devil. Can you imagine being a ten-year-old and while all of your friends are outside Halloween night interacting with one another, showing off costumes, and gathering all of the treats, you're stuck upstairs in your house with the lights off, being forced to ignore all of the fun? It seems to me something devilish and mean-spirited to deny your kids that kind of fun, which is kind of ironic given the beliefs of a fundamentalist Christian.

As a one-time seminarian studying to be a Catholic priest for nine years of my life, I'm very familiar with belief in the Devil. Nowadays, in light of the advances in science, many would claim that believing in the Devil is as crazy as that fundamentalist Christian mom I just spoke about. Such nonbelievers may be convinced by Sigmund Freud's ideas, arguments, and psychoanalytic diagnosis that God, the Devil, Heaven, and Hell are just figments of a child-like imagination projected onto reality for purposes of comfort and making sense out of a senseless universe (God, Heaven), or for keeping people in moral check, delivering justice, and punishing evildoers (Devil, Hell). Freud thinks we need to wake up, *grow* up, and realize that—working alongside purely material parts and processes—we're the only things in the universe with any power to design or destroy, praise or punish, and free or fetter.

Part of me is actually scared of even talking about the Devil, let alone putting together a book about the Prince of Darkness. No bull. Why? Because the irrational kid in me still thinks that there is this knowing, willing, evil being that exists and is powerful enough to possess me, or cause pain and suffering to befall me, like you find in Hollywood movies. In other words, the emotional part of me fears messing with, and possibly pissing off, the Devil, while the rational part of me realizes this isn't possible because there's likely no such being. In the very first philosophy class I ever took in the college seminary back in 1988, the topic of tarot cards, amulets, and Ouija boards came up before class started one day, and the professor for the course, Fr. Pat, told us simply, "Listen to me. That stuff is of the Devil. Don't look at it. Don't touch it. Don't do that shit." I will never forget his words, partially because it was one of the only times I've ever heard a Catholic priest swear, but mostly because a man of God, an authority concerning the supernatural, was confirming the existence of the Devil and the likelihood that I would be in big trouble if I toyed with any devilish devices.

The seminarians in my first philosophy class took it for granted that the Devil exists and in that sense weren't very good philosophers. You should never hold any belief—especially the belief in the Devil(!)—without first considering the arguments and evidence associated with it. One of the questions a book like this one forces you to ask is, "Are there any good arguments for the existence of the Devil?" We know there are plenty of stories and pictures, but is there any good evidence, solid grounds, or believable, rational justification for such a being?

One argument from the Christian perspective that I have heard numerous times goes something like this: In this world, some people go through life and do horrible things, yet die not having been punished for their evildoing, or die not having been punished *enough* for their evildoing. Consider Adolf Hitler (1889–1945), described by biographer Ian Kershaw as "the main author of a war leaving over fifty million dead and millions more grieving their lost ones." When laid out in pictures, stories, and videos, the atrocities he's responsible for between 1934 and 1945 can literally bring the most macho of men to tears. I admit that I teared up and was *very* depressed after having gone through the United States Holocaust Memorial Museum in Washington, DC, the first time back in 1993. Hitler got off easy by shooting himself in the head at the end of World War II.

Professor Emeritus at the University of Hawaii, R.J. Rummel, has estimated that Joseph Stalin's (1878–1953) policies in the Soviet Union from the late 1920s to the early 1950s led to the murder or indirect unjust killing of upwards of sixty million people, far more than the twenty million estimate that is now commonplace. Stalin got off easy, too, dying of a massive stroke (or possibly poisoning in combination with a stroke) in 1953. As one of the Lithuanian characters in Ruta Sepetys's 2011 historical novel, *Between Shades of Grey*, notes of Hitler and Stalin while she's being forced to dig for beets by Stalin's police force in 1941, "We're dealing with two devils who both want to rule Hell." So there was a time when the Devil wore *Pravda*.

While we're on the whole "mid-twentieth-century evil dictator" topic, some researchers say that the founding father of the People's Republic of China, Mao Zedong (1893–1976), was responsible for more deaths than Hitler or Stalin. In one of his speeches from 1958, Mao joyfully boasted that he sentenced 46,000 Chinese scholars who challenged his authority to death by being buried alive. Can you imagine that? Because of your nonconformist thinking in a university environment, being thrown into a hole, and having dirt thrown over you to the point where you have to breathe the dirt into your lungs and suffocate on it? Add a third devil that wants to rule Hell to the mix. Mao got off easy like the others, dying after a massive heart attack in 1976.

I could go on and on with examples of sinister SOBs who perpetrated, and essentially got away with, unbelievably evil things, but you get the picture. In the same way that Christians believe that Jesus Christ was the physical embodiment of a good, truthful, just, loving God, so too, it's easy to see how you can think that a Hitler, Stalin, or Mao is the physical embodiment of an evil, lying, unjust, hateful Devil. In fact, in the past fifty years each one of these dictators has been likened to the Devil incarnate—a living, breathing antichrist—by some writer, speaker, or researcher.

Speaking of Jesus, he's a great example of just the opposite of the evildoers who "got away with it" unpunished. Recall Job from the Bible, or the end of Socrates's life, or the famous book from Rabbi Harold Kushner, *When Bad Things Happen to Good People* (1978). Along with Job, Socrates, and Rabbi Kushner, we also notice in this world that good people get the shaft. They go through life doing good things but don't get rewarded for their goodness; in fact, they get unjustly persecuted, ridiculed, taunted, tortured, killed, and any combination thereof. Besides Job, Socrates, and Jesus Christ—and along Christian lines—a good example is Sir Thomas More (1478–1535), who was an important counselor to King Henry VIII. When King Henry wanted to separate from the Catholic Church to become Supreme Head of the Church of England, More opposed this, which many throughout history have claimed to be not only a good thing, but also downright heroic. (BTW: Henry VIII could be considered another one of those SOBs who hurt a lot of people and got off easy, albeit his victims were far fewer than those of the twentieth-century dictators.) But what did More get for his goodness, his righteous courage and heroism? He was tried for treason and then beheaded, apparently after several attempts, given that the executioner was so nervous. The poor guy couldn't even get a swift execution, and you know he suffered a lot while the executioner axed at his head and throat to get the job done. More's famous last words supposedly were, "I died the King's good servant, but God's first."

The point is this: Evil people go through life and aren't punished appropriately, and this isn't right. And good people go through life and aren't rewarded appropriately, and this isn't right either. Yet, in this world, we are aware of "just deserts," we can make things right, and we do witness people getting what they deserve. There is justice, at times, where wrongs are righted and good deeds are rewarded appropriately. Given these facts thus far, the argument for the existence of the Devil concludes that there must be beings who are powerful enough to mete out rewards and punishments, as well as a "place" where the souls/minds of people can "serve their sentences" so to speak. This life simply can't be the end of the story; we can't be left hanging without the happy ending of a just balance in the universe. God, then, must exist as the Head Honcho of Heaven where souls ultimately are rewarded and get their just deserts (especially if they didn't get those deserts on Earth), while the Devil must exist as the Head Honcho of Hell where souls ultimately are punished, getting their just deserts too.

We can respond to this argument by saying something like this: It's a fallacious move to think that from premises having to do with the reality of injustice in this world, we can therefore conclude to the existence of things like God, the Devil, Heaven, and Hell. Christians have merely invented these things to make themselves feel better about a life that is simply unfair, at times. It's all just wishful thinking and projection in a Freudian fashion to believe that these things really, truly exist, so the response goes. Wouldn't it be nice if God and the Devil existed to help make things right? Maybe so. But believing it doesn't make it so. Life's a bitch (sometimes), and then you die.

The Christian has another problem to overcome, too, if the whole God, Devil, Heaven, and Hell argument is going to work. And that's the idea that your soul/mind actually survives the death of your body. Nowadays, although most people think that a person's mental states—like consciousness, awareness, and feelings—really do exist as part of a person, they also think that mental states are wholly dependent upon a functioning brain and nervous system. So, once the brain and nervous system die and disintegrate, the soul/mind ceases to exist. In other

words, once the brain starts to go, the mind that is wholly
dependent on that brain starts to go, too. The overwhelming
amount of evidence from neuroscience and psychology pointing
to this dependency seems to be undisputed. As Roger Sperry so
eloquently put it back in 1980, "Consciousness is a functional
property of brain processing, constituted of neuronal and
physicochemical activity, and embodied in, and inseparable
from, the active brain." Assuming the Christian's argument for
the existence of God, the Devil, Heaven, and Hell works, one
still has to prove that there's actually going to be a soul/mind
that will inhabit Heaven or Hell to "serve the sentence" so to
speak. And many would say that the argument for the existence of a soul/mind without a brain just doesn't work. Souls
without bodies, disembodied minds, ghosts, spirits, and the like
are all a bunch of BS—so the argument goes—wholly fabricated by the imagining mind, which in itself may be ironic since
the mind in reality doesn't outlive the body.

There are a whole host of other philosophical issues surrounding the Devil in this book. In these pages you'll find:
metaphysical issues regarding the existence and nature of the
Devil, Hell, and evil; epistemological issues concerning knowledge and belief in the Devil and other immaterial beings; logical issues pertaining to the Father of All Lies who tricks and
deceives people into believing false claims and fallacious, irrational reasoning; ethical issues about devilish behavior, resisting the Devil, and even the possibility of a demon remaining a
demon while abiding by moral principles; issues in political
philosophy having to do with devilish democracies and the
wickedness of injustice; and, of course, an argument for why
Satanic heavy metal is better when it's produced by actual
Satanists!

By the way, the contributors in this book and I all know that
there are straightforward as well as subtle distinctions that
can be made between the Judeo-Islamic-Christian conception
of the Devil and Satan—and other demonic, evil figures—as
many have done throughout history. For example, the German
bishop and theologian, Peter Binsfeld (around 1540–1603),
divvied up demons according to the seven deadly sins: Lucifer
is the demon associated with pride; Satan with anger;
Beelzebub with gluttony; Asmodeus with lust; Leviathan with
envy; Mammon with greed; and Belphegor with sloth. And

most of us have heard of, and read, John Milton's (1608–1674) *Paradise Lost* (1667) where he equates Satan with Lucifer, who's aided by other demons such as Beelzebub, Belial, Mammon, and Moloch. In most cases, throughout this book the Devil, Satan, and Lucifer refer to the same being.

I could go on and on about all of the fascinating and stimulating chapters in this book, but won't because I need to take my kids to Target so they can pick out costumes for Halloween. We *won't be* worshipping the Devil Halloween night, but we *will be* up super late having consumed a lot of chocolate. Happy reading . . . and Halloween too!

I

The Devil Defined

1
Can You Guess My Name?

Nicolas Michaud

When dealing with the Devil, it's a good idea to know who you're dealing with. When you start thinking about all of the names we use to identify his Royal Evilness—Satan, Beelzebub, the Lord of the Flies, Lucifer, just to name of a few— it's easy to confuse them. In fact, you might even get them wrong! After all, if you simply *must* sell your soul for talent, fame, sex, or some other fun (though fleeting) amusement, you wouldn't want to make the mistake of selling it to one of his low-level minions.

And for those of you who are preparing to do battle with El Diablo himself, wouldn't it be helpful to know who is just a one-horned low-level mischievous imp, and who is the sulfur-belching tub-o'-evilness likely to suck the marrow out of your bones after beating you with them? There is, after all, quite the hellish pecking order. . . . So pick up your fiddle, put on your fire-resistant undies, and let's figure out who exactly is who downstairs. Because in naming them, we might come to know their nature—for better or worse!

Keep in mind that we're dealing with a pretty powerful idea. Sometimes we forget what power names have. We're told that summoning a demon requires knowing its name (not that that ever goes well!). But even just in our day-to-day lives, think about how powerful a name can be. If you have access to someone's name, you have access to *them*. So, as we consider these names, we have to realize that names are somehow fundamental—they determine what something *is*. Think about a time when you remembered someone's name but they didn't remember yours. Didn't that give you the upper hand in the relationship? Names are no joke, especially when they come to the Devil. In fact, I'd be willing to argue that what name we use for the Devil determines whether or not he's a good guy, or a bad guy.

Incubi, Succubi, and Familiars . . . Oh, My!

Let's start with just a basic catalogue. After all, there are numerous kinds of demons who have been catalogued in books, comics, movies, and TV shows. Some of you may remember the game *Dungeon Keeper*: In it, you play the demonic lord of a dungeon who has to kill off the heroes who try to steal your gold. I remember that one particular demon you would summon to do your bidding in the game was the "Dark Mistress"—she was a succubus and the only character in the game that would scream with delight when you threw her in the torture chamber. So, to put it simply, there are a bunch of different kinds of demons, ranging from lowly imps all the way up to arch demons.

The Catholic Bishop Alfonso de Spina (who lived around 1430–1491) put together a pretty useful little guide in 1467. He classified numerous kinds of demons; the most well-known to us are goblins, incubi, succubi, and familiars. There were also drudes, cambions, and mischievous demon-like imps. He included discussion of demons that specifically attack saints and demons that try to sucker little old ladies into attending a "Witches' Sabbath." I can't imagine what would tempt a happy old grandmother to such a demonic event, but I assume they must have promised them free punch and little hard candies.

De Spina's goblins are still pretty popular today. Generally, they are considered to be ugly as sin, mischievous, and greedy. J.R.R. Tolkien used them in *The Lord of the Rings* (they are those little freaky dudes that like to scurry around dark places). Spider-Man deals with a special kind of Green Goblin whose qualities—maniacal laughter, envy, and bloodlust—capture the nature of the demon he names himself after. I assume that it is their greed and deviousness that inspired J.K. Rowling to employ goblins as bankers in the Harry Potter stories.

Incubi are male demons and succubi are female demons who appear in dreams and seduce their victims through their sexual powers. It was said that having too much sex with a succubus wasn't a good thing and would eventually drain the victim of life. The Dark Mistress from *Dungeon Keeper* was a succubus (dressed in all black leather and carrying a whip). Today you find gamers summoning succubi in *World of Warcraft*—ironically enough—to fight evil. It was incubi and succubi, according to de Spina, who were responsible for cambions, the children of humans and demons.

Drudes and familiars were pretty common in European folklore. Drudes most often appeared as little old ladies who were obese (it was not a good time to be a granny when de Spina was writing). They were said to sneak into tiny cracks in peoples' houses while they were sleeping and sit on the victims' chests, giving them nightmares and possessing them. Familiars were fairy-like creatures that would help witches with their evil magicks. Often the witches thought the familiars were helpful or good, but more often than not they were malicious little creatures that would take the shape of a friendly animal like a cat or bird. If you remember "The Smurfs," Gargamel's cat, "Azrael" probably comes to mind when you think of a familiar.

I Laid Traps for Troubadours

There's also the question of where the different categories of demons live. Dante Alighieri (1265–1321) wrote *The Divine Comedy*. The only part of the book that anyone seems to care to remember is the "Inferno." In the *Inferno*, Dante writes that he is given a tour of Hell, which has nine levels. Each level corresponds to worse and worse sins starting with Limbo (which isn't as fun as it sounds) and ending with Treachery, the worst of sins. Between the two you find Lust, Gluttony, Greed, Anger, Heresy, Violence, and Fraud. And in each level of Hell, sinners are found being tormented in the way most appropriate. Those who indulge in lust, for example, are eternally buffeted by a horrible storm representing their inability to control their naughty urges. Today, Dante's *Inferno* most often brings to our mind a pretty awesome video game where Dante has to battle the demons of Hell to save his lost love.

The original Dante's *Inferno* gives some interesting information about its demonic inhabitants. In the Eighth Level the

Malebranche (Evil Claws) can be found—you'll love this— keeping the politicians boiling in a lake of super-heated tar. The leader of these demons is named Malacoda (meaning "Evil-Tail," which is a good deal less intimidating a name than one would hope for an archdemon). Malacoda and his evil troop are pretty darned evil and they do their damnedest to trick Dante and his guide Virgil, hoping to capture them in Hell for eternity. Thankfully, our heroes manage to escape.

And All the Sinners Saints

Now that we've gotten around to the names of one of the nastier demons, let's consider some of the others. We find that many of the names that we normally attribute to the Devil originally belonged to various high-level demons identified by medieval scholars. Some thought that these archdemons each corresponded to a particular month, others a particular kind of person or evil occupation. And of course, there is a demon for each of the seven deadly sins.

Peter Binsfeld (1545–1598), a German bishop, put together his classification of the big bad guys according to the seven deadly sins. I'm sure you'll recognize some of the names:

PRIDE: *Lucifer*

GREED: *Mammon*

LUST: *Asmodeus*

ENVY: *Leviathan*

GLUTTONY: *Beelzebub*

WRATH: *Satan*

SLOTH: *Belphegor*

So it's Beelzebub who laughs throatily when I stuff my face with too much cake! These seven princes of Hell, answering to the Devil himself, tempt humans with the sins.

You might have seen the movie *Seven*. In it a serial killer punishes violators of the seven deadly sins. The film is pretty friggin' terrifying, and when a glamor model kills herself rather than live with having her face horribly disfigured, we realize those sins are still pretty popular today. It's a good piece of advice, though, to not try to indulge in all of them; in today's busy world we simply don't have enough time. If you must indulge, pick one and excel! Just be prepared for some unpleasant consequences.

Notice that many of the names Binsfeld uses are names that we generally treat as interchangeable with "The Devil." But back in the day different names were often used to identify different entities. For example, the Hebrews did not identify the serpent in the Garden of Eden with the Devil, and they did not believe in Hell in the same way many Christians do today. Satan was, to the Hebrews, often best described as "the adversary." We assume that means God's adversary. But many Hebrews believed it was the role the angel was given, to be our adversary. Basically, you could think of Satan as the prosecutor in God's trial of your life. . . . Kind of makes you hope you can hire Perry Mason, doesn't it?

I'll Lay Your Soul to Waste

You might be wondering, though: "Weren't the demons fallen angels?" Sebastien Michaelis (1543–1618) certainly thought so. He identified three hierarchies of demons as coming directly from the hierarchies of angels. The first hierarchy was made up of demons who used to be Seraphim, Cherubim, and Thrones. According to Michaelis, Beelzebub was a fallen seraph who tempts humans with pride, second in command to Lucifer. Leviathan was also a prince of the Seraphim, tempting people with heresy. Seraphim were the highest of God's angels in the Catholic tradition, attending God's throne directly. The other two hierarchies including Powers, Dominions, Virtues, Principalities, Archangels, and Angels, which were, generally, farther from direct contact with God—though it was also possible for an Archangel to be a seraph, as in the case of Michael the Archangel (Yes, as portrayed by John Travolta!).

Not all ideas of demons come from a Catholic tradition. Really, we don't need to look any further than the nearest comic book store or movie theater to find categorizations of demons. In the *Hellraiser* series, there are the cenobites, which to this day still make my skin crawl. Originally written as extra-dimensional beings, the cenobites are sexless creatures that indulge themselves in extreme sadomasochism as a form of pleasure. By torturing themselves and others, they find physical fulfillment resulting in scars covering their bodies and disturbing piercings. Pinhead, whose piercings cover his head like a steroidal hedgehog, becomes increasingly evil through the series and eventually becomes a demon bent on enslaving all of humanity.

Not all portrayals of demons in pop mythology are quite so evil, though. There's always the gruff but funny Hellboy, whose goal is specifically to prevent Hell on Earth. Hellboy, who is basically what de Spina would describe as a cambion (a human demon crossbreed), goes so far as to file his horns down to look more human while fighting off minions of evil. There are also demons that were initially human, like Spawn, who sold his soul to a demon in order to see his wife again after his death. Because of his deal with the devil, Spawn gains extraordinary powers that he uses to fight the minions of Hell (and occasionally Heaven). Despite gaining superpowers, though, being destined for Hell doesn't seem to go well for anyone who can't play the fiddle; Spawn leads a seriously tragic life/death. The advice the movies and comics seem to give us seems to be to be good, don't sell your soul, and quit smoking. Just ask Constantine. . . .

What's Puzzling You Is the Nature of My Game

So what's in a name? After all, I did seem to promise at the beginning that I could prove that there was more to all of this than just learning a few names. It's ironic, though, that anyone reading a book about the Devil would expect me to keep my promises. . . . But I shall, though you may not like it! We are doing something here called "ontology," which isn't nearly as occultish as it sounds—it is the study of what it means "to be" and "to exist" (okay, so maybe it's a *little* occultish!).

I hinted originally at the possibility that knowing names gives us power. And that's true, at least to a degree. When we know someone else's name we can, literally, call them—summon them, in other words. For example, I once was a waiter at a restaurant . . . I always wanted to bring a pox down on the people who would snap their fingers at me and say, "Hey Nick." They knew my name because I had a nametag. I of course didn't know their names, so I would have to answer, "Yes sir, how can I help you?" That damnable customer had a power over me, and because he could use my name he could "summon" me, though I could not summon him. But names are even more important than that.

Names reveal what we believe about a person or thing. And they determine how we'll act. For example, when Christopher Columbus arrived in the Americas he used to torture natives, force them to find him gold, cut off their hands, have dogs tear them to pieces, and hang them in the town square while lighting them on fire. Columbus died a rich man by basically starting the slave trade in the Americas. If someone deserves his own little festering corner of Hell, it's Columbus. But think about it: this devilish man has cities and countries named after him. In fact, Washington DC (the District of *Columbia*) is in part named after him! So are Colombia, in South America, and the Costa Rican currency, the colon. He has his own damned holiday. And if you ask the natives, what did Columbus "discover?" Nothing! They were already there! You can't discover something someone already lives on.

So why does Columbus have his own holiday? Why do little children all around the US learn to revere rather than revile this demon? Because we *named* his invasion a "discovery." Discovery takes all of the teeth out of what he did; it's such a friendly word, and it shows whose side we have chosen. He *discovered the land and the natives*, rather than running into it and meeting them. The natives became his because he *found* them. And so we give him, and ourselves, power over the people who lived here long before us!

Just Call Me Lucifer

So what about the Devil himself? Surely naming can't have an impact on our view of incarnate evil. Well, I beg to differ! If we can find a way to make a mass-murdering, genocidal, slave-trading maniac a national hero, we can find a way to make our red-bottomed foe not such a bad guy. We've already hinted at one way of doing this. The Devil, to the Hebrews, was known as "the adversary." He didn't choose to take up the mantle of prosecutor (or persecutor); he was appointed that task as an angel. The Hebrew translation of Satan's name makes him sound far more like our opponent than the incarnate evil opponent of God. In fact, it makes him sound like the guy who's doing God's bidding by prosecuting those who deserve it.

But the naming problem gets even worse. "Lucifer," today, is synonymous with the Devil, though it has not always been. The translation of Lucifer means "bringer of light." It was a reference to the morning star that comes right before the dawn. The "Lu" in "Lucifer" shares with it words like *luminous*, *luminescent*, and *lumens*, all words meaning "light." If we look at the book of Genesis, the fall of Lucifer is the verbal equivalent of "light-bringing." And what happens as a result of Lucifer's fall? Well, we're all damned, but also, we're granted knowledge: tremendous knowledge of Good and Evil. In other words, the darkness of our minds is il*lu*minated!

The Greeks had a story a lot like this one. Prometheus, a Titan, defies the gods and gifts humanity with—go figure—fire . . . light! As a result, he's damned to a daily dose of torture by having his liver ripped out by an eagle. But the Greeks looked at Prometheus in a very different way than we look at Lucifer; for better or worse they were grateful for the knowledge they were granted, even though both they and Prometheus were punished mightily. We, on the other hand, are ashamed of our ill-gotten, demon-granted knowledge. The Greeks took that knowledge and thought it made them special, believing in the amazing ability of humans to overcome any obstacle. Today, we seem pretty afraid of illumination. We're terrified of the dangers knowledge can bring. We're wary of scientists who interfere in God's domain by cloning and genetic engineering, we're suspicious of philosophers who question our deeply-held beliefs, and more and more politicians are suggesting college isn't necessary and just leads our children astray.

So, why do names matter? Because they determine how we think of what we know. The way we think about knowledge, the way we understand that knowledge—as a blessing or as a curse—depends on a name. Was it gifted to us by a light-bringer, helping us cast out the darkness of ignorance? Or was it afflicted upon us by the Devil, a foul temptation meant to lead us astray?

2
My Long-Lost Lover the Antichrist

SHARON M. KAYE

When I was a girl I dreamed that the Antichrist came to my bed and kissed me on the lips.

Yep.

It was a long, hard, hot, and heavy kiss, so vivid that, even after I woke up, I couldn't help wondering if it was somehow real.

Bothered by the experience, I told my older sister. She remains to this day convinced that it was real and that it was meant to convey a very important message to me. I have since decided, however, that the dream was caused by the high fever I had that night.

Still, I suppose my sister was right in a way since I went on, some fifteen years later, to write my PhD thesis about the Antichrist. It felt like a fresh encounter by then. I was minding my own business in college studying philosophy when I came across a strange debate: three of the greatest minds of the fourteenth century passionately discussing some crazy question about the Antichrist.

How extraordinary! I thought. Is this really what smart people spent their time thinking about in those days? Who is this Antichrist anyway? And could he really exist? Perhaps my pubescent rendezvous subconsciously fueled my determination to get to the bottom of the issue.

The Issue

So, I learned Latin, Greek, and paleography, sat a few exams, wrote a few term papers, and then buried myself in research. I found out the Antichrist is the man charged with the task of bringing about the end of the world. First-ranking servant of the Devil, perhaps even the Devil's son, he's expected to appear on Earth and seduce the nations into the final, apocalyptic rebellion against God.

This, at any rate, is what Jesus himself is believed to have prophesied and what prompted my medieval philosophers' intense debate. They were panicking, you see, because they realized the foretold coming of the Antichrist revealed a contradiction so glaring that it could damage their religion beyond repair.

The contradiction arises through the following three assertions:

1. Jesus prophesied that the Antichrist will come.

2. Jesus can speak only the truth.

3. The Antichrist is free to choose not to come.

In other words, what happens if the Antichrist has a change of heart? If he's a man—and therefore responsible for what he does—then he has the right to choose. What if he decides to bag the Apocalypse and do something else instead? For instance, *just for instance*, what if he meets me, sweeps me off my feet, and we live happily ever after? That would leave some serious egg on Jesus's face.

And so, three great medieval minds, who could have been busy—I don't know—inventing penicillin or something, threw their considerable energy into this issue. Did they do it because they really wanted to solve the problem or because they wanted to show the world (in the only way they could, without being burned at the stake or whatever) that, in fact, the problem *can't be solved*?

You decide.

Solution One

Before we get to Peter Aureoli, fourteenth-century French philosopher, and first contender in our debate, I have to tell you right now that I'm completely convinced that the end of the world will be upon us within the next twenty to thirty years.

Come on—with all the nuclear bombs, global warming, and super germs floating around, we're already living on borrowed time.

One thing I always admired about the medievals is they never took it for granted that they would live to see another day. Ironically, the measly four-hundred million people on the planet in those days really had no basis for worrying, while we *seven billion* can't be bothered. (I have an iPod and an Xbox—what could possibly go wrong?)

Anyhow, I mention this in order to explain why I speak as though the Antichrist is already living and breathing among us. No spring chicken is gonna be in a position to seduce the nations. He'll have to be at least a little bit gray around the temples, already well into his career, yep, right around my age. . . .

So let's take a moment to consider the most crucial question of all: Does the Antichrist wear boxers or briefs? It's got to be one or the other, right?

Wrong! I'm sorry—I swear you can trust me about everything else, but that last bit was a devil's snare. The truth is that the Antichrist may very well "go commando"—with nothing on at all—under tight designer jeans.

I set you up on that one to illustrate the Fallacy of False Dilemma, a very common logical error human beings are prone to make. (Republican or Democrat? Coffee or tea? Men or women?) When someone tries to force a choice like that down your throat, your job, as philosopher, is to say, "neither!" or "both!"

Even philosophers are human, however, and there is one either/or to which they have almost always remained loyal, namely, bivalence. Bivalence is the logical "law" that every well-formed statement has to be either true or false.

Consider the following statement: "The Antichrist locked lips with Sharon Kaye at midnight on February 7, 1983." While we may not know whether it's true or false, most of us think that it has to be one or the other. Aureoli is happy to agree so far. He argues, however, that statements about the *future*, though perfectly well-formed, are neither true nor false. In other words, he boldly rejects the law of bivalence.

So, suppose that, back in 1982, I made the following prediction: "The Antichrist will lock lips with me at midnight on February 7th, 1983." This sentence was not true, according to

Aureoli, because the future is contingent—it hadn't been decided yet. Facts about the world make sentences true. If there is no fact yet, then there is no truth yet.

So, what happens if the Antichrist chooses not to come? According to Aureoli, Jesus's words, which represented God's perfect knowledge without being true or false, must not have meant what they seemed to mean.

As an infallible predictor (unlike the rest of us schmucks), Jesus gets to mean whatever ends up happening. For him, the statement "The Antichrist is going to come" can mean "The Antichrist is *NOT* going to come."

Hmmmmm . . .

On the one hand, we have to give Aureoli credit for recognizing that prophecies are supposed to be vague and mysterious. Think of an example from your favorite astrology column: "You will be lucky in love this week." This could mean absolutely anything and the true believer can easily match it up with something that actually happens. Likewise, Aureoli insists, the passages in the Bible in which Jesus is supposed to predict the coming of the Antichrist are open to a wide variety of interpretations.

On the other hand, it'd be hard to defend Aureoli from the charge that his view is self-defeating. Saying someone could mean the *exact opposite* of what they seem to mean has a way of undermining their ability to communicate anything at all.

I should know, because I'm a mom and children practice this mind-bending form of communication all the time. Consider the following exchange between my daughter and me:

> **ME:** Would you like cheesie pizzies or yum burgers for dinner?
>
> **HER:** Cheesie pizzies!
>
> **ME:** Okay! [*Two minutes later*] Here's your cheesie pizzie!
>
> **HER:** [*Pouty face*] Mom! I wanted a yum burger!
>
> **ME:** But you said you wanted cheesie pizzies.
>
> **HER:** No, I didn't! [*Look of genuine outrage*] I meant I *didn't*

want that.

Who am I to question my daughter's ability to retroactively mean whatever she pleases? But when you start playing the game that way, no one's gonna wanna play with you. I've stopped asking my daughter what she wants for dinner. Would anyone bother reading the Bible if they knew God was acting like a three year-old?

Aureoli earned the title *"Doctor Facundus"* (Eloquent Teacher) for his contribution. I don't know about you, but I'll take meaningful over eloquent any day.

Solution Two

Thomas Bradwardine, our second contender, was a fourteenth-century English philosopher with a flair for physics, astronomy, and mathematics. Helping to formulate fundamental laws of nature that Galileo later took credit for, he earned the title *"Doctor Profundus"* (Deep Teacher). His magnum opus—a treatise more than eight-hundred pages long—was an effort to save human free will within an omnipotent God's master plan. It may have been a more challenging mental exercise for him than his pioneering work in trigonometry.

Suppose, just for a moment, that the Antichrist is driving his Mercedes convertible to the airport so that he can fly his private jet to Hollywood (well, he would have to be very rich as well as very handsome in order to seduce the nations, wouldn't he?) and he rear-ends my Mazda on my way home from work. It's just a scratch . . . no problem . . . he's very apologetic and charming . . . he buys me a drink . . . we get to talking . . . things lead to things . . . and before you know it, we decide to ditch our lives and run away together. . . .

Now, if this should happen, say, next week—or, how about tomorrow?—then that's what God always knew. But— ooooops!—that's not what Jesus said. Does this mean it can't happen? The Antichrist isn't free to choose me over the Apocalypse after all? Bradwardine insists on preserving this choice. The Antichrist is still free because God has the power to bring it about that Jesus's prophecy never happened.

What?!

At first it may sound like Bradwardine is saying God can change the past. Like the editor of a movie, he can go back to the beginning and cut out a scene here or there without doing any damage to the storyline. But that can't be right. In real life, even one tiny change in the past could have untold effects into the future. For instance: if Jesus never made that prophecy, then I wouldn't have come across it as a girl, and wouldn't have had that dream about the Antichrist kissing me, and wouldn't have been so intrigued by the fourteenth-century debate I ran across later, and so I would have become a hair stylist or something instead of a philosophy professor.

No, when Bradwardine says God can bring it about that the prophecy never happened, what he means is that God can switch the movie.

What?!

You better believe it. If the Antichrist decides to become a lover rather than a fighter, then God will switch the movie to the one in which Jesus makes no prophecy and I become a hair stylist.

Do you really think God would make just one dinky movie of the history of the world? Come on! We're talking about an omnipotent being here. Naturally, he produced a myriad of movies—hey, why not an infinite number? Each one is a "possible world." Which movie becomes the actual world depends on our choices.

Points for creativity. But this infinite possible world scenario—even if we manage to get our minds around it—has a serious defect. It feels to us humans, as we move through time, that the past is real, closed, over and done with, while the future is wide open. If Bradwardine is right, then this experience of time passing is a *massive illusion*. God ultimately picks the winning movie as a timeless whole from his eternal vantage point.

Perhaps the passage of time is an illusion. Fine. I could deal with that, I really could, if it didn't render choice itself an illusion. Which movie God picks is supposed to depend on our choices, but choice itself requires the passage of time. Think about how you make a choice: first you're thirsty, then you take a drink of beer. One state is succeeded by another.

Bradwardine tried to claim that you could have a succession *in nature* without a succession *in time*. Two instants of nature for every instant of time. But he just made that up to keep from losing the game.

I don't go for *ad hoc*. Do you?

Solution Three

Fortunately, we have a third contender. John of Mirecourt, another fourteenth-century French philosopher, asserts that, if the Antichrist chooses not to come, then (against Aureoli) Jesus spoke a falsehood, and (against Bradwardine) it can't be undone; therefore, Jesus must have *lied*.

While the idea of Jesus lying may come as a shocker to some, it didn't bother Mirecourt at all. He was part of a group of progressive thinkers who followed the lead of William of Ockham. You may have heard of Ockham due to his "Razor." Ockham's Razor is an epistemic principle—a tool theorists use to come up with better theories.

What a useful thing to have! Because everything is theory, you know. From the weather forecast, to what you learn in chemistry class, to what your preacher proclaims from the pulpit, to what your psychologist advises, to the latest political analyses on TV, to what your doctor diagnoses, to what your mother taught you as a child. It's all based on various made-up stories about the world. Some are better than others. The epistemic question is: How can we identify the better ones?

Ockham's Razor says that the simpler theory is more likely to be true. Simpler, meaning fewer assumptions. Every assumption, you see, is a liability because it could possibly be false. The more assumptions you have, the more likely your theory is false. For example, it could be that the name "Antichrist" refers, not to an individual man, but rather, to a lot of different people who freely conspire to bring on the Apocalypse. But adding more people doesn't help at all. Since every single one of the conspirators is free, every single one could have a change of heart, still leaving us without anyone to fulfill the prophecy! So, it's simpler just to stick with one man.

The Razor is named after Ockham, not because he invented it (it can be found in earlier thinkers going back to Aristotle), but because he used it so often and with such devastating effect. Ockham slashed away the elaborate metaphysics his predecessors had built up to support their old-fashioned ideas. One of the things he attacked was the idea of universal moral laws. Right and wrong are a function of what God commands individuals to do, in Ockham's view. God doesn't need some higher principle in order to know what to command. He's already God. His will is sufficient, and there's no limiting it.

So, God can lie and he can command someone else to lie, and whatever he commands is right. Moreover, God's individual commands (which come to us mortals mostly through our conscience) can override anything he ever said in the Bible or to the Pope.

Wow. Pretty gutsy for a couple of monks.

While I applaud Ockham and Mirecourt for presenting the most realistic of the three solutions, I still can't lay the problem to rest. Look at it this way: if God can reveal the future to Jesus, then he can just as easily write it on a rock. Last time I checked, rocks can't lie. So, there sits the statement about what the Antichrist is going to do. And he hasn't made that choice. Give the poor guy a chance!

Once we start walking down this road, things start getting really sketchy really fast. Think about it. If God can write one thing about the future on a rock, then (being omnipotent) he can write everything. Give him a big enough rock (or, hell, a giant database, if you like) and he could nail down the whole history of the world for us before any of it ever happened. Every choice you ever think you're making: already there. Not a choice after all. This would really take the fun out of carrying on, wouldn't it?

Mirecourt's proposal not only fails as a solution, it was also condemned as heresy. Sadly, he didn't earn any special titles and he disappeared from record shortly after his condemnation.

No Solution

So, the contradiction with which we began turns out to be a real stinker:

1. Jesus prophesied that the Antichrist will come.

2. Jesus can speak only the truth.

3. The Antichrist is free to choose not to come.

Aureoli and Bradwardine tried denying the first assertion and

Mirecourt tried denying the second, creating a Bermuda triangle of bizarre and unacceptable options for the believer. It's no surprise to find, therefore, that the third assertion was next on the chopping block. By the end of the fourteenth century, the Protestant Reformation was born. Its dominant theme—explicit in the likes of Martin Luther and John Calvin—is theological determinism.

In recent years, I've made the reluctant admission that *physical* determinism is probably true. But the idea that there is a God who makes a bunch of people do a bunch of bad stuff and then gets really mad about it—that just doesn't make any sense, no matter how much metaphysics you throw at it.

So, it's time for me to get back to Antichrist-watch. I promise that, if I find him, I'll do my very best to lure him into my lovin' arms and thereby save the world.

Meanwhile, if *you* see him, be sure to thank him. At the very least, Jesus's famous prophecy about him served to permanently discredit Christianity (and, by extension, Judaism and Islam as well, since they also involve prophecy) for late medieval intellectuals and anyone who stopped to think about it ever since. It thereby ushered in a more secular age in which we can all write what we want without having to worry about being condemned as heretics.

Not that I'd mind going to Hell if you're going to be there, Loverboy . . .

3

Satan—Romantic Hero or Just Another Asshole?

JAMES MORSE MCLACHLAN

Let's think back to 1956 when Cecille B. DeMille had Moses/Charlton Heston climb the mountain and meet the burning bush. If you haven't seen *The Ten Commandments*, go watch it and come back. I'll wait.

Back? Okay. In the biblical version of the story, when Moses asks God who he is, the bush (God) answers, *"eyheh asher eyheh."* This usually gets translated as "I am that I am." Sort of like when Popeye says, "I yam what I yam" and then goes on to kick ass because he was the toughest guy around, at least after he ate spinach. God doesn't need spinach, though. He's the toughest of all time, all of the time. He's the unchanging, the ultimate power in the universe and nothing you or I or anyone can do can ever change Him even in the slightest bit. He's even more in control of things than Sinatra ever was. He does it *His* way.

But this is supposed to be a chapter about Satan, or the Devil. However, the way Christian theology has always painted things, you have to start out talking about the other guy, the anti-Satan if you will, and this is probably because God created him in the first place, as well as because the bad guy always needs to be contrasted with the good guy.

Two Romantic Satans

Satan was viewed as a really bad guy throughout most of medieval Christian history. The traditional Devil, the guy from feudal times was a rebel against his liege lord. He'd broken his covenant and was going to pay for it.

Then, somewhere in the 1700s, Satan started to look kind of coolly rebellious and "Romantic." By the times of the French and American Revolutions, the idea that Satan had rebelled against his Lord actually turned from a minus to a plus. This idea of Satan culminated in the Romantic era, an intellectual, literary, and artistic movement that originated in Europe toward the end of the eighteenth century and advocated emotion as an authentic source of aesthetic experience—a reaction to the Scientific and Industrial Revolutions.

During this Romantic period, Satan is envisioned as rebelling against the supreme tyrant, the great king God who wouldn't change for anything even if you were being starved to death by some earthly tyrant that He'd placed there to be your king. After all, God had created the Great Chain of Being and placed the King and the nobles up near the top, and a little tin snipper like you down on the bottom. You were above most of the animals and plants, to be sure, but still pretty far down there, so you shouldn't be mouthing off to your betters. If you're good and do what you're told by your betters, you'll be able to sing God's praises for eternity in the heavenly choir.

Against this tyranny, the Devil is a romantic rebel, fighting the power, a loner against the unjust order of the world. He's a rebel and he rebels against anything that blocks the way of progress to liberty, beauty, and love, like the King and God. The status of a lot of people, including literary and religious characters, changed in the revolutions. The medieval poet Dante had placed that assassin Brutus down in the sixth circle of hell where Satan munched on him for eternity. The revolutionaries turned him from an assassin and traitor into a revolutionary hero. He'd killed the tyrant Caesar! Call this version of the Devil, Satan the Rebel.

But the Devil could also be a total asshole. A real arrogant bastard who thought only of himself, had a heart like a rock, and loved no one. He talks a good line about creativity, but doesn't ever really make anything though he does destroy a whole lot of stuff. Lord Byron, in his poems, had the Devil tell Cain that humans should rebel against God, but only so they could serve Satan. So, on this second idea of Satan, God might be somewhat of a tyrant, but Satan is a wannabe tyrant asshole because he wants to be just like God, the one big power in the universe. Call this version of the Devil, Satan the Asshole.

Satan the Rebel

William Blake (1757–1827), who was really good at turning a phrase and is widely considered one of the fathers of Romanticism, said that we really need religion somehow or other and if we don't have the religion of Jesus, we'll have the religion of Satan. Blake, like the other Romantics, liked Milton but the problem with *Paradise Lost* (1667) was that the Devil comes out far better than God. Blake wrote:

> The reason Milton wrote in fetters when he wrote of Angels & God, and at liberty when of Devils & Hell, is because he was a true Poet and of the Devil's party without knowing it.

Milton himself was a rebel, a soldier in the army of Satan, in rebellion against tyrants in Heaven and Earth. On Earth he helped the folks who separated Charles I's head from his body. Blake has both takes on Satan—the rebel-hero and the asshole who just wants to replace God—but then for Blake God or "Nobodaddy" is really just an asshole Himself.

Percy Bysshe Shelley (1792–1822) read Milton's *Paradise Lost* and re-created Satan as the first romantic hero. Satan, the romantic rebel has inspired countless Heavy Metal bands and kids who like to dress in black outfits and talk about how meaningless it all is as they rebel against "the Man." This is repeated in countless vampire movies with their incredibly sexy vampires. (Of course the new sparkly vampires are much nicer but also less awesome). Dracula's given a tragic past where he's lost the woman who would have made him a very nice guy had God not stolen her away in death. The 1979 *Dracula*, for example, had the tagline: "Throughout history he has filled the hearts of men with terror, and the hearts of women with desire." How can you not be drawn to such dark, tortured, coolness? Satan rebels against the tyrant God just as humanity rebels against the tyrant kings, and he's soooooooooo misunderstood.

Later, Shelley couldn't quite bring himself to make Satan his hero, so he shifted the satanic rebellion to Greek mythology and, bingo, Satan became Prometheus and God/Jehovah became Jupiter. The point's pretty clear: God is the tyrant of the universe who runs everything. It's better to get strapped to a rock and have your guts eaten out for eternity by some vulture than just go along. At least you have guts. If we only worship God because we're afraid he's going to zap us with cancer or the Black Death, wouldn't the courageous thing be to rebel against the jerk? Even if Satan's a jerk too, at least he has the guts to rebel against God. It's *Scarface* on the cosmic level. Satan is like Tony Montana—he's an asshole but at least he doesn't kiss ass. Even if we can't win, it's still worth rebelling. God's the maker of all that is. He's the chairman of the board. He does things his way and his way is the best way no matter how screwed up it might seem to rebels. That's why even ass-kissers like Milton are secretly on Satan's side. God's such a jerk that the French writer Stendahl (1783–1842) once quipped, "God's only excuse is that he does not exist."

Satan the Asshole

Besides Milton, the Romantics (especially William Blake) also liked the seventeenth-century mystic and shoemaker, the mysterious Jacob Böhme (1575–1624). Böhme famously thought that Hell was the place where everyone blamed everyone else for his being there. People in Hell wanted to be like they imagined God to be—someone who was a completely independent being beyond time, change, and relation to anyone else. Someone who could say "I am that I am." This kind of egoistic self-admiration led people to Hell because of their complete self-love and demonic egotism. People in Hell were assholes in life, but they become *complete* assholes in Hell. Böhme's idea that God was the opposite of these folks actually got him in trouble. People like a very powerful God.

Let's go back to Mt. Sinai and Moses Heston before the burning bush. *"Eyheh asher eyheh"* can be read as, "I am that I am." That's the way it usually gets read. But it isn't always read that way. Rashi (1040–1105), a medieval rabbi, thought it should read more like, "I shall be what I shall be." It's a promise about the future. God says He's going to be with Israel during their troubles and subjugation. More like "I will be there for you" than "I am what I am." Böhme thought God was someone who makes promises and is going to keep them. But then God is someone who actually is related to the folks to whom God made the promises.

Satan wants to be Yul Brynner, the pharaoh in Demille's movie. He imagines himself God, the chairman of the board, above the world, and all must worship him. Pharaoh is mad at God because God is just bigger and badder than he is. This "demonic" attitude refuses to accept the existence of others as others and sees itself as the unique center of its world. The Devil wants it to be his world. We just live in it. But the problem is that others don't go along with the story so Hell is that darkness where each of the damned blames the others there for his despair.

The Foundation Ass-holiness

Perhaps the most famous description of Hell to come out of the twentieth century was Garcin's famous declaration near the end of Jean-Paul Sartre's play *No Exit* that "Hell is other people." Sartre, like Blake, was a great turner of phrases. Not only did he say that, "Hell is other people" but that "Man is a useless passion." All that sounds pretty depressing but Sartre's point is that we all seem to have a little of the Satan bug within us, we all "desire to be God." We desire to be complete beings, to be "what we are." We want to say with Popeye and Jehovah "I am that I am." The problem is that "others" always remind us that we're not the self-made men we think we are. Other people constantly remind me that I'm not who I imagine myself to be. I might think I'm the greatest and wittiest philosopher but people who read my stuff remind me that isn't the case. We imagine our heroes like God, Popeye, and James Bond. They are complete, never threatened, and always cool. Bluto's, Blofeld's, Goldfinger's, and Satan's frustration is that they can't complete their projects. They are blocked by others, in this case Popeye, Bond, and God.

But this is really an illusion—Popeye, Bond, and God are just projections of our own desire to live out the fantasy, to be God. We only enjoy the stories by deceiving ourselves into thinking that there is a chance that Bluto could beat up Popeye, Goldfinger might laser Bond in half, Satan's rebellion could win. We also know they don't have a chance, but this self-deception is what allows the fun.

We all want to be badasses. But notice the problem to be complete would be that you are finished, completed. To be alive, to be conscious, is not to be complete, it's to be aware of something outside yourself and to be changed. Thus hoping to be both alive and conscious and "perfect being" is "a useless passion." It's this desire we have to be God, to possess Godness that is the source of Hell. Others, simply by their otherness, constantly remind me of my lack of Godness, my lack of totality, of completeness, that I can't even complete my little projects to be a smart philosopher much less the conquest of being. This is why the really mega-assholes of the Marquis de Sade–type fantasize not only about torturing flies, dogs, cats, and people to death, but also their friends. Eventually they even fantasize about destroying the universe.

Hell Isn't Other People

One of the Romantics who said he really liked Böhme was the philosopher Friedrich Wilhelm Joseph von Schelling (1775–1854). In 1809 he decided to write a book about human freedom with the incredibly catchy title *Philosophical Investigations into the Essence of Human Freedom and Related Matters*. This also turned out to be a book about evil. He thought romanticism provided an alternative view of perfection and also of evil, Hell, and Satan. Freedom is life and life is movement so life is better than completion, it changes. If God is a life, God isn't complete.

Schelling maintained that you could think of perfection that was beyond the world of change, that was eternal, infinite, and One; pure bliss. The problem with this is that it's more like death. It couldn't possibly even know itself because we do this by looking in the mirror of other people. It couldn't love, for love requires a beloved. The perfect One knows nothing, feels nothing, loves nothing; it is without passions. In addition, religiously we should only be devoted to this perfection. Such a perfection is "dead." For there to be any knowledge, feeling, experience, or love—in short, any life—there must be otherness, something or someone who is experienced, known or loved.

God becomes a person in relation to another mirror of God— us. Schelling thought that God comes to know Himself in dialogue with beings like him who are free and acting on their own. Schelling declares: "He speaks, and they are there." The statement is obviously an allusion to Genesis 1 and John 1; and it's a stunning rereading of those oft-quoted texts. But it's not saying that God just created everything from nothing so everything could worship Him. All speech demands another person, the one who is spoken to. All language is between persons, so for God to speak there must be another. The aim of existence should not be to return to a bliss beyond otherness, to be one with everything. That would be to return to nothing.

Schelling thinks there are two wills in all of us. He calls them the will of the basis and the will to love. We can just call them self love and love of others. Both are necessary, and it would be wrong to say that either is evil. For love and unity to exist, they must exist *between* individuals so there has to be some self-love/individuality or the other person would just swallow me whole. The will of the basis is the human desire to create a space for itself, to express itself. This is necessary to be a self but it carries with it temptations toward egoism and self-isolation. If this *freedom from* others, the will for individuality, is too strong, the result is egoism. Satan loves no one, only himself, like Ayn Rand's John Galt, another famous asshole, he sees himself as a completely self-made being. These guys want to be the center of the universe. They want to be everything.

But really God and everyone else only come to know themselves through their relation to others, through love. For love to exist there must be at least two beings, there must be a self and another person. For the other to be a real other, one must have some element of real choice and real independence. Otherwise, love is merely a mechanical relation—God would be talking to Herself or just playing with Himself. Real love has to be a free response, not one commanded by omnipotent power. Real love must even run the risk that the other will reject its suit.

Never Quite Achieving Ass-holiness

According to Schelling, God created a being free enough that it could rebel against God. That humanity can say *no* as well as *yes* is the basis of love; but also the possibility of evil. Evil is a positive disease, not simply a lack. One chooses not simply to reverse the order of things but to create a new perverted order. Satan and vampires like Dracula create a false immortality and community, a pyramid scheme, in which the first in the con becomes a God to the others. They are the complete parasites and imagine themselves creative and powerful. Satan and Dracula resemble the torturers of the Marquis de Sade's *120 Days in Sodom* (1785), who end up killing each other and finally fantasize the destroying the universe. This is a pure egomania that can't endure that anything exist that is not completely controlled by them. The demonic attitude refuses to accept the existence of the other as another, and sees itself as the unique center of its world.

Whether it is God or human, demon or angel, the independent other is the source of continual pain to the wanna-be Devil. We exist in relation to one another, and the other eliminates the possibility of fulfilling the ass-holiness fantasy. Were we to pursue individuality to the extreme, we would have the perfect chaos—billions of little Gods each living in their own private universe. But this would be the end of existence. We can't be totally alone. Not even Satan can be the total asshole he wants to be.

II

Can the Devil
Make You?

4
The Devil Made Me Do It

Elizabeth Butterfield

"You set me up! You played me!" screams Kevin Lomax at the Devil in the 1997 movie *The Devil's Advocate*. Kevin is pissed because he thinks the Devil is the reason for his own poor choices. Up to that point, Kevin had been living selfishly, ignoring his wife and many a moral duty, acting like a sleazy scumbag, and when he's finally forced to confront the consequences of his choices, he denies any responsibility. He makes the same lame excuse so many people have used: "It's not my fault—the Devil made me do it."

So, why don't we take the blame for the stupid or immoral things we do? And why in the Hell (pun intended) would we blame the Devil for the so-called "evil that men do"? It's a useful defense, really—after all, if I couldn't help myself, if my behavior was determined by a force greater than my own, if I didn't freely choose this act, then I can't be held accountable for it. If the Devil made me do it, then I don't have to take any responsibility for my own choices. But can we really blame the Devil for our bad behavior?

Existentialist philosophers of the last two centuries have drawn attention to the fact that many of us go through our daily lives trying to deny that we have free will, and not taking responsibility for the difficult choices we have to make. These philosophers claim that we often try to flee from facing the consequences of our choices, and we are usually more responsible than we would like to acknowledge. One of the greatest existentialist philosophers was Jean-Paul Sartre (1905–1980), and we can use his ideas to examine *and cross-examine*—Hah! Get it? He's a lawyer in the movie—Kevin's defense in *The Devil's Advocate*, asking all the while about the extent and importance of human free will.

Freedom Is Radical, Dude

Sartre was an iconoclastic philosopher in many ways, but perhaps the most important philosophical tradition he broke with was the belief in a pre-determined human nature. Whereas most Western philosophers had believed in some sort of fixed human essence that determines who we become and how we will live—in a sense laying out the paths of our lives for us in advance—Sartre unequivocally rejects this idea. Instead, he argues that we humans are profoundly free—to an extent much greater than we recognize. Who we will become and how we will live depends upon the choices that we ourselves make. Certainly we also exist within a situation that shapes and limits our options, but within that situation, we're always also free to make something of ourselves.

When Sartre claims that we're radically free, he isn't talking about a practical or political freedom to do things in the world. Rather, he's thinking of the freedom of consciousness to interpret our lives, and to assign value and meanings to what we experience. Sartre argues that how we come to understand our experiences depends upon our own choices. No matter what situation I find myself in, as long as I'm alive and conscious, I'm free. This extreme human freedom also entails an extreme responsibility. Sartre points out that we are actually responsible for much more of our lives than we would often like to admit.

Just like many existentialist philosophers before him, Sartre gives a great deal of attention to the topic of anxiety. When I face the open-endedness of my freedom, and the fact that no one else can tell me how to live—that ultimately I must make my own decisions—this can seem overwhelming and lead to anxiety. When we feel anxiety, we humans often react by attempting to flee. Sartre names the attempt to flee my anxiety, and thus my own freedom, *bad faith*. Bad faith can be understood as any attempt to lie to myself about my responsibility. The person who chooses to live in bad faith lies to himself or herself, making excuses for the choices that were made, or denying that they were free choices at all. Ultimately, at its core, bad faith is an intentional, chosen strategy of dealing dishonestly with myself, and a rejection of my own responsibility.

Rising Star

In *The Devil's Advocate*, the story of the main character Kevin Lomax can be understood as a journey through a series of moral dilemmas. When we first meet Kevin, he's a young and cocky small-town defense lawyer in Gainesville, Florida. We learn that he has developed quite a reputation because so far he has a perfect record and has never lost a case. However, this perfect record looks to be in danger, because Kevin is facing a situation in which it looks like he is sure to lose. Kevin is defending a man named Gettys, who's accused of child molestation, and he comes to believe that Gettys is actually guilty of the crime. Here he must face the first of many moral dilemmas in the film: should he sacrifice his perfect record and resign from the case, or should he keep going? Kevin decides to push on, and ultimately wins the case and gets Gettys acquitted, though doing so required destroying the testimony of the young female victim while she was on the stand. It appears that Kevin easily brushes off Gettys's guilt, ignoring the possibility of the child's suffering, and moves on to bask in the glory of winning an unwinnable case.

As news of Kevin's success spreads, he's offered a job at a big New York law firm called Milton, Chadwick and Waters. Kevin's very religious mother urges him not to go, fearing the sinfulness of the big city. But Kevin accepts the offer, which seems like the big break he deserves, and he and his wife MaryAnn move to the Big Apple.

From the beginning, Kevin is very driven and very successful in his work at the firm. He is the young rising star, and as such he receives a lot of special attention from the head of the firm, John Milton. John introduces Kevin to the high life in the big city and a life full of parties, drinking, and sex. Kevin, while remaining faithful to his wife MaryAnn, has a strong attraction to another lawyer at the firm, Christabella Andreoli.

As Kevin gives himself over to his work and is away from home more and more, MaryAnn begins to have problems. At first it seems she's just lonely or depressed, missing Kevin when he is away, and feeling lost in a new city. But these problems soon turn darker, as MaryAnn claims to have seen the other wives turn into demons, and she dreams that someone has stolen her ovaries. Kevin's mother then comes from Florida to care for her.

Another Guilty Bastard

At this point, Milton presents Kevin with another moral choice. As his boss, Milton clearly says to Kevin, you don't have to work this hard. Why don't you step down from the case, take a break, and spend more time taking care of MaryAnn instead? Milton actively tries to talk Kevin out of it. He says, don't you love her? This is your wife, man, she's sick. What are you doing? I'm taking you off the case. But in response, Kevin actively fights to stay on his current case, and to continue along the same path. He chooses to put his work first, and his marriage second.

The case that Kevin fights to keep is the defense of a billionaire named Cullen who is accused of murdering his own wife, child, and maid. While preparing for the trial, Kevin again becomes convinced that Cullen is actually guilty. Here Kevin faces another moral dilemma. Should he continue with the case? When Kevin talks with Milton about the situation, Milton offers to support Kevin no matter what happens. Milton puts no pressure on Kevin whatsoever to continue. But as a driven young lawyer who's out to win, Kevin chooses to go on. He chooses to put a witness whom he knows is lying on the stand, and due to the false alibi she provides, he's able to get Cullen acquitted. Again, he seems ignorant of his own culpability in helping a murderer to walk free, which is easy to do when he's exhilarated by his own growing success.

Later, Kevin's approached by someone from the US Attorney's Office, asking him if he would be willing to go on record about illegal activity at Milton's firm. Kevin had begun to suspect early on that Milton's law firm was involved in some illegal enterprises, as he had walked in on a late-night shredding session that was destroying evidence of foul play. Again, he faces a moral dilemma: should he speak openly about violations of the law, even if it might compromise his own rising star of success? Kevin chooses to say nothing and walks away.

Back to Bite You in the Ass

Eventually, however, the consequences of Kevin's choices seem to fall into his view in quick succession. First, he learns from the US Attorney that his client Gettys—the one he got acquitted for child molestation—was found with a dead girl in his car trunk. Kevin then witnesses his other client, Cullen, touching his own young stepdaughter inappropriately, implying that he's sexually abusing her as well, and explaining the motive for the murders. Finally, Kevin confronts the consequences of his choices in his personal life. He returns home to find MaryAnn physically injured and out of her mind. She tells Kevin that it was Milton who harmed her in this way, but Kevin refuses to believe her and has her committed to a mental hospital, where she soon commits suicide.

Shortly before MaryAnn takes her own life, she explains that she knows why she is having so many problems. It seems that while Kevin continues to throw any concern for his own responsibility to the curb, MaryAnn has begun to realize their own guilt. She explains to Kevin that she's suffering because of the "blood money." She says, "We just kept drinking it down, both of us. We knew it. Winning those cases, and taking the money. We knew they were guilty." MaryAnn explains that because of this, she has come to see herself as a monster. But Kevin refuses to listen, and he has an excuse to dismiss what she says, since he can attribute it to her mental breakdown.

However, after MaryAnn's suicide, Kevin's mother reveals to him that John Milton is actually Kevin's father. Still with the blood from MaryAnn's suicide on his clothes, Kevin storms into Milton's office. At this point, Milton admits that he had depraved sex with MaryAnn, and that what she said about him was true. Kevin in his anger shoots Milton in the chest, but instead of injuring him, the gunshot causes only a few white feathers to fly into the air. This is when Kevin realizes that John Milton is actually the Devil himself.

Accusing the Devil

It's in the climax of this final scene, the confrontation between Kevin and the Devil, that the philosophical themes of existential freedom and bad faith emerge so profoundly.

When Kevin first arrives in Milton's office, he's come to accuse him. At first, he tries to blame Milton for MaryAnn's death. Milton responds, "Oh I hope you're kidding. You coulda saved her anytime you liked, all she wanted was love. But hey, you were too busy." Milton reminds him that he offered him a chance to step away from the case. Firmly rooted in a position of bad faith, Kevin responds by calling Milton a liar. He still wants to refuse to acknowledge that he had any role to play in MaryAnn's anguish or death. He still wants to refuse that his free choices had consequences that affected her.

Milton points out that Kevin hadn't been committed to MaryAnn for a long time, and that he had "started looking for a better deal," meaning a new lover, as soon as he arrived in New York City. Milton is referring to Kevin's attraction to Christabella. Again, Kevin says that's not true and that Milton is lying. Again, Kevin is continuing to lie to himself about his own motivations. Again, he's in bad faith and refusing to take responsibility for what were actually his own free choices.

Kevin then directly accuses Milton, saying, "You set me up! You played me!" Kevin is arguing that he didn't make his own decisions, that Milton is responsible for forcing Kevin's hand, as if Milton determined Kevin's fate, and Kevin had no free choices to make. After all, this is at the root of bad faith—if Kevin had no free will, and didn't freely choose, then he can't be held responsible for these choices.

The Devil Knows Best

It's the god-damned (pun intended) *Devil* who helps to bring Kevin to an awareness of his own freedom, and consequently, of his own guilt! Milton lists all of the decisions that Kevin made all on his own—Gettys, Cullen, putting a witness who would lie on the stand. Kevin responds to the mention of the witness by arguing, "You did that, you made her lie!" But the Devil responds by saying, "I don't do that, Kevin." Milton explains, "I'm no puppeteer, Kevin. I don't make things happen. It doesn't work like that." "Free will, it's like butterfly wings, once touched they never get off the ground. No, I only set the stage. You pull your own strings."

The Evil Existentialist?

Essentially, the Devil is explaining that we humans have no grounds for arguing that "the Devil made me do it." The Devil always faces his limit in human free will. He can't interfere with free will. All he can do is set the stage, create situations, bring humans to face temptation and moral dilemmas, and then watch to see what choices the humans themselves make. At this point, the Devil is an existentialist, arguing that humans have no excuses. Humans freely choose, even when we don't want to admit to ourselves that we are freely choosing, and what follows is our responsibility alone.

Milton reminds Kevin that with the Cullen case, when he was urging him to drop the case and care for MaryAnn instead, he told Kevin, "What did I say to you, maybe it was your time to lose." To this, Kevin responds with fury and passion as if it's coming from the very core of his being, and he screams, "Lose? I don't lose! I win, I win, I'm a lawyer, that's my job, that's what I do!" Kevin's impassioned response seems to shock even himself, and it jolts him into realizing that yes, it was the power of his drive to win that was motivating him the whole time. He finally comes to realize that *yes*, he was the one who was freely making these choices, and freely choosing to disregard the consequences.

Milton describes this as Kevin's vanity: "Vanity is definitely my favorite sin. It's so basic. Self-love, the natural opiate. You know, it's not that you didn't care for MaryAnn, Kevin, it's just that you were a little bit more involved with someone else—yourself." In response to this, Kevin finally seems to abandon his bad faith. He stops choosing to lie to himself, and instead finally admits that yes, he chose these things. He says, "Yes, you're right, I left her behind and just kept going."

Vanity can be understood as pride, excessive self-love, or a desire to be better than others. Traditionally, vanity was one of the seven cardinal or deadly sins as defined by the Catholic Church. It's a cardinal sin in the sense that it is the root cause of other sinful behaviors. And this is true in Kevin's case, as he comes to see how his vanity, his drive to win, caused him to sacrifice everything else, including morality, commitment, and love. Kevin finally recognizes his existential freedom, and that he himself was freely choosing this path all along.

Free Will—It Is a Bitch

The story doesn't end there, however. We learn that Milton, the Devil, wants something from Kevin. We learn that the Devil has fathered many children on Earth, but all of the others have let him down. But he's particularly proud of the potential he sees in Kevin. And he wants Kevin to mate with Christabella, who is also a child of the Devil and Kevin's half-sister, so that they can conceive the anti-Christ. Milton invites Kevin to join him, and to claim what is his own. If Kevin will agree to the Devil's plan and have sex with Christabella, which he has wanted to do all along anyway, he can have wealth, power, pleasure, anything he wants.

The one hitch in Milton's plan, however—and the limit that the Devil must always come up against—is human free will. As we have learned, the Devil cannot compel Kevin to do anything. Kevin must freely choose his own path. Milton explains that he can't do this on his own, because "Free will—it is a bitch."

What we have learned about Kevin throughout the movie is that what he cares about most is *winning*, coming out on top. More than family, more than moral goodness, more than love or commitment, he values winning, and the defining feature of his character is the vanity of caring about his success more than anything else. When Milton then offers Kevin a place of power in the Devil's reign on Earth, Kevin's response may at first seem surprising, but turns out to actually be completely consistent with what he have learned of his character.

Recall that Kevin's anger with Milton earlier in the scene wasn't due to the fact that Milton had had violent depraved sex with MaryAnn, but rather, his anger was rooted in the fact that he felt he had "been played." To join Milton, Kevin would always be number two, the son to the father who rules. As Milton invites Kevin to join him, he says, "It's time to step up and take what's yours." Kevin responds by saying, "You're right. It's time. Free will, right?" as he pulls out the revolver and shoots himself in his head.

On Top

In the end, Kevin is still determined to come out the winner. Rather than giving in to Milton and playing along with his plan, Kevin exercises his free will to take what is his—his own life. Kevin doesn't do this because he's worried about the moral consequences of choosing to join the Devil. No, he chooses to take his own life as the supreme exercise of free will, asserting his freedom in order to win this struggle of wills, to show that he'll still come out on top.

In response, the Devil explodes in rage, destroying everything in sight with the flames of his anger. Free will is a bitch to the Devil because it's central to our being, always remaining beyond his grasp. Thank God for that!

5
After All, It Was You and Me

JIM BERTI

I'm dozing in my chair, thinking of the house I'm about to purchase when I hear a voice coming from my left shoulder. In a raspy whisper it says, "Go on Jimmy, take the money and run. This is your money, you deserve it, take it, it's all yours, and it's okay. You deserve to be happy."

I rub the blur from my eye only to see, of all freaking people, *the Devil*! He opens a briefcase and shows me seven neatly arranged bottles and hands me a prescription, it reads, "These pills are to be taken when the path of righteousness is too difficult and you need a quick fix." And with a smile and a sip of a martini He's gone, leaving me to figure out what just happened.

Those who own homes know how exciting it is to buy a house, especially your first one. House purchasing also means the depletion of bank accounts. My closing costs alone are through the roof! (pun intended). Long story short, I'm a little strapped for cash, and I'm worried that I won't have enough money left over to pay my bills, purchase food and gas, or buy a couple of brews at happy hour. For the past three weeks, I have debated whether or not to purchase this house.

Five minutes after my strange interaction, something hits me. I feel a strange pang in my stomach, the same feeling I get right before a girl I've been seeing is about to drop the words, "It's just not working, Jim." Feeling nauseated, I go to my medicine cabinet for some Pepto-Bismol. Inside the cabinet there is another note: "Hey there, Jimbo, do you wanna feel better? I've got a little something that can ease your pain." Maybe the stress of purchasing the home has cracked me. There's no way

I'm having conversations with the Devil, and He sure as heck can't be leaving me notes in my cabinet. I'm just going to chug the Pepto and lay down for a bit.

Did I Have a Dream or Did the Dream Have Me?

I wake up with my heart pounding under my cold sweat-soaked shirt. I just had the most vivid dream. The Devil offered me a one-time opportunity to get some extra money to help in my closing procedures by robbing a bank. He provides me with a ready supply of pills and one Hell of a plan to rob a bank. Step by step, He crafts out everything from scoping the bank out, to the weapon of choice—right down to the getaway. Just as I enter the bank and step up to the counter, I wake up. The Devil's final words, "Good luck Jimbo."

Now here I am, drenched in a cold stench of sweat, hoping this is part of a weird dream or some residue effect of chemicals ingested at concerts in the past. I can't tell if I'm possessed or completely losing it. I check my e-mail to clear my head. I have a job offer to work a few hours tutoring students after school. Though the job pays good money and would substantially help my economic dilemma, I don't want to work two jobs. It's tough enough waking up in the morning, teaching an entire day, without having then to go work with kids for three more hours! I think about my dream and my encounters with the Devil. I work my ass off at my job and I feel like I have so little to show for it. Fourteen years of teaching and I'm still living in my small apartment that makes immigrant tenements in New York City look like the *Titanic*.

Maybe the Devil is onto something. Wait, what the Hell am I saying?! I was brought up in a Catholic house, went to Sunday school, memorized my Commandments, learned to do right and not do wrong. Besides some juvenile run-ins with the law, I have a clean record. I'm not a bad person, so why am I actually thinking about robbing this bank? What's happening to me? And why is the thought of walking out of the bank with a bag full of money so tempting?

Robin Hood-esque?

It appears Jim is in the mist of a moral-spiritual dilemma stuck between good and evil. Though he knows stealing is wrong, it seems as if the Devil has already dosed one of his drinks with the pill of greed. Greed, characterized as the sin of excessive wanting and desire, blinds and binds one into unhealthy wanting. The Devil has provided Jim with a quick fix to his financial situation. Instead of working for the money, the Devil's pill of greed makes stealing the money appear to be Robin Hood-esque. Jim would be stealing from the rich to give to the poor, himself! If he wants to own a house he can work a second job, meaning more work and longer days, but he would have the satisfaction of earning money, legally. But greed manipulates one into seeing only what they want to see. The Devil has done nothing more than to provide Jim with an alternative path. Never has He forced Jim to choose sin over doing the right thing, but He has preyed on Jim's growing weakness.

If You Meet Me, Have Some Courtesy

I awake to the shout of a prison guard, "Berti! Prisoner #58435." I am shackled and in a cold prison cell. The guard opens the door to my cell and walks me down a dark corridor leading into the courtroom. Twelve peers eye me up and down with stoic faces. My family and friends, even ex-girlfriends, have come to see me plead not guilty on the charges of armed robbery and assault. My only defense was that the Devil made me do it. In my closing argument, I plead for forgiveness, begging the jurors to have some sympathy for me. On the witness chair I told the story of the Devil coming to me, tempting me with the thoughts of easy money. I can only hope for a sympathetic juror, one out of twelve is all I need.

"We the jury find the defendant, James Matthew Berti . . . *guilty* on all charges of premeditated armed robbery and assault." Bowing my head in shameful disbelief, I feel an itch on my left shoulder. The Devil's back. "Where the Hell were you when I needed you at the bank?" I ask. "Oh Jimbo, where is all your well-learned politeness? It was always you and me, and now it's your soul to waste." He lights up a fat cigar and proudly struts down the center isle of the courtroom singing, "Tell me baby, what's my name?" as I am handcuffed and brought to the Albany County Correctional Facility, my new home.

That Shady Dude

Go ahead and listen to The Rolling Stones' "Sympathy for the Devil" which can be found on the album *Beggars Banquet*. Crank up the volume, dance in the comfort of your home, and relax the mind before we get our philosophy on. Whether it's your first time listening or the hundredth, you're sure to be singing "woo, woo" for the next three hours. When I listen to the song, I envision the Devil with a coy grin plastered on His face, smirking at me while He dances to the rhythmic grooves. Though He never directly introduces Himself by name in the song, listeners can infer who it is through the association of crimes and atrocities committed throughout history.

He's the Devil, and He's a shady dude. He's been at the sites of evil, but He leaves behind no fingerprints, no bloody footprints, and no bloody gloves. He's never fired a shot in war or on the streets. He's never stolen, whether it was another's identity or a pack of condoms from Wal-Mart. Like a shadow, He lurks in the background watching every move, laughing because He knows He'll never serve a day in prison or on death row. The Devil knows He has a buffet selection of participants who are ready to bloody their hands in His name.

Where There's Smoke . . .

"But, the Devil made me do it!" or "It was the Devil, He possessed me!" We've heard this excuse before, usually in the aftermath of a hellish crime. In "Sympathy for the Devil," the Devil proudly boasts of his presence at the great tragedies in history. From hearing the cries of Anastasia upon the execution of her mother and father during the Russian Revolution, to riding shotgun with the Nazi Blitzkrieg in World War II. Though the song ends around 1968 with the assassination of Robert F. Kennedy, Mick Jagger and Keith Richards could pick up today where they left off. As long as there are humans, there will be evil—and as long as there is evil, the Devil will be close by. One cannot spell *Devil* without the word *evil*.

We can liken the connection between evil and the Devil using the old adage, "where there's smoke, there's fire." Where there's evil, there's the Devil. It's not the Devil, however, who lights the fire. While He provides the lighter fluid (gasoline) and match, He stands back and watches His personal arsonists strike the match and ignite the flame. In "Sympathy for the Devil" the Devil makes no excuse—He's proud of all the evil acts committed under his guidance. But He's got a little bug up his crawl about the failure of humankind to accept responsibility for the crimes that are committed. Although the tempter, He's not the one committing the evil acts.

Thanking God (and the Devil) for Making This Happen

It's common in our society today to see open praise toward God and religion. What used to be practiced in the confines of places of worship and one's home has now taken center stage in sporting arenas, Hollywood, and in suburban neighborhoods and playgrounds. Whether it's the Tebow kneel, the point to the sky and sign of the cross, the "I would like to thank God for making this happen," or signs on places of worship asking if we have found God and thanked Him for all the good we have on this earth, religion and spirituality have found their way into many corners of modern living.

Let's assume that the Judeo-Islamic-Christian God and the Devil exist, and that they're in a constant tug of war for our attention. Both want us to be the executers for their plan for Earth. Whereas God wants us to do His will so as to bring about goodness, peace, harmony, and all that is life-giving, the Devil is on the lookout for recruits to foster his plan to destroy all that's good about humankind. When we thank God for a positive achievement, it's seen by most as a socially acceptable act. Though we may feel awkward in the presence of open worship of religion, we tend not to label someone as crazy for Tebow-type beliefs. When someone blames the Devil for an evil act, however, we scoff at them: "Get 'em a straight jacket because . . . Es muy loco!" And herein lies the conundrum. Is it possible that we give too much credit to God for the good and too much blame to the Devil for the evil humans are engaged in? By doing so, we omit ourselves as the ones responsible for those acts.

The Drug Dealer of Sin

The Ten Commandments of Christianity, the Four Noble Truths of Buddhism, the Five Pillars of Islam, and the Eight

Limbs of Yoga are examples of spiritual moral codes. They all share a belief in a higher spiritual power of good and provide an outline of how to live in harmony on this Earth. They're examples of moral codes sharing the common themes: don't harm yourself or others, don't steal, give compassion to those in need, treat the world we have inherited with respect, and treat others with respect. They are codes of righteous behavior, providing followers with a path to follow, the yellow brick road to salvation.

The path of righteousness, however, isn't an easy path to follow. To build on the metaphor of the yellow brick road, think of the trials and tribulations Dorothy and her friends encountered on the way to see Oz. If the path was easy, I'm confident there would have been more company for Dorothy besides the Tin Man, Scarecrow, and Cowardly Lion. If the commandment, "thou shall not kill" was easy, there would probably be fewer murders and random acts of violence committed. To live a moral life takes conscious effort on the part of people to choose to do right thing; and that isn't easy when the temptation of an easier path exists.

To put this concept into perspective, let's use the drug epidemic as an example. Drug use is a perceived easier path to happiness. Why do people do drugs? For many, it's to ease a distress, to avoid and alleviate pain, and to find a happiness that isn't found in sobriety. Drugs provide a false sense of security and pain relief, but they're an escape, an easy way out. Let's say my girlfriend breaks up with me (after many breakups you would think I'd be used to it, but I'm not!), and I feel like crap. There is a nagging pain in my head, and I want to get rid of it. I have choices. While I could throw down a few Xanax, or drown myself in a couple twelve packs, I could also go outside for a run or a bike ride, maybe take a yoga class or meet up with some friends for karaoke night. Finding healthy alternatives to drugs take effort. Engagement in physical activity means I have to get off the couch, put on my sneakers, and put my feet to the pavement. If I choose to do drugs, my pain is gone in seconds, and I can stay here on the couch. Drugs aren't healers so much as temporary reprievers. The pain of my breakup will return once the drug wears off, meaning I'll have to face the choice again. Drug dealers—and probably pharmaceutical companies, too—feed off the pain of society, preying on the cycle of healing symptoms rather than the cause.

The Devil is the drug dealer of sin. He enjoys seeing the world in turmoil and takes great pride when evil prevails over good. Though he has no moral codes or commandments, the Devil does carry seven bottles labeled greed, lust, gluttony, sloth, hate, wrath, envy, and pride. These are the Seven Deadly Sins, the drugs the Devil looks to provide those who have tired of the path of righteous goodness. He won't force-feed anyone sins, but with a market of willing guinea pigs he doesn't have to. Say what you will about the Devil, but you can't say he doesn't allow free will.

It's Your Soul to Waste

There's no easy way out and there is no shortcut home. Rocky Balboa knew this in *Rocky IV*. While his opponent, the Russian gargantuan Ivan Drago was shooting roids, Rocky was in the Siberian forest chopping down trees and running up mountains. In the end, good triumphed over evil. Rocky's path to victory was difficult, but anything worthwhile takes effort.

To live a good life, whether adhering to a specific moral code or your own moral compass, takes effort. The path of goodness is easy when life is going good, just as it's easy to sail a ship on calm waters. But what happens when the storms arrive and the waters get choppy? We can curse Mother Nature or we can right the ship ourselves. In the toughest times we can seek a quick and easy resolve from the difficulties facing us or we can push on through the day. For some, it may be easier to hate than to love, to steal than to work, to lust than to accept.

There will be those who choose the path of the Devil, and for those who do, remember to "have some taste because it's not the Devil's soul that will waste." While those who have done the blood work for the Devil waste away, His song continues on. Just remember His name and not to use it in vain; after all, He didn't commit the crimes, it was you and me.

6
You Did That

JENNIFER BAKER

When I was visiting my Evangelical Christian cousin, she asked, "You know, Christian couples have the highest rates of divorce?" I was surprised. "They do?" "Well yeah," she laughed, "who else is the Devil going to bother to tempt?"

Oh. Interesting. The Devil.

That's the first time I heard someone characterize the Devil as a player! Of course, I'd heard of Hell. And like all kids growing up the 1980s, I had a healthy respect for teenage Satan worshippers. It's just that I had never thought of the Devil as an agent, playing a role in our lives. Not the lives of people who didn't wear black concert T-shirts and eyeliner, anyway.

At my cousin's Sunday school I joined the kids in a song that involved something about the Devil being in a box, the Devil being taken out of a box, the Devil being punched in the face—this had me looking around to see if anyone else found this a bit weird. Nope.

According to a 2007 Harris poll, sixty-two percent of Americans believe in the Devil. So some of us are raised to think that the Devil is a person, with a face, who can be punched, and who even bothers to tempt us from our marriages. And some of us aren't raised to think this way. So my question is this: Does the Devil do us any good? I don't care if He's real or not, so setting that issue aside (which I know a Christian might not be able to), does the idea of a Devil help us to be good? Or to be responsible for our own actions?

Ethics is the branch of philosophy that considers whether actions are right or wrong, what it means to be a good person,

49

and why we should be held responsible for our own actions, among other things. *Virtue ethics* refers to ethical theories that are concerned with making you into a good person, so that you can do right and good things. In traditional virtue ethics, having to do with the ethical theories of Plato, Aristotle, the Stoics, and the Epicureans, there's no Devil. If you ruin your marriage, that's just you—you did that.

Even according to Christians, you're still the one making the decision to act in the way the Devil wants. The Devil doesn't really force you to do any bad things; he's not punching anyone in the face. He merely manipulates or tempts you into doing the wrong thing, and *knowingly*. (I can feel the guilt from here.) He does the manipulating and leaves you holding the bag. Yet we still blame Him, at times, for *tempting* us, as if "The Devil made me do it" could account for our own wicked behavior.

Perks and Downsides

It seems to me that there are at least two perks or benefits to thinking of ethics as involving the Devil. The first is that the Devil provides an ultimate explanation for the evil in this World. If we can blame the Devil for the immeasurable assortment of horrors out there, we've done something, at least. The Devil functions as a kind of placeholder for why evil exists. Another perk to thinking that ethics involves the Devil has to do with bad decision making on our part. The Devil reminds us that we're not perfect and, at times, shouldn't be trusted in our judgments. The Devil is generally represented as a tempter, and when he tempts us, it's a reminder that we're weak, we rationalize away our evil deeds, and we aren't to be trusted.

But there are downsides or disadvantages to thinking that ethics involves the Devil. The first is that, yes, the Devil is *an* explanation of evil, and I've mentioned that something might be better than nothing in this regard. But He is just *one* explanation out of a whole lot of explanations. Even if we narrow our focus to how we can personally go wrong, you see the problem. We go wrong in all sorts of ways! Some of us knowingly, some of us for reasons for self-advancement and rebellion. But we also go wrong because we do something stupid or because we lack perspective or experience. The Devil simply doesn't explain all of the bad things we do.

And the standard representation of the Devil isn't a good picture of the threats to us that really exist out there in the World. Most of the people we fear are just bullies, ready to punch us in the face to get what they want. (That's not just me, right?) The Devil is so much more non-realistic. Why doesn't He use force? Why does He *just* tempt us? And what's in this for Him?

Another major downside to thinking that ethics involves the Devil is that this Devil business makes bad behavior more fascinating than it actually is. Christians associate sin with this incredibly dramatic, scary personage, one who fought a heavenly war. Is this association necessary? Why can't we just recognize that plenty of us are plenty dumb and plenty mean? Isn't sin really the easiest thing to understand in the world? Like young children, we can be dumb and thoughtless and doing harm to others can feel good. Is there any mystery here?

Scary Satan

Yet another reason to think that ethics involving the Devil isn't a good idea is the simple fact that we can terrify other people with good intentions. It's just a part of raising children. We tell them about ghosts and (where I live) boo hags that will get you if you move in your sleep.

The Epicurean virtue ethicists thought there was something wrong with this. With our cheap little stories and stay-in-bed tricks, we get children used to reacting emotionally to something that isn't there. The habit stays in place and adults enjoy murders on *Dateline* for the same effects. What's wrong with this? The Epicureans thought this interest in scaring ourselves was a prime explanation for why we couldn't figure out that the point of our lives was to just do the right thing and, thereby, become happy.

The Devil is supposed terrify us—that's clear. Is terrifying people an effective way to develop strong and clear agency? That isn't so clear, not even if we leave the Epicureans aside. Perhaps, like the overly-stern propaganda of the past (on drugs and various things) when you find out what you've been frightened of isn't as bad as you were told, you become distrustful of every other message you received, well-intentioned or not.

So Glamorous

A final downside to this whole Satan business is that He's envisioned as being glamorous. Remember in high school (or college) when you had to read the poems and prose of William Blake (1757–1827), Lord Byron (1788–1824), and Milton's *Paradise Lost* (1667)? Remember how totally cool Satan seemed defying a tyrant God and living the free and rebellious life?

In her book, *The Power of Glamour: Longing and the Art of Visual Persuasion* (2013), Virginia Postrel makes the case for how glamorous someone like model Kate Moss has remained. What has Moss done particularly well, really? Nothing. She's hardly given any interviews. Satan never gave interviews, either, but remains elusively silent. We see visual representations of Him and get to read about Him but we never get the kind of access to Him that would render Him anything other than a "most fascinating person" candidate.

Glamor appeals to us in aspirational ways. Postrel describes candy as glamorous to a very poor child, as it represents "a gilded world, much fancier than our everyday, dull life." Everyday life can be dull—our indulgences no more than sugar and flour, an affair nothing more than a pathetic way to distract yourself. Thinking that the Devil Himself is involved is a way to jazz it all up. Certainly part of the appeal of the rebel is his glamor, the idea that, no matter how short-term, we can leave normal rules and restrictions behind.

The Virtue Ethics Alternative

Virtue ethicists like Plato, Aristotle, the Stoics, and the Epicureans saw happiness as our highest good. As a result, we were best off if we organized our aims around the happiness of our lives as a whole, rather than around shorter-term aims. Power, wealth, fame, and glamor aren't things that could reliably guarantee happiness. This was a matter of our psychology, which would not be satisfied with any level of, for example, fame. But it was also a matter of the goods themselves. Power, wealth, fame, and glamor never really become part of us, as much as we might want them to. They could so easily be taken away. Their care could so easily consume us with worry and attention.

On the other hand, a life lived for the sake of being moral was something that would psychologically satisfy (once the hard work of becoming committed to such a life is over, at least.) And a life lived for the sake of being moral would make the (inevitable) losses of any lesser goods easier to prepare for.

The consequence of committing to such a life would be the development of the virtues. The virtue ethicists' central idea is that if you have a virtuous character, then not only will you likely perform morally right actions, but also these actions likely will have good consequences. And, after all, we want to not only perform right actions that have good consequences, we also want to be *virtuous persons* performing right actions that have good consequences. You can get a demon to do the right thing yielding good consequences; however, he's still a demon.

Virtues and Vices

Virtue ethicists see virtue as a good habit where you foster a kind of balance in your psychological disposition (also read as personality or character). The idea is to promote the "not too much" or "not too little," but the "just right" in your dispositions so that your actions and reactions to situations reflect this hitting of the mean between two extremes.

The virtuous person has cultivated the kind of healthy disposition whereby they know how to act and react in the right way, at the right time, in the right manner, and for the right reasons in each and every moral situation encountered. However, the way in which you cultivate this virtuous disposition is through constantly choosing virtue-building actions. So for example, if you want to cultivate the virtue of honesty so that you can actually be an honest person, then you need to act honestly time and time again so that the virtue can "sink in" to the person's psyche. The more Johnny actually tells the truth when asked whether he has done something wrong, the more Johnny cultivates the virtue of honesty. You gotta be like George Washington every single time. The more Suzy lies when asked whether she has done something wrong, the more she cultivates the vice of dishonesty. Virtue ethicists have a general list of virtues, including honesty, courage, prudence, generosity, integrity, affability, and respect, to name just a few.

Honoring your commitments is another virtue that my Evangelical cousin and others like her should consciously practice so as to remain faithful in their marriages, or they should get out of the marriage. That's her conscious choice to cheat or not to cheat, and the Devil shouldn't be the fall guy in the event she does cheat (which hopefully she won't).

The ancient schools were all convinced that the process of developing virtue would have to be active and acutely conscious. In other words, no one's surprised to find themselves virtuous. It's not the sort of thing you could attain without being aware that to do so was your primary agenda. To be naturally brave isn't to be truly brave, according to the ancient philosophers, because bravery requires awareness of the point of your activity, as well as doing it over and over and over again. Without this conscious awareness, your actions are still not virtuous. To be truly courageous, you need to have an understanding of why and when courage is appropriate.

Luther on Lucifer

If ancient virtue ethics is right, we can't all be equally susceptible to evil, as the Christian Devil story would have us believe. The idea that we all contain equal potential to do terrible things is just plain false. Someone who tortures an animal or a child, or commits a rape, has that behavior modeled somewhere in their history—torturers usually were tortured, rapists tend to have been raped, abusers were abused. It's not the Devil making you do it, it's your messed up environment in the past that influences—though it doesn't determine—your actions.

How about the guidance we get from those who tell us to focus on the Devil? Martin Luther (1483–1546) gave some famous advice, and suggested that we outsmart the Devil. Here's what he wrote in *To Spite the Devil* (1530):

We are conquered if we try too conscientiously not to sin at all. So when the Devil says to you, "Do not drink," answer him, "I will drink, and right freely, just because you tell me not to." One must always do what Satan forbids. What other cause do you think that I have for drinking so much strong drink, talking so freely and making merry so often, except that I wish to mock and harass the Devil who is wont to mock and harass me. Would that I could contrive some great sin to spite the Devil, that he might understand that I would not even then acknowledge it and that I was conscious of no sin whatever. We, whom the Devil thus seeks to annoy, should remove the whole Decalogue from our hearts and minds.

For Luther, we have to be wily and out-strategize the Devil, throwing Him off His game.

But this type of approach to being good is misguided. It places too much emphasis on the Devil as the reason for *your* bad behavior. The Devil is an ethical crutch. "The Devil made me do it!" you say. No!!! You did that! Let's contrast that lack of ethical responsibility with what Plato would tell us to do.

What Would Plato Do?

As there is no Devil in Plato's metaphysics or moral philosophy, Plato would say: Let's focus on you, and what you're aiming for. Do you feel conflicted? Imagine you're made up of various sets of goals. Some are very short term, like getting donuts, drugs, or that bit of glee that comes from one-upping someone else. Other goals are based on how others see us. They concern our reputation above all else. These goals of yours might get you interested in perhaps even being miserable, as somehow that might prop up whatever self-conception you are clinging to. Now imagine that these two types of goals will also seem appealing, but, even when satisfied cannot make you content. A final set of goals would be those that involve a long-term per-spective on your life. These can encourage you to put off the donut or resist the pleasure of lashing out at someone.

Plato describes us in this way, using various analogies, in order to get us to resist the pull of short and mid-range goals. This approach gets us to focus on what our actual motivations are. They're often not very clear to us. Where the Devil is a master of surprising us with new temptations, ones for which we can't be prepared, traditional virtue ethics suggests that the cause of our own bad behavior is better understood if we think about why we do what we do, and whether it's right and wrong, bearing in mind our goals.

We're the Ones

Traditional virtue ethicists would even have something to say to Satan himself. It would tell Him that His plan to rebel against goodness has no chance of success. No matter how powerful He becomes, no matter how much misery He reaps, the real path to contentment is just a matter of becoming motivated to do what you can simply see is best. He's off course. He's to be pitied. He's like a small child or a rabid animal. There's no lesson in Him and there's no reason to be surprised by His villainy.

So the answer to the question I asked at the beginning of this chapter, "Does the Devil do us any good?" is *no*, not really. The Devil distracts us from the fact that we're the ones who punch people in the face. We're the ones who knowingly and willingly cause pain and suffering. We're the ones who are, at times, plenty dumb and plenty mean. We're the ones who screw up our marriages. And we're the ones who give the lame and surely false excuse: "It's not really my fault—the Devil tempted me."

III

Sussing Out Satan

7
What the Devil Do We Really Know?

JOHN V. KARAVITIS AND LUCIFER

Roman Polanksi's *The Ninth Gate* is the story of Dean Corso, an unscrupulous book dealer tasked with determining the authenticity of a rare book, *The Nine Gates of the Kingdom of Shadows*. This book, we're told, was written by someone named Aristide Torchia, in 1666, allegedly in collaboration with the Devil, just before Torchia was burned alive at the stake. *The Nine Gates* is reputed to allow one to summon the Devil.

The idea of the Devil has existed throughout history, and He has been referred to by many names—Satan, Lucifer, the Prince of Darkness. For Christians, the Devil appears in the Book of Genesis, where, as the serpent, He tempted Eve to eat fruit from the Tree of Knowledge of Good and Evil. The story of Faust is also well known in Western literature. Faust wanted total knowledge of the world, and was willing to trade his immortal soul to obtain it.

Although the Devil has played a prominent role in Western history and religion, the source of this belief isn't readily apparent. Curiously, people feel compelled to go to great lengths to create logical arguments to prove the existence of God, yet seem to accept without question that the Devil exists.

What reliable evidence do you have for your opinions and beliefs? How do you know that your opinions and beliefs are true? What do you really *know*? These are fundamental questions in epistemology, the branch of philosophy that deals with knowledge. The word epistemology comes from *episteme*, the Greek word for knowledge. As we look at the characters in *The Ninth Gate*, we'll examine their beliefs, the evidence they have for their beliefs, and determine whether they really have knowledge of the Devil.

By a Long and Circuitous Route

Dean Corso begins his journey toward knowledge of the Devil in a seminar room at the New York headquarters of Balkan Press. He has an appointment to meet with Boris Balkan, PhD, the founder and owner, who is also a wealthy collector of rare books. Corso falls asleep at the back of the seminar room while Balkan lectures on "Demons and Medieval Literature." At the end of the lecture, Balkan awakens Corso and takes him to his private library, where he reveals the purpose of their meeting. Balkan apparently has acquired one of the three extant copies of *The Nine Gates of the Kingdom of Shadows*. He wants Corso to compare his recently acquired copy with the other two remaining copies, and to either confirm his copy's authenticity, or to get his hands on one that is authentic.

Sense experience is a basic way that we come to know things, and this is probably why Corso first uses his senses of sight, touch, and hearing when examining Balkan's copy. Riffling the pages close to his ear, Corso notes that he believes that the book is indeed authentic. "Even the paper sounds kosher." But seeing is not believing, or knowing, in this case. Corso's next step is to go to the New York City Library, where he refers to the catalog of rare books that acts as the definitive reference resource for his field. He thus further confirms his opinions and expands his knowledge of the book by relying on the evidence of an established authority.

But sometimes seeing something or relying on established authority is not enough evidence to convince you—especially in the case where a certain book can not only summon the Devil, but whose creation was allegedly collaborated on by Him. In his search to confirm the authenticity of Balkan's copy, Corso begins to interview former and current owners of the book to gather more evidence. In New York, Corso meets with the widow of the previous owner of Balkan's copy, Liana Telfer. In Toledo, Spain, he meets the twin book dealers, the Ceniza brothers, who had sold Balkan's copy to Andrew Telfer. He then travels to Sintra, Portugal, to meet Victor Fargas, and then to Paris, France, to meet with Baroness Kessler. Throughout his journey, Corso encounters a mysterious green-eyed girl and strange situations that seem to parallel the engravings in Torchia's book.

By the end of Corso's journey, Andrew Telfer, Liana Telfer, Boris Balkan, Victor Fargas, and Baroness Kessler are all dead. The Ceniza brothers have vanished. Thus, everyone who has owned a copy of *The Nine Gates* is gone. Only Corso is left, and all that remains of the three copies of Torchia's book are nine engravings signed "LCF."

To Believe or Not to Believe

As budding epistemologists, we can look at the main characters and ask whether each one believes in the Devil, and why. Andrew Telfer's beliefs are unknown—since he committed suicide within the first few minutes of the movie, we can only speculate. We know that he sold his copy of *The Nine Gates* to Balkan right before he committed suicide. If Telfer truly believed in the Devil, one would think that he would have used Torchia's book to solve any problems that might drive him to such a final act. When Corso interviews Telfer's widow, Liana, about whether her husband had ever used the book in a ritual, she laughs. "I certainly can't see him chanting 'mumbo-jumbo', or trying to raise the dead." Corso replies, "The Devil, Mrs. Telfer. This book is designed to raise the Devil." Her look of incredulity speaks volumes about her belief—or lack thereof. Baroness Kessler later tells Corso that Telfer bought the book specifically for his wife. The evidence we have implies that Andrew Telfer probably didn't believe in the Devil.

We do find out that Liana Telfer is a member of The Order of the Silver Serpent, and that she presides over a black mass at her family's chateau in France once a year, on the anniversary of Torchia's death! According to Baroness Kessler, The Order is more of a "social club for bored millionaires and celebrities. . . . They are under the illusion that they owe their money and success to membership in The Order." It looks as if Liana Telfer neither truly believes in the Devil nor in the power of the book to summon Him.

The Ceniza brothers know about the discrepancies in the engravings in Torchia's book, and they claim that Torchia's "illustrious collaborator" is none other than Lucifer Himself.

Although they may seem serious at first, their casual and jovial attitude suggests more playful badinage than belief in either the Devil or the power of the book to summon Him. With such a book in their possession, they would never have parted with it.

Victor Fargas is an "unbeliever," as Baroness Kessler informs Corso. However, he must at the very least believe in the existence of evil, regardless of its source. He warns Corso: "Some books are dangerous . . . not to be opened with impunity." There is no indication that Victor Fargas truly believes in the Prince of Darkness or His literary aspirations.

Baroness Kessler is a great source of information for Corso. When Corso meets her for the first time, she tells him that she's in the middle of writing a biography of the Devil, and that she in fact saw Him when she was only fifteen years old. "I saw Him as plain as I see you now," she reveals to Corso. With regard to Torchia's book, she claims that her knowledge is "profound." This is to be expected, given that she'd also written a biography of its author, Aristide Torchia. Kessler also confides in Corso what she knows about Liana Telfer and The Order of the Silver Serpent. Prior to Liana Telfer acquiring her own book, Kessler had loaned her copy to Liana. "But not that it has ever worked," she notes. If Kessler believed in the power of the book, she surely would never have loaned it. Kessler must also be acquainted with Balkan, as Corso later finds a postcard from him in her copy of the book. It may be safe to conclude that Baroness Kessler does believe that the Devil exists, but not that the book has the power to actually summon Him.

Boris Balkan is single-minded in his pursuit of the Devil. Of all the owners of Torchia's book, we know without question that he is a true believer. He is quite knowledgeable about the occult, as shown by both the lecture that he gave prior to meeting Corso, and also by his large collection of rare books about the Devil. It is perhaps the greatest collection of such books, and one that has taken him a lifetime to amass. When he explains that he wants Corso to verify the authenticity of his copy of *The Nine Gates*, or to procure a copy that is authentic, Corso quips, "You mean the Devil won't show up?" Balkan truly believes; Corso does not. Toward the end of the story, we see Balkan inside the Chateau de Puivert, arranging in proper order those copies of the nine engravings signed "LCF," prior to pledging himself to the Devil. Balkan beseeches the Devil: "Erase me from the Book of Life; inscribe me in the black Book of Death." Unfortunately for Balkan, the Devil doesn't make an appearance. Balkan, engulfed in flames, perishes.

The characters in *The Ninth Gate* have varying degrees of belief in the Devil. Whether they have *knowledge* of the Devil is the real issue. But what is knowledge exactly? A common mistake is to equate knowledge with absolute certainty regarding a statement of fact about the world. Such can never be the case. People are fallible. Yet still we seek some kind of objective truth. We seek *knowledge* about the world.

What Do We Know about Knowledge?

In one of Plato's famous dialogues, *Theaetetus*, Socrates and Theaetetus discuss the nature of knowledge. They first consider whether knowledge can be equated with *perception*. This would seem reasonable. Our senses collect data from the real world, and our mind consolidates these sensations into perceptions that we weave into a web of facts about how the world works. However, this definition is found to be insufficient, as people may differ in their perception of the same event. Different perceptions can't be considered knowledge.

The next definition proposed is that knowledge is a *true belief*. If a belief isn't true, then it can't accurately describe the real world, or be considered knowledge. Yet even this definition is found wanting because one could accidentally know that something is true, or guess that it is, and be correct. But surely knowledge can't be the result of accident or guesswork. There has to be something more substantial before one can claim knowledge of something.

Finally, knowledge is proposed to be true belief with a reason, explanation, or argument backing it up—a *justified* true belief. However, even this definition is found to be lacking. What makes a reason, explanation, or argument good enough to allow one to claim knowledge of something? Although Plato's *Theaetetus* ends without a final resolution to the question of what knowledge is, the idea of knowledge as a justified true belief has remained with us ever since.

Who Can Claim Knowledge of the Devil?

Balkan certainly *believes* in the Devil's existence. He has spent his whole life tracking Him down, and he has built a library of rare books written about Him. In the end, Balkan dies trying to summon Him. But even given all this, the question is whether Balkan has *knowledge* of the Devil. We need to see whether Balkan can rightly claim to have a *justified true belief* about the Devil's existence.

Balkan believed in the Devil and in the power of Torchia's book to summon Him because he had woven a web of internal beliefs that reinforced each other. This system of beliefs that Balkan had created over the decades, while collecting rare books about the Devil, and researching Him, reinforced each other in a coherent whole. Balkan informs Corso at the beginning why he wants to confirm the authenticity of his copy of Torchia's book. "*According to my own research*, only one is authentic." Balkan's justification was internal to himself and rested on this internal, coherent system of beliefs that he had built throughout his lifetime researching the Devil.

After Balkan's death, Corso asks the mysterious girl who had accompanied him throughout his journey of discovery, "Is that it?" She replies, "For Balkan yes. Not for you." Given the arguments in Plato's *Theaetetus*, we see that Balkan may have *believed* in the Devil, but he can't be said to have had *knowledge* of Him. A coherent set of beliefs may make sense to someone, but you need to have evidence. So, Corso's companion is correct. We aren't done yet. Does anyone in *The Ninth Gate* have knowledge of the Devil?

The Greatest Trick the Devil Ever Pulled . . .

Whereas Balkan's justification for his belief in the Devil is based on his own internal, coherent set of beliefs, Corso seeks justification that is external to himself. Corso begins his journey motivated by nothing more than the monetary remuneration, the "hard cash" that Balkan presumed would guarantee his allegiance. "Do you believe in the supernatural?" Balkan asks Corso. "I believe in my percentage," he replies. Using his senses, Corso first physically examines the book, and then he consults a catalog of rare books. Next he interviews former and current owners of Torchia's book. Corso begins to have doubts about the authenticity of all three of the extant copies when he observes that six of the nine engravings in each copy are signed "AT" (Aristide Torchia), whereas the remaining three are signed "LCF" (Lucifer).

Toward the end, Corso finds himself at the Chateau de Puivert, where Balkan believes he will summon the Devil by using the nine engravings signed "LCF" in a ritual. As Corso descends the stairs to where Balkan is standing, he informs Balkan, "I'm the only apparition you'll see tonight." Thus, even at this point, Corso neither believes in the Devil, nor in the power of the book (or rather just the nine surviving engravings) to summon Him. Corso wanted the engravings for what they represented, not because he believed in their power to summon the Devil. "You killed for those. They're worth more than money." After Balkan's death, we see Corso and the mysterious girl coupling just outside the burning chateau. In the flickering light of the raging fire, we seem to see the mysterious girl's face morphing, at times angelic, and at times demonic. Corso's expression is definitely one of shock and awe.

A short while later, driving along the highway, Corso asks "Why didn't it work for Balkan?" Now we see that Corso finally believes. For Corso, by the end of the story, the Devil does indeed exist, and Torchia's book is the key to summoning Him.

But whether Corso can be said to have knowledge of the Devil depends on whether he had a justified true belief. The central issue here is Corso's *justification* for his belief. Corso's justification was external to him. He came to this justification through his experiences in trying to determine the authenticity of Balkan's copy of Torchia's book. In a sense, yes, he does have knowledge of the Devil. Corso relies on his senses, his perceptions, his expertise in rare books, an established catalog, his reasoning powers, and his interviews with other people, but above all, his direct experiences. If Corso can reasonably believe that these sources of information are generally reliable, and that they provide strong evidence of the Devil's presence being made manifest throughout *The Ninth Gate*, then Corso can indeed be said to have knowledge of the Devil, even though the Devil never appeared in *The Ninth Gate*.

Do You Have Knowledge of the Devil?

Disregarding the fact that *The Ninth Gate* is a work of fiction, you might wonder whether there could be any rational explanation for what Corso experienced. I ask this because there's another person who's a part of this story: *you*. As Descartes argued, your senses can be mistaken, or you could have a dream that you mistake for reality. Perhaps even a demon is deceiving you. Skepticism like this is important, as it provides a third path to understanding the claims to knowledge of Balkan and Corso. Balkan came to *believe* because of what he had read in books and researched over the years. Corso came to *believe* because of what he had experienced. However, the audience clearly remains skeptical, given that the Devil never showed up. Not one event in the movie directly provided hard evidence of the Devil's existence. Even though the viewer is led to believe that the tragic events in *The Ninth Gate* are the direct result of the Devil's influence, these events could easily be explained as the result of plain bad luck. Driven and blinded by greed, people tend to put themselves in harm's way, and they need a way to explain their bad luck without laying blame at their own feet.

Also, as a challenge to the knowledge claims of both Balkan and Corso, the viewer can point out how the scenes and faces in the engravings from Torchia's book matched Corso's experiences of events and the people he met throughout his journey. That Corso could see all of these engravings in a single sitting—indeed, as he must have reviewed them repeatedly throughout his journey, and then experienced the events that the engravings displayed—point to Corso's experiences as being part of an elaborate dream. Seeing pictures in a disjointed and repetitive fashion is one hallmark of dreaming. After Corso arrived at Balkan's lecture, he noticed the mysterious green-eyed girl sitting nearby, and then fell asleep while Balkan was lecturing on the occult. Could the entire movie have just been Corso's dream? Or is such skepticism really just the easy way out?

In terms of justifying their beliefs about the Devil's existence, Balkan's justification for believing was internal, and Corso's was external. And given the final outcome, perhaps the movie hints that Corso's justification is superior to Balkan's.

Regardless, the viewer knows better, and remains skeptical through and through, and rightly so. For it may have all been just Corso's dream.

So worry not, gentle reader. Regardless of what you might have come to believe, or think, or have read, or been told by someone, or seen in a movie, there's no such thing as the Devil. No such thing. Keep repeating that to yourself. No such thing. No such thing.

—*"LCF"*

8
What Possessed Emily Rose?

GREGORY L. BOCK AND JEFFREY L. BOCK

The Exorcism of Emily Rose (2005) is part horror movie, part courtroom drama, based on the true story of a young German girl who died in 1976. The setting of the movie is the trial of Father Moore (Tom Wilkinson), who has been charged with negligent homicide after the failed exorcism of Emily Rose (Jennifer Carpenter).

His defense attorney (Laura Linney) makes the argument that an exorcism is a legitimate form of treatment and care. The prosecutor (Campbell Scott) believes that Father Moore's belief about demon possession is "archaic and irrational superstition." Is the prosecutor right? Is it simply a bunch of nonsense drummed up by the easily fooled masses to explain away some strange and hard-to-understand ailments that should be addressed by modern medicine and psychology?

In Father Moore's trial, the prosecution insists that Emily was mentally ill but that Moore ignored Emily's medical needs by abandoning treatment and pushing a naive and reckless religious alternative. The prosecutor calls to the stand a number of experts who testify that Emily most likely suffered from epilepsy, which involves visions and intense bodily contortions.

The medical examiner testifies that it was severe malnutrition that led to her death, making her body unable to withstand the repeated damage caused by the epileptic seizures and self-inflicted injuries. The examiner's conclusion is that Emily's epilepsy had digressed to a more severe condition he calls "psychotic-epileptic disorder," which means that her seizures would have been accompanied by schizophrenic symptoms such as auditory and visual hallucinations, and sometimes extreme paranoia.

The defense attorney argues, on the other hand, that an exorcism is a legitimate alternative when all medical options fail. She explains that Father Moore and Emily's family sincerely believed her problems were supernaturally caused and that Emily even believed this herself and consented to the exorcism. In the words of Father Moore: "We [he and Emily] both felt that she was beyond medical care and that she had to see this through to the end by faith alone." The defense attorney argues that this was not negligence but was, in fact, deep care rooted in the family's belief system. To those who were with Emily, what they witnessed seemed beyond the bounds of science and medicine.

The Power of Christ Compels You!

Perhaps the strongest evidence of the supernatural is contained in the audiotape recording that Father Moore brings to the stand. On the tape, we hear Emily (or the demon inside her) resisting all of Father Moore's efforts and speaking in two simultaneous voices. During the recorded ritual, Father Moore has three assistants or witnesses: Emily's father, Emily's college friend, and a medical doctor. Emily's wrists are tied with cloth to the bedposts. When Father Moore sprinkles holy water on Emily, her pupils turn black, and she snarls in fluent German at her father (Emily's native language in the film is English): "Dolls and kisses and crosses and wishes. You think that can save your little girl?" Other strange things occur in this scene: a crucifix on the wall breaks free and swings upside down. The lights go out. Three cats enter the room and attack Father Moore. Emily then breaks free from her restraints, jumps through a second-story glass window, and runs through the storm to the barn where the others catch up with her.

In the midst of Emily's growling, screaming, and thrashing, Father Moore starts reading from the Bible. Insects, rats, snakes, and spiders start to emerge from their hiding places, and in one case a snake flies through the air and lands on Moore's shoulder. He places a small crucifix on Emily's chest, which makes a burning sound when it comes into contact with her flesh. Emily lets out a scream and starts writhing. The doctor runs to her aid, but Emily grabs him by the neck and over-powers him. It takes the strength of all three men to free the doctor. Father Moore commands the demon to tell him its name. Emily (in growling demonic voices) counts to six and in six different languages says:

"We are the ones who dwell within."

[in Hebrew] **"I am the one who dwelt within CAIN!"**

[in Latin] **"I am the one who dwelt within NERO!"**

[in Greek] **"I once dwelt within JUDAS!"**

[in German] **"I was with Legion!"**

[In Assyrian Neo-Aramaic] **"I am Belial!"**

[In English] **"and I am Lucifer, the Devil in the flesh!"** (from IMDB.com)

After this, Emily collapses to the floor. The horses in the barn break out of their stalls, and the ritual comes to an unsuccessful end.

The prosecutor argues that this evidence isn't sufficient to establish a supernatural cause and suggests that natural causes can explain Emily's behavior. For one, Emily, in her catechism, would have been exposed to all of these languages. Second, human vocal cords can be trained to vocalize different voices at the same time. In addition, many of the reported events aren't recorded on the audio tape; the jury is left to trust Father Moore's "biased" testimony (although this overlooks the testimony of other witnesses).

Facts Leave No Room for Possibility

The trial in *The Exorcism of Emily Rose* nicely illustrates the fact that demon possession cases often contain ambiguity and are open to interpretation. The same strange behavior can be explained in terms of natural or supernatural causes depending on the worldview of the one doing the interpretation.

The two main worldviews here are naturalism and supernaturalism. Naturalism is the view that the natural world is all that there is. Supernaturalism is the view that reality includes more than just physical things. For someone who accepts naturalism, attributing the cause of an event to a demon will seem naive and superstitious. For someone who accepts supernaturalism, it will seem narrow-minded to insist that every event must have a natural cause.

While having a worldview is inescapable, it is an epistemic virtue to be open to the evidence. Naturalists should consider evidence to the contrary, as should supernaturalists. However, this doesn't mean people must change their beliefs every time counterevidence appears. As Thomas Kuhn describes in *The Structure of Scientific Revolutions*, scientists don't abandon their theories at the first sign of problems. They work within paradigms and hold on to their beliefs and hypotheses even in the face of anomalies or counterevidence. This epistemic resolve is appropriate in science and in other affairs of life; however, it can be taken too far. In other words, at some point the counterevidence may become so overwhelming that the most rational thing to do is to abandon the old theory or paradigm and adopt a new one. The difficulty is in knowing when this point has been reached.

A significant amount of evidence would be required to be justified in believing someone is demon-possessed. For someone who accepts naturalism, recent videos of exorcisms on the Internet probably don't amount to sufficient evidence, for example the exorcism of entertainer John Safran or the one conducted by Pope Francis in Vatican City. Even supernaturalists, at least of the mainstream Christian kind, require a sufficient amount of evidence of the demonic because in addition to supernatural causes, they also accept medical and psychological explanations of weird behavior. Would a case like Emily's constitute sufficient evidence?

Proof of the Supernatural?

Can anyone ever be justified in believing that someone is demon-possessed? Consider the following evidence from the movie:

1. **Emily herself reports being attacked by an invisible assailant**

2. **Emily appears to have extraordinary visual and auditory perceptions**

3. **Emily demonstrates fluency in languages that she didn't seem to know before**

4. **Emily has extraordinary strength**

5. **A crucifix in Emily's house swings upside down during the exorcism ritual**

6. **Animals display erratic behavior during the exorcism**

7. **A snake goes airborne and lands on Father Moore's shoulder**

8. **A common crucifix makes a burning sound when touched to Emily's flesh**

9. **Father Moore reports seeing a ghost-like hooded figure**

10. **The above phenomena are corroborated by other witnesses to the exorcism**

The first two points might easily be attributed to natural causes since they could be classified as delusions produced by unbalanced neurochemistry. The following eight points, however, are not so easily dismissed. Mental disequilibrium cannot explain language acquisition, extraordinary strength, and levitation.

In his *Religious Studies* article from 2004, "Finite Spirits as Theoretical Entities," Phillip H. Wiebe says, "Phenomena that involve changes to the spatio-temporal order require an explanation that describes realities beyond those that are implicated when only subjective phenomena are involved." The case that Wiebe considers is an exorcism in the gospels. A man is possessed by many demons ("Legion"), who beg Jesus not to send them to the Abyss but into a herd of pigs instead. Jesus sends them into the herd, which then charges into a nearby lake, drowning them. Wiebe calls this "transfer of behavior from one being to another." In short, Wiebe argues that this case contains some elements that can't be explained by psychiatry because it isn't reasonable to think that mental illness can affect objects in the world this way.

Likewise, if we were witnessing Emily's exorcism and personally saw the events as they were depicted in the movie, proposing natural causes would be a stretch. Perhaps the hardened skeptic would propose that Emily had been lifting weights and working on her Hebrew, Latin, Greek, German, and Assyrian Neo-Aramaic pronunciation in her spare time. Someone might speculate that Emily had an accomplice helping her orchestrate special effects at her house such as attaching strings to crucifixes, timing the release of multiple feral animals, and setting up contraptions to fling reptiles. Perhaps in the case of the possessed man in the gospel story, Jesus's disciples were hiding under bushes and spooked the pigs. Of course, if Hollywood can make it look convincing, so could someone else. But is such a possibility the best explanation of the phenomena? How much skepticism can we tolerate before we cry foul?

The Skeptical Spirit of David Hume

Although David Hume (1711–1776) seems to have never directly addressed the question of demon possession, he most certainly would have considered it a superstition. We might be able to conjure a Humean argument against being justified in believing someone is demon-possessed by looking at his argument against miracles in *An Enquiry Concerning Human Understanding* (1748). There is quite a bit of debate over what exactly Hume's argument is, but for the time being, let's just assume that Michael Levine's interpretation of Hume is correct and use it to construct an argument for our purposes (Levine authored an archived *Stanford Encyclopedia of Philosophy* article on miracles).

Hume says, "A wise man . . . proportions his belief to the evidence," and this evidence comes through experience. Through experience we become acquainted with the laws of nature, and through experience we come to trust what other people tell us (testimony). However, sometimes people report extraordinary things that contradict our experience of nature. In such situations, Hume says, we should proportion our belief to the evidence and always believe our own experience over someone's testimony "unless the testimony be of such a kind, that its falsehood would be more miraculous, than the fact, which it endeavors to establish."

Hume thinks that in cases where an extraordinary testimony is widely confirmed, we should accept the fact that the event occurred and look for a naturalistic explanation. Hume's illustration of this is an Indian prince who is incredulous about the reports of water freezing. Since such a phenomenon is widely confirmed, Hume says, the prince should accept the reports and look for a natural explanation.

Hume rejects supernatural causes because the only things that qualify as causes for Hume are things that can be perceived in terms of sense impressions. Spirits can't be perceived in this way, so spirits would not qualify as possible causes. Levine explains that if Hume witnessed a so-called "miracle" himself, he would be constrained by his theory of causation to attribute to it a natural cause.

In response to Hume's argument, Levine proposes the following thought experiment: Hume is standing with Moses on the edge of the Red Sea and events transpire just as they do in the film *The Ten Commandments* (1956). Levine says that Hume couldn't consistently grant that he's just witnessed a miracle. Hume would be forced by his principles to admit only that he has witnessed something extraordinary and to start searching for a natural cause. He'd have to turn to Moses and say something like, "That was amazing! How'd you do it?" Levine considers this a weakness in Hume's argument.

In the same way, we could imagine Hume in Emily's barn during the exorcism, witnessing the extraordinary events that transpired. No matter how spectacularly the scene played out, Hume would be forced by his principles to reject out of hand the suggestion that there was anything supernatural about it, but we think this demonstrates that Hume is not genuinely open to the evidence.

The Ghost of René Descartes

Someone might say that demon possession can be ruled out because such an explanation would require a theory of mind that is untenable, namely substance dualism. Substance dualism is the view that human nature is essentially dualistic: we are minds that inhabit bodies like ghosts in machines. This argument would go as follows:

1. **If demon possession is possible, then the ghost-in-the-machine view of human nature must be true.**

2. The ghost-in-the-machine view of human nature is false.

3. Therefore, demon possession isn't possible.

On any other view of the mind, there is no room for an inhabiting ghost or demon, the mind just is the brain. For anything like demon possession to occur on a materialistic account of the mind, something like a brain transplant would have to occur. Of course, this isn't possible yet, and most materialists would probably explain demon possession in terms of unbalanced neurochemistry.

The theory that we are all 'ghosts in machines' is called substance dualism—because it claims that the mind and the body are two entirely different and separate 'substances'. Substance dualism is usually traced to René Descartes (1596–1650), who used doubt to investigate the foundation of knowledge. He determined to doubt everything until he could find one thing that couldn't be doubted, and eventually he realized that he couldn't doubt that he was doubting, which led to his key statement, "Cogito ergo sum" (Latin for 'I think therefore I am').

Descartes viewed himself as a thinking thing (mental substance) separate from his body, a ghost in the machine. He says in *The Meditations* (1641):

> On the one hand I have a clear and distinct idea of myself, in so far as I am simply a thinking, non-extended thing; and on the other hand I have a distinct idea of a body, in so far as this is simply an extended, non-thinking thing. And accordingly, it's certain that I am really distinct from my body, and can exist without it.

Substance dualism is not very popular with philosophers these days. The main objection to it is simply that if the mind and the brain are different substances, we don't know how they could interact. Dualists respond that we don't need to know *how* something works to know *that* it works. Anyway, substance dualism has a lot going for it, not the least of which is that it's the common-sense view. It also may be better at explaining the mystery of consciousness and the privacy and feel of mental events.

In the end, it may just come down to empirical evidence. An equally valid argument can be constructed on the other side:

1. **If demon possession is possible, then the ghost-in-the-machine view of human nature must be true.**

2. **Demon possession is possible.**

3. **Therefore, the ghost-in-the-machine view of human nature must be true.**

Of course, such an argument would require sufficient evidence for the second premise.

Aliens as Natural Causes

Perhaps there's an explanation for Emily's symptoms that we've overlooked, one that is both naturalistic and more plausible than the demonic: aliens. In *Men in Black* (1997), the character Edgar is inhabited by a "bug" from outer space. His wife says, "I know Edgar, and that wasn't Edgar. It's like something was wearing Edgar, like a suit, an Edgar suit."

An alien abduction of this kind might be able to explain the language acquisition and extraordinary strength in Emily's case within a naturalistic framework; however, it doesn't seem to be the best explanation. Many aspects of Emily's case were religious in nature, for example the crucifix and prayer. In addition, the "demons" seemed to be bothered by the religious rite of exorcism and constrained by the invocation of the name of Jesus Christ. Why would aliens care about such things? If Emily were abducted by aliens and aliens were influenced by Christian rituals, then this would provide support for the existence of the Christian God, which would in turn provide support for believing that demons exist.

What we're claiming is rather modest, and we have nothing to say about actual reports of demon possession since neither of us has witnessed cases that were as unambiguous as Emily's. All we're saying is that it's possible that someone could be justified in believing that someone was demon-possessed, as in the case of Emily Rose.

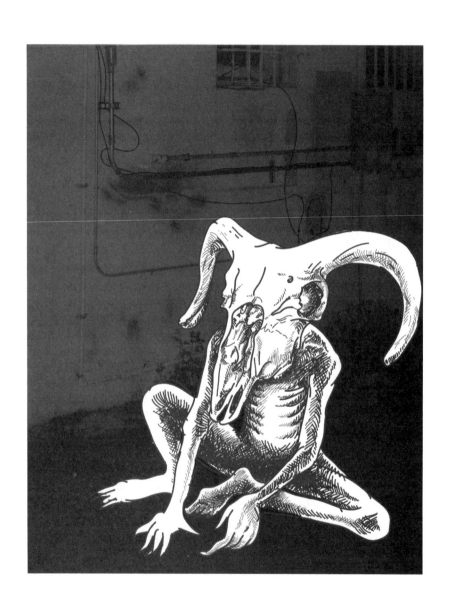

IV

In Search of
Pure Evil

9
The Joker and Diabolical Evil

DANNY SMITH

Why are audiences so fascinated with the character of The Joker, the main antagonist in Christopher Nolan's 2008 movie, *The Dark Knight*? Why are we so much more intrigued by him than by the other numerous bad guys in the film, like the mob boss, or the terrifying Two-Face?

It's because he's so much more evil than they are. His evil isn't a lust for power or money, like the mob, nor is it a thirst for vengeance, like Two-Face. His evil is something much more terrifying, much more diabolical.

Normal Evil

In his 1793 book, *Religion within the Limits of Reason Alone*, Immanuel Kant divided evil into three different kinds: normal, radical, and diabolical evil. So let's start with normal evil.

Our first example of evil comes from Batman himself. The Joker kidnaps Harvey Dent, the charismatic mayor of Gotham, and Rachel, with whom both Harvey and Batman are in love. He then gives Batman a choice: both of them are strapped to timed bombs, and Batman will only have enough time to save one of them. Batman chooses to save Rachel, but The Joker has left him with another surprise: when he arrives at her location, he finds Harvey, not Rachel there.

So what would Kant make of Batman's decision? In many ways, intending to do what's right is at the basis of Kant's ethics. If we want to understand someone's moral character, then it's their intentions that are important, according to Kant, not the actual outcomes of their actions. And further than this, you have to intend to do what's right just because it's what's right, not because of a personal desire, or because it'll bring about good consequences. In fact, when you act according to your own personal desires, rather than dutifully intending to do what's right, you're actually doing something immoral.

Now, even though Batman did in fact save Harvey, he had intended to save Rachel. And while Batman was personally very attached to Rachel, it seems pretty clear that, from the perspective of Gotham city, she was hardly an important figure when compared to Harvey Dent. If he was trying to do his duty as the self-proclaimed savior of Gotham, Batman really ought to have picked Harvey. Batman allowed a personal attachment, a private interest of his own to get the better of doing his duty, which is, according to Kant, not only immoral, but is also the definition of normal evil, or human frailty. There's nothing wrong with having personal interests, it's only when we favor them over doing the right thing that they become, to use Kant's term, pathological. Batman's attachment to Rachel was clearly pathological in this sense, because it led him to make what most of us would probably agree was the wrong choice.

Kant would have had other problems with Batman's behavior. True, Batman does maintain an absolute commitment to his maxim "never kill," which might seem to be an admirable example of sticking to one's moral principles. But even a positive principle like this one can turn into something pathological, in Kant's view. True, Batman never kills, but he apparently has no problem with torture, with the destruction of huge chunks of the public services in the city, or even of setting up an extraordinary surveillance network spying on every citizen in the city—all the collateral damage of his principle for which he is apparently not willing to assume responsibility.

His tendency towards holier-than-thou moralism comes through clearest in a scene where he deals with a group of vigilantes dressed up like him, one of the few times Bruce Wayne/Batman meets the "real people" of Gotham (as opposed to the super-rich friends he invites to lavish parties). You might expect him to praise people following his lead in fighting crime in a situation of such social chaos, but when he sees they are using guns (hence sacrificing their ethical dignity), he starts to fight them, not the criminals.

When they ask him: "what's the difference between you and me? What gives you the right?" rather than properly justifying himself in response to these perfectly reasonable questions, he quips: "I'm not wearing hockey pads." But of course, ordinary people simply don't have the money for Batman's fancy gadgets, and so can't afford to never kill—guns and hockey pads are a lot cheaper than Batsuits (and let's not forget that much of Bruce Wayne's wealth comes from producing and selling high-tech weaponry).

His commitment to his moral principle might be admirable in itself, but it's pretty clear that in Batman's case, this principle has been led to the point of becoming a pathological self-satisfaction, which, rather than inspiring him to perform good actions, in fact leads him to absolve himself of moral responsibility in other areas.

Radical Evil

Well, that was normal evil. How about radical evil?

When Batman arrives at the building where he thinks The Joker is holding Rachel, Harvey (who is in radio contact with Rachel) is incensed that he was saved instead of Rachel. In the ensuing explosion, half of his face is burnt off. With this, he's transformed from Harvey Dent, the White Knight of Gotham city, into Two-Face, the classic comic-book villain.

According to Kant's account, the transition from good to radically evil is always a kind of epiphany like this, a decisive moment where all your previous aims and desires are transformed, and you come out of it literally as a new person; marked in this case by his change in name. Harvey was basically a good person, morally speaking: if we judge him to have failed in that, it will be because we disagree with his conception of the good, or because he failed to live up to that conception in some way. Perhaps he made some decisions we might disagree with, perhaps from time to time he let his own interests stop him from properly carrying out his duty (that would be normal evil).

But with the transition to radical evil, what changed wasn't at the level of his actions but something in his very personality. So while Harvey basically wants to do good, Two-Face no longer cares about doing the right thing. He knows that what he's doing is wrong—at one point he almost kills Commissioner Gordon's innocent young son—but he's so consumed by hatred that "the good" simply stops being a motivating force for him.

It's not that, as in normal evil, his personal interests are sometimes able to overcome his desire to do the right thing: more drastically, he lets his actions be entirely determined by his one pathological concern—namely, his desire for vengeance—giving up entirely on the idea that he might ever act according to what is right.

One of the key features of radical evil, according to Kant, is the way it denies the freedom of the ethical subject. We see this shift in Harvey/Two-face's use of the coin toss. As Harvey, his two-headed coin was used as a trick to make people think that he was taking risks, whereas in reality he was just another schemer, who would never leave important things to chance. Kant, who famously argued that lying is always wrong, would no doubt have disapproved of Harvey's deceptive use of the double-sided coin. But it was clearly a case of normal evil, where Harvey simply violated a moral principle he ought to have followed. After the explosion that burns Harvey's face also blackens one half of the coin, he begins to use it in a very different way. Rather than using it to deceive other people, Two-Face uses the now fair coin to deny his own moral responsibility. When faced with a moral choice, rather than following the normal procedure of reasoning about it, weighing up the pros and cons of each side, he "outsources" his responsibility to the coin, which effectively makes his decisions for him.

For Kant, this is much more serious than merely deceiving other people: in leaving his important decisions to chance, Two-Face is completely denying his own ability to act as a free moral being. In radical evil, the ethical subject denies that they ever could be moved by moral reasons, only ever allowing their actions to be determined pathologically.

Diabolical Evil

The most interesting category in Kant's theory of evil is diabolical evil, which he models on the Devil. The difference between radical and diabolical is subtle, but crucial if we are to properly understand what's so terrifying about The Joker.

Whereas in radical evil, the moral agent completely gives up on the good, in diabolical evil they deliberately do the opposite of what they take to be good (The Devil's "Evil, be thou my good"). Where a radically evil agent acts only on their pathological interests, ignoring all moral motivation, a diabolical agent ignores their pathological interests, acting only in opposition to the good, no matter how much this might hurt their own interests!

What makes The Joker so horrifying, and surely what makes him such a fascinating character, is that he seems to follow this model of pursuing evil "just for the Hell of it" (pun intended), with a total indifference towards what happens to him personally. In one of the most memorable scenes in the film, he burns a huge pile of his own money, surely the ultimate symbol of pathological personal interests, apparently for no reason. In another, he gives Two-Face the opportunity to kill him, just because it would "make things more interesting."

A crucial diabolical aspect of The Joker's character is his psychology. At several points in the film, he explains how he got his scars: each time, the explanation evokes a traumatic scene, which might go some way to explaining his psychological make-up. However, the explanations are all inconsistent with one another. His point is to demonstrate to us that he can't be "accounted for" in this way, to mock this kind of psychological explanation of his character. Like we often see in depictions of the Devil, The Joker is not portrayed as a psychologically deep character, whose perverse attitude is to be explained by a "difficult childhood." He is simply a malevolent force of nature that cannot be accounted for by its history, a pure surface with no depth.

Another indication of this is the way he relates to his mask. Whereas a normal person puts on a mask to play a role, with the truth remaining in the real person behind the mask, for The Joker, any truth is to be found in the mask itself, not in anything we suppose to be behind it. Significantly, the only time he takes off his mask, his real face is supposed to function as a disguise.

When we inquire into what it is The Joker wants, the answer is equally demonic: total chaos, an end to the entire ruling order of Gotham City. In fact, his pursuit of chaos gives us a useful point of difference between him and the radical evil of

Two-Face. Two-Face, as we've already seen, also uses chance, tossing a coin to decide whether or not he should kill each of his victims, effectively using the coin so he doesn't have to assume responsibility for the decision himself.

The Joker's use of chance is quite different. Rather than using chance as a way of negating his freedom, of handing over his moral responsibility to a coin, he positively values chance, using it to enforce his belief that "chaos is fair." He has no problem taking full responsibility for the outcome of the chaos he creates, whatever it is, which we see from the way he constantly addresses himself to the population at large. He isn't trying to hide his actions—he wants people to hold him to account for the chaos he creates. He isn't a tortured soul or a tragic hero, deeply suffering while he does the terrible things he feels that fate is forcing him to do, but a free spirit who carries out his plans with joy. This, of course, only makes him all the more diabolical.

Beyond Good and Evil

Some philosophers have noticed a massive and deeply embarrassing problem with Kant's account of diabolical evil. Kant's moral theory requires us to do our duty, but it doesn't specify exactly what our duty is.

Our duty isn't to be found somewhere outside, like the Ten Commandments, waiting for us to discover it. On the contrary, it is we free moral beings who decide what is to be our duty. We will of course disagree with one another, each having a slightly different idea of what duty requires of us, but this never-ending process of arguing and re-negotiating is what ethics is all about (consider the discussions between Commissioner Gordon and Harvey Dent about the proper role and scope of the police).

When it comes to ethical action, then, the goal should be to renounce all of our pathological motivations completely, and act purely out of principle. The devastating argument is that this is exactly what happens in diabolical evil. A diabolically evil agent doesn't act for pathological reasons, in fact they have to have the strength of will to renounce all of that so that they can commit fully to carrying out evil, no matter the cost (this is why it's so difficult to achieve this level of evilness). Like someone carrying out the good, they act purely on principle—but as we have seen, these principles aren't written in the stars waiting for us to discover them, they are freely created by us. A normally evil agent like Batman won't put their principles to the test of discussion, but the same isn't true of the diabolical agent, who has no problem making a case for what they're doing. This leads us, then, to the only possible conclusion: diabolical evil is identical to the highest good.

Topsy-Turvy

This is a pretty distressing result, one that might quickly lead us to abandon Kant's way of thinking about ethics entirely. But couldn't we rather apply another turn of the screw and treat this outcome not as a criticism of Kant's position, but as a result to be fully endorsed? In our discussion of The Joker's diabolical evil we noted a number of things: his total indifference towards money; his lack of concern for his own life; his lack of a deep inner psychological life; his total identification with his mask persona; his wish to destroy the entire order of Gotham; his wish to create chaos. Couldn't we try to re-interpret all of these features as positive virtues to be admired?

With regard to money and his own life, these are pathological features that a truly ethical actor ought not to be too attached—isn't there something noble in being prepared to die for one's cause if necessary? With regard to his psychology residing wholly in his mask, this simply shows us that he is unwilling to have his behavior explained by external factors: he wants to assume full responsibility for all of his actions, something that Batman never does. With regard to his wish to destroy the ruling order and create chaos, he says it himself: chaos is fair. Gotham is in a situation of absolute social disarray, and yet Bruce Wayne and his other elite friends continue to live their extraordinarily lavish lives unaffected. When dressed up as Batman, Bruce Wayne tries to save Gotham, but as we have already seen, he doesn't appear to show any kind of respect for the actual people of Gotham. In contrast to Batman, who treats the people as passive victims who need to be saved by being spied on and duped by "noble lies," The Joker frequently speaks to them directly and honestly (as he says three times: "I'm a man of my word"), not only taking responsibility for his own actions, but asking them to do the same.

Most ordinary people are already living in a situation of chaos, and so The Joker's aim is really just to shake things up at the top, where the corruption is at its worst. Significantly, he doesn't only target Batman and the police, the mob is also an important part of the degenerate social hierarchy, and he manages to throw them into more of a panicky disarray than Dent ever did. When it comes to building his own gang, they are remarkably disciplined and loyal (even when one of the Joker's minions is tortured by the good guys, he doesn't give up the information), recruited from those who are excluded from the system—garbage collectors, truck drivers, those locked up in Arkham asylum—that is, those who have the most to gain from a complete reorganization of the social order.

Watch It Burn

Our final clue comes from Alfred, who says this when describing The Joker's motivations: "Some people aren't looking for anything logical, like money. They can't be bought, bullied, reasoned, or negotiated with. Some people just want to watch the world burn." This might seem to be another way of saying that The Joker is diabolically evil—he can't be motivated by anything pathological, he's a pure demonic force who wants nothing but to destroy.

But things look very different once we've heard the rest of the story. In Burma, Alfred had encountered a similarly motive-less character, a thief who stole jewels from the British colonialists and then immediately threw them away (they learned this when the British soldiers discovered a small child in the forest playing with an enormous ruby). Hoping to gain some insight into how to tackle The Joker, Bruce Wayne asks how they finally caught the thief, and Alfred tells him: "We burned down the forest." Who is it, then, who really wants to see the world burn?

10
Simply Watching the World Burn

GEORGE A. DUNN

In *Batman Begins*, Bruce Wayne finds himself in a Bhutanese prison, face to face with an enormous thug who's itching for a fight with the foreign newcomer. "You're in Hell, little man," sneers the brute as he launches into a violent assault on our hero, "and I am the Devil!"

Wayne's answer is more prescient than he could have possibly realized at the time: "You're not the Devil," he growls, fighting back with a ferocious skill that makes short work of the thug and five of his confederates. "You're practice." But no amount of "practice" beating up Bhutanese goons could possibly prepare Wayne for the diabolical figure he encounters in *The Dark Knight*, a psychopathic clown whose evil seems to possess a purity that puts him in an entirely different class from any other criminal that the Batman has faced.

Is The Joker a Satanic figure? There are strong indications that we're meant to view him that way. There's so much that's downright uncanny about him, starting with the fact that he seems to have appeared mysteriously out of nowhere. As Lieutenant Jim Gordon remarks after taking The Joker into custody, he seems to have no criminal record or, for that matter, any other trace of a prior existence, as unlikely as that would be for someone so flamboyantly wicked: "No DNA, no fingerprints. Clothing is custom, no tags or brand labels. Nothing in his pockets but knives and lint. No name, no other alias." His lack of history is also indicated by his two different accounts of how he got his scars—were they inflicted by his sadistic father, as he tells the gangster Gambol, or were they self-inflicted in an ill-conceived effort to put a smile on his wife's face, as he tells Rachel Dawes? His story changes to suit his different audiences, as though he has no real past, only various fictive pasts fabricated on the spot to serve whatever he takes to be the needs of the moment.

But the strongest evidence for the Satanic nature of The Joker lies not in the obscurity of his origins but in the mystery of his motivations. What makes him appear so Satanic is not just that his crimes are worse or his methods more depraved. Rather, what separates him from your garden-variety criminal is the nature of his motives—or rather his seeming lack of *any* sensible motive other than the desire to do evil for its own sake. While other denizens of Gotham's underworld act from amoral but otherwise perfectly understandable motives, such as greed or revenge, The Joker's wickedness seems entirely gratuitous, indulged out of sheer delight in sowing chaos and inflicting suffering. There's something inhuman about him. Perhaps Bruce Wayne really is up against the Devil this time.

Watching the World Burn

The Joker has threatened to kill someone every day until Batman accedes to the demand that he unmask himself. The Joker has already slain a Batman impersonator, a judge, and the police commissioner, in addition to making an attempt on the life of crusading "white knight" prosecuting attorney Harvey Dent. Now Bruce Wayne is trying to puzzle out his new adversary's motives for this killing spree, as a first step toward working out a plan to apprehend him. "Criminals aren't complicated," Wayne assures his valet and confidant, Alfred Pennyworth. "We just need to figure out what he's after."

Wayne's assumption is, on its face, eminently reasonable. Criminal behavior, like most other forms of human conduct, is goal-directed, a means to an end. If you're trying to understand why someone does something, whatever it might be, first figure out what he or she wants or hopes to accomplish. That's where you'll find the motive. Criminals differ from the rest of us in their willingness to employ certain *means* that most people ordinarily find abhorrent—such as violence, intimidation, and deceit—but the *ends* they pursue are, generally speaking, no different than those of most law-abiding folks.

Most people hew fairly closely to the straight and narrow, while others take shortcuts along the path of crime, but the things that matter to us are pretty much the same: wealth, power, and status, along with the pleasures to which they grant us access. As the notorious bank robber Willie Sutton is reported (perhaps apocryphally) to have responded to someone who was silly enough to ask him why he robbed banks, "Because that's where the money is." Willie Sutton and Bruce Wayne may be on opposite sides of the law, but they have a shared view of what primarily motivates moral transgression: the impetus to crime is best understood in "instrumental" terms, as a wicked means to achieving some otherwise perfectly comprehensible end that the miscreant regards as good (for himself, at least). The criminal differs from the rest of us only in his willingness to overstep ordinary moral boundaries in order to get the sort of things that all people want—or, since we all overstep moral boundaries on occasion, in his willingness to do so more regularly or egregiously.

Gratuitous Evil

But Alfred suspects that The Joker may be a different breed of criminal, one for whom such an instrumental explanation may not apply: "With respect, Master Wayne, perhaps this is a man that you don't fully understand either. A long time ago, I was in Burma, and my friends and I were working for the local government. They were trying to buy the loyalty of tribal leaders by bribing them with precious stones. But their caravans were being raided in a forest north of Rangoon by a bandit, so we went looking for the stones, but in six months we never met anybody who traded with him. One day, I saw a child playing with a ruby the size of a tangerine. The bandit had been throwing them away.

"So why steal them?" asks Wayne, puzzled. "Well, because he thought it was good sport," replies Alfred, "because some men aren't looking for anything logical like money. They can't be bought, bullied, reasoned, or negotiated with. Some men just want to watch the world burn." Unlike the ordinary criminal, whose aim is to acquire good things, the man described by Alfred is a devil who wants only to lay waste to everything good, which, in The Joker's case, includes even the moral goodness of

Gotham's "white knight," Harvey Dent and the hope for a better future that he inspires. Such an individual is possessed by a diabolical desire to cause harm for its own sake, toppling our ordinary patterns of life and destabilizing our orderly world just because he can. As The Joker succinctly describes himself to Harvey, "I'm an agent of chaos."

We call such a desire diabolical because it is precisely the sort of motivation that has typically been ascribed to the Devil within Western civilization. Historian Jeffery Burton Russell, author of a five-volume series of books on the history of the Devil, notes in his *The Prince of Darkness: Radical Evil and the Power of Good in History* that popular religion in the West has traditionally defined the Devil as a "person or personality with consciousness, will, and intelligence whose intent is entirely focused on causing suffering and misery for their own sake."

What this definition emphasizes is not just that the Devil is bent on doing harm. It also highlights the *gratuitous* nature of his evil, the complete absence of intelligible motives like greed or revenge that help us make sense of the crimes committed by ordinary mortal lawbreakers. We may not approve of the actions of mob boss Salvatore Maroni or rampaging vigilante Harvey "Two-Face" Dent, but at least we have some sense of what makes them tick. Perhaps we can even imagine ourselves doing similar things given sufficient incentive or provocation. But to choose evil *not* as an expedient but, as it were, just for the *Hell* of it—that may require a motivational structure so monstrous and perverse as to be no longer even recognizably human.

That's the Devil of popular religion, as well as much popular culture. As Russell observes, "Inflicting suffering for suffering's sake, evil for evil's sake, the Devil is by definition the personification of cosmic evil." In his work *Evil: Inside Human Violence and Cruelty* (1999), psychologist Roy Baumeister discusses what he calls the Myth of Pure Evil, the view of evil most often depicted in popular cartoons, movies, and religious stories. Baumeister asks: "What drives Satan and other evil figures? Apart from some vague ambition to gain power, the answer appears to be: nothing. Or rather, nothing beyond the sheer satisfaction of doing evil." Such a description seems to fit The Joker to a tee, except that it's not clear that The Joker is even very interested in power except as a tool for the commission of more evil.

A Better Class of Criminals?

We're first introduced to The Joker in the course of a bank robbery, which is just the sort of conduct one would expect from an amoral (and audacious) villain whose greed is not held in check by respect for the law or the property of others. Were Willie Sutton to witness this scene, he would undoubtedly be nodding in recognition. Depending on how unscrupulous Willie was, he might even feel some admiration for the elaborate knavery by means of which The Joker eliminated all of his confederates in order to keep the entire haul for himself. But when The Joker torches that towering pile of loot in the presence of the Chechen, Willie would surely gaze upon that act with the same stunned disbelief as the Chechen does. How insane! One spark becomes a conflagration and in the next moment the Joker's brilliantly executed heist has been rendered *all for nothing*.

We're reminded of Alfred's Rangoon bandit, who tossed away precious jewels because he "wasn't interested in anything logical like money," but only wanted "to watch the world burn." But this gratuitous act of destruction only demonstrates the truly diabolical depths of The Joker's evil. For just as someone who exhibits true moral virtue doesn't seek a reward for his good deeds, so too The Joker cares nothing for the spoils of crime. And just as the genuinely good person disdains the man of conventional respectability for whom virtue is just an expedient for acquiring a good reputation, so too The Joker has nothing but contempt for criminals whose wickedness is merely a means to tawdry ends such as lining their pockets with cash. "All you care about is money," he berates the Chechen. "This town deserves a better class of criminals."

Like the Devil, The Joker seems to have a diabolical commitment to evil for its own sake, evident in his willingness to sacrifice everything, even his own life, to fulfill his mission of corruption. He invites Batman to mow him down with the Batpod and even hands Harvey Dent a gun and helps him hold it to his head, ready to offer himself up as a sacrificial victim if that will further the cause of corrupting Gotham's finest. In a telling scene, an enraged Batman savagely pummels The Joker in the police interrogation room, as he simply laughs, "You have nothing, nothing to threaten me with. Nothing to do with all of your strength!"

Like some kind of saint of evil, The Joker scorns the material goods and pleasures that motivate ordinary people, including ordinary criminals of Gotham. He seems to have elevated evil to the status of an inviolable moral principle. According to the philosopher Immanuel Kant (1724–1804), what distinguishes the demands of morality from the dictates of prudence is the unconditional character of the former, meaning that a genuinely moral person treats morality as an end itself to which he is prepared to sacrifice everything else. The Joker's diabolical commitment to evil appears to involve the same sort of unconditional demand, which is the reason why he "can't be bought, bullied, reasoned, or negotiated with." He's like a warped mirror image of the incorruptibly good person, an anti-moral hero whose maxim is always to oppose the good regardless of the cost to himself.

Pure Evil Is a Myth

But does aspiring to evil as an end in itself, rather than as a means to satisfy some natural human desire for pleasure, power, or happiness, even make sense? We previously mentioned psychologist Roy Baumeister's discussion of the Myth of Pure Evil on display in cinematic and religious depictions of evil figures who delight in inflicting harm on others just because they can. Without such villains, movies like *The Dark Knight* would be much less interesting, but that doesn't mean that the purely diabolical motives we like to ascribe to characters like The Joker are ever found in the real world.

Baumeister maintains that our belief in the possibilility of pure evil and in all things Satanic has little correspondence with reality. Rather, these beliefs stem from our psychological need to drive a wedge between "good guys" and "bad guys" and to perceive the perpetrators of evil as belonging to a fundamentally different class than the rest of us—the victims of evil who, of course, dwell among the angels. And this last point is the flip side of the Myth of Pure Evil: the victim of evil is as "innocent and good" as the perpetrator is dastardly. But the truth, according to Baumeister, is very different. So-called "evil" people are typically seeking the same things as the rest of us—money, power, status—though they're often less hampered by moral scruples, good judgment, self-control, and other buzz-kills that keep most of us out of trouble. Baumeister would undoubtedly agree with Bruce Wayne's statement, "Criminals aren't that complicated." Or at least not any more complicated than the rest of us.

Baumeister's view is shared by most of the philosophers of the Western tradition, dating back to the ancient Greek philosophers Socrates (469–399 B.C.E.) and Aristotle (384–322 B.C.E.), both of whom argued that the aim of every human action aims is procuring something that we judge to be good. The good we seek may be just short-term pleasure and the gratification of our lower appetites, which is what most of the crooks in Gotham are after. On the other hand, it might be the deeper, long-term happiness that Aristotle believed could come only from a life of noble or virtuous actions, like those performed by Bruce Wayne or Jim Gordon. But if people choose wickedness, it's not because they find evil inherently attractive—because there's nothing attractive about it. Lacking the inspiring luster of virtue, wickedness can be deliberately chosen only as a shortcut to obtaining pleasure or perhaps out of ignorance of what's truly good. That's why Aristotle believed that bad men harbor a secret contempt for themselves, at least to the extent that they are able to recognize themselves as bad.

Are There Diabolical Humans?

Likewise, Immanuel Kant, who believed that true moral goodness meant choosing to do the right thing without any thought of reward, agrees with Socrates and Aristotle that people *never* choose to do the wrong thing *unless* they think that there's something else in it for them. Every rational being is aware of the demands of morality, according to Kant, which is why no one—with the exception of those who are truly insane, such as the victims of the Scarecrow's "fear toxin"—can escape accountability for his or her actions.

But we also possess what Kant calls *pathological* motivations that they have their source in our feelings and desires. "Pathological" doesn't imply that these desires are somehow diseased. Kant uses this term merely to highlight the fact that we are *passive* in relation to them. We can't help it that we feel a certain way or have certain desires, though Kant insists that we do have a choice whether to act on those feelings or pursue those desires. The evil person is someone who lets these *pathological* motivations, which may even include concern for our loved ones, override the strict demand of morality to do the right thing no matter what. And the fact that we *all* let our personal feelings and desires trump morality from time to time suggests to Kant that human beings in general have a "natural propensity toward evil."

While fully acknowledging the depths of human depravity, Kant insists that the concept of "diabolical being"—a being for whom resistance to the moral law would itself be elevated to an incentive for acting—is not applicable to the humans. Despite what the Myth of Pure Evil would have us believe, there are no devils among us who delight in evil for its own sake, only weak and deluded human beings for whom morality routinely takes a backseat to other concerns that are more urgently felt. The most monstrous cruelty springs from the same source as our smallest daily trespasses. Kant would almost certainly have agreed with philosopher Karl Jaspers when he wrote in a letter to Hannah Arendt that it's a terrible mistake to ascribe "Satanic greatness" to human wickedness, even to the most horrendous crimes: "It seems to me that we have to see these things in their total banality, in their prosaic triviality, because that's what truly characterizes them." And, notwithstanding The Joker's lament, that's as a good a class of criminals as we're ever going to get.

The Battle for the Soul of Gotham

Even if no one delights in evil for its own sake, there might be other definitions of "diabolical" that apply to The Joker. In her 2002 book, *The Atrocity Paradigm*, Claudia Card gives this definition of 'diabolical'. Doesn't it fit The Joker like one of his custom-made suits?

> Suppose we define diabolical evil as knowingly and culpably seeking others' moral corruption, putting them in situations where in order to survive they must, by their own choices, risk their own moral deterioration or moral death . . . Diabolical evil . . . consists of putting others

under the extreme stress, even the extreme duress, of having to
choose between grave risks of suffering or death (not necessarily
their own) and equally grave risks of severe moral compromise, the
loss of moral integrity, or even moral death.

This definition reflects the traditional picture of the Devil as
the tempter par excellence, a creature who not only inflicts
physical suffering and distress, but, worse still, strikes at the
very souls of his victims by sowing the seeds of moral corruption. And, indeed, this is precisely how The Joker's own words
suggest that we ought to view him when he tells Batman that
the two of them are engaged in a "battle for the soul of
Gotham."

The Joker's primary stratagem in that battle is to engineer
various situations that force the ostensibly good, law-abiding
people of Gotham City to decide whether being morally upright
is really their first priority. So, for example, rather than personally killing Coleman Reese, the hapless Wayne Enterprises
accountant who discovered Batman's true identity, The Joker
threatens to blow up a Gotham hospital unless someone else
does the deed for him, thus forcing many otherwise "good" citizens to contemplate doing something that under ordinary cir-
cumstances would almost certainly never cross their minds,
namely, killing an innocent person.

But the image of the Devil as a tempter who foments moral
corruption doesn't quite fit The Joker either. The Joker seems to
view himself more as a revealer than an instigator of evil—a
tempter, indeed, but not because he tempts good folks to stray
onto the path of iniquity, but rather because he tempts false pre-
tenders to virtue to show their true colors. And, in The Joker's
mind, that's all of us. His "social experiment" with the detona-
tors on the ferries is designed to demonstrate that despicable
felons and so-called decent citizens are in the same boat morally
speaking, at least when placed in a situation of extreme duress.
If genuine virtue means doing the right thing no matter the
cost, then The Joker believes that the closest thing to virtue
you'll ever find in this world is a simulacrum of goodness among
those whose moral fiber has never really been seriously tested.
"When the chips are down, these civilized people, they'll eat
each other," he opines and then sets out to prove it.

If the Myth of Pure Evil would have us believe that so-called "evil" people are an entirely different species than the rest of us—and that we "civilized people" are pure and innocent lovers of the good, for whom virtue is its own reward—then the Joker's aim is to strip that illusion away. People are "only as good as their world *allows* them to be," he tells Batman. Our virtue is fragile and tentative at best, "a bad joke. Dropped at the first sign of trouble." And in The Joker's dedication to proving that claim regardless of the cost in human suffering, he resembles another famous diabolical figure—Satan, as he appears in the biblical book of Job.

Readers of Job may be surprised to discover that this Satan, whose name in Hebrew could be translated as "the Accuser," is not an inveterate enemy of God bent on destroying everything good, but rather appears to be a member of God's heavenly court, where he acts as something like an overzealous prosecuting attorney. This Devil has more in common with Kenneth Starr than with Lucifer, the "morning star" who was allegedly expelled from heaven.

After hearing God praise Job as a perfectly upright man, Satan suggests that perhaps Job is just a wily sycophant who obeys God only because God has blessed him with abundant prosperity. "Does Job fear God for nothing?" Satan asks, insinuating that Job's righteousness is more calculated than sincere. Satan then proposes a wager: Let's take away Job's prosperity, murder his loved ones, afflict his flesh, and let his true motivations stand revealed when he deserts his faux-piety and curses God.

Just as the biblical Satan targets Job, said to be the most upright man, so The Joker sets his sights on the heroic Harvey Dent, "Gotham's white knight," who is also said to be "the best of us." And as with Job, the battle for the soul of Harvey Dent involves both the murder of a loved one (Rachel Dawes) and a cruel affliction of his flesh (disfiguring burns). But here the similarity ends, for, unlike Job, Harvey lets his rage at the injustice of what has been done to him burn out of control, reducing his moral scruples and his esteem for the law to cinders, until there's nothing left but a homicidal craving for vengeance. Thus The Joker seems to have whipped up a fairly convincing proof of Kant's thesis that even among the best of us, our commitment to morality doesn't run as deep as we'd like to believe.

Is the Joker Banal After All?

Seen in this light, The Joker and Satan begin to look a little bit like high-minded moralists, crusading against the smug complacency of all those so-called decent people who are able to persuade themselves of their moral goodness only because their virtue has never been put to the test. And that would explain why The Joker—who's prepared to sacrifice everything, even his own life, in his single-minded campaign to expose moral hypocrisy and exploit moral weakness—regards himself as superior to everyone else in Gotham, law-abiding citizens, cops, and "uncomplicated" criminals alike. They're all "schemers," too preoccupied with things like money, power, and status to warrant any respect. He clearly sees himself as better than them, having risen above the tawdry desire for worldly gain to enjoy a degree of freedom that eludes those who remain slaves to "pathological" motivations. That's why he feels free to treat those who are beneath him as mere things who can be manipulated and sacrificed to send a message to the schemers—a message that in the end is simply the claim that human beings are slavish creatures who lack the dignity that would entitle them to any better treatment. "When I say that you and your girlfriend was nothing personal, you know that I'm telling the truth," The Joker tells Harvey. But if that's true, it's only because The Joker hardly regards Harvey and Rachel as *persons* at all, at least not in the sense of being rational creatures who are entitled to respect.

If our guess about what's going on with The Joker is right, however, there's at least one "pathological" motivation to which he *does* remain enslaved, one that also associates him very closely with the figure of Devil—namely, pride. In his pride, the Devil flouted the authority of God, just as The Joker aspires to "live without rules." And, according to Baumeister, the belief that pride or inflated self-esteem lies at the root of evil may in fact be one aspect of the popular perception of evil in which we see an actual "infusion of reality into a psychological fabrication." The Joker does seem to believe that his actions exhibit something like "Satanic greatness" and it's easy to recognize self-glorification as an important piece of his motivation. He doesn't "just want to watch the world burn." Rather, he wants credit for starting the conflagration. The irony is that to the extent that his supposedly "diabolical" evil is fueled by an all-too-human pride, it has a lot in common with many our most petty vices and failings. Evil for The Joker turns out to be instrumental, pathological, and banal after all.

The cure for pride, according to Kant, is the sort of humility that arises from a proper appreciation of our own moral failings and a refusal to make excuses for ourselves. And he believes that it's through admitting our own moral culpability and abandoning our self-righteous insistence on our own goodness that we most nearly approximate the genuine moral virtue that's otherwise out of our reach.

Ironically, we get our most compelling glimpse of the power of this moral humility in one of the situations that The Joker had contrived to expose the feebleness of our morality. On one of the ferries that The Joker has rigged to blow up, the one carrying the prisoners, a large inmate confronts the guard, intimidating him into handing over the detonator to blow up the other ferry. "Give it to me," the prisoner demands, "and I'll do what you should have done ten minutes ago." The guard complies—noticeably relieved that the responsibility for committing an act of mass murder has been lifted off his shoulders—and the prisoner promptly tosses the detonator out the window.

Perhaps some criminals are complicated after all.

11
How (Not) to Train Your Demon

NICOLE R. PRAMIK

In the world of Brandon Mull's fantasy series *Fablehaven* (2006–2010), encountering magical creatures is everyday business. You can eavesdrop on fairies; play tennis with satyrs; pick fights with centaurs; and, of course, banter with demons.

Make no mistake—demons aren't your friends in *Fablehaven*, and you'd have an easier time trying to have lunch with a zombie (as in *not at all*). But does that mean you can't teach a demon at least a little something? Like how to be good, for instance? After all, the only fate any demon gets in Mull's universe is either eternal damnation or imprisonment in Zzyzx (and no, not the former California settlement).

Grandpa Sorenson, the caretaker of Fablehaven, asserts that magical creatures don't follow the same rules of morality humans do. Instead, such beings, including demons, act in accordance with their natures and not necessarily for morally right reasons.

But what makes an act moral anyway? Luckily for us, we don't have to guess. We have one dearly departed famous philosopher to give us his posthumous take and two Shadow Charmers to provide us with clues as to whether or not *Fablehaven*'s notorious denizens are capable of learning any lessons in morality.

Of Duty and Demons

Immanuel Kant (1724–1804) was a lead thinker in a view of ethics called *deontology*, which focuses on duty or *why* you act the way you do. In other words, Kant was more interested in why people would do something (right motivation) rather than what happened after they did it (good consequences). Duty-based ethics, then, says we should do what's right because it's right, and we should avoid doing what's wrong because it's wrong based on *principle*.

Kant summed up this very idea in what he called the *categorical imperative*, which applies to all rational beings and is more concerned with commanding (that's why it's *imperative*) that you act morally more so than giving you a list of strict Do's and Don't's. But it also draws two conclusions. First, the categorical imperative claims moral rules are universal. Therefore, you should always act in a way so your actions could, in theory, become universal moral law. If you aren't willing for others to behave as you do, then your actions aren't moral.

Secondly, it asserts people should be treated with respect and always as an end in and of themselves, never as a means to achieve something else. Thus, deceiving, manipulating, coercing, or bullying someone to do what you want are always wrong. According to Kant, using people isn't necessarily wrong but it's definitely immoral if they're treated *only* as a means to an end.

So what does duty-based ethics look like in action? Let's say you're thinking of snitching your best pal's leftover candy bar and lying about its whereabouts later. (I trust you wouldn't but let's just pretend you're as devious as a demon). According to the categorical imperative, you would test yourself by asking whether or not lying to your friend about taking something that was his should become a universal moral law that *everyone* should do. If you can't condone your actions to allow others to treat you in the same fashion (allowing others to take your candy and lying to you about it), then it would be wrong for you to lie and steal. Likewise, if lying to your friend would mean using him as a means to get his candy for yourself, then that would also be immoral. So either way you slice it, you're acting wrongly by Kant's standards.

All potential candy stealing aside, it's fair to say that the demons of *Fablehaven* have committed far more heinous acts than snitching sweets. These fiends, despite their demonic origins, are rational beings, so they're subject to the categorical imperative just as we are. But since they're wicked by nature, does that mean their actions will, at some point, revert to evil?

It's a fair question and there are two lessons we can learn from two different demons, Graulas and Nagi Luna, when it comes to trying to train a demon to do what's right.

Demons Make Strange (and Destructive) Bedfellows

When Seth Sorenson, one of the young protagonists, first encounters Graulas in *Grip of the Shadow Plague*, he remains a consistent moral agent towards the demon. So it makes sense he would have some sort of ethical influence over Graulas.

Well, we can at least hope.

After Seth makes contact with a powerful talisman that marks him with dark magic, he catches the attention and interest of Graulas, formerly one of the most powerful demons in the world. Now Graulas is confined to a small realm inside Fablehaven thanks to the guidelines of the preserve's treaty. When Seth visits Graulas, he seems willing to help uncover the origin of a dastardly plague transforming the preserve's creatures into shadowy beings.

Unlike what most sane kids his age would do, Seth tries to befriend the demon. While Kant and his imperative don't have anything to say about trying to make friends with demons, they would assume Seth is acting morally. Instead of trying to hurt Graulas for no reason, Seth approaches Graulas with a sense of congeniality. And since Seth's attempts to be nice to Graulas create a moral law that says something like "be kind to your enemies," Seth's actions are moral. Likewise, Seth never treats Graulas as a means, even when the demon offers insight into matters beyond Seth's realm of knowledge. Instead, he views Graulas as his own person (or demon), not just a resource to use and toss aside.

So Seth is clearly the good guy (or kid). But what about Graulas? Since Graulas is a rational being, just like Seth, then the categorical imperative applies to him, too. When warning Seth about the shadow plague, Graulas does share as much information as he knows that he senses will be beneficial to finding a cure. Under deontological principles, if sharing information about a potentially dangerous situation saves others and prevents disaster, it could stand as moral law since most people would agree that doing both things are out of a sense of duty to others and the greater good. Hence, Graulas acts rightly. Likewise, Graulas doesn't appear to use Seth as a means in this case. He simply tells Seth what he knows about the plague and leaves Seth to go about his business to stop it. So far, so good.

The second interaction Graulas has with Seth is in *Secrets of the Dragon Sanctuary*. This time, the demon extends his assistance when Seth's family needs to obtain a unicorn horn guarded by centaurs living on the preserve. Likewise, Graulas finally makes Seth a Shadow Charmer, magically sealing the talisman's power residing in Seth, enabling him to talk to dark creatures, render himself invisible, and become immune to emotional manipulation.

While Seth worries being a Shadow Charmer will make him evil, Graulus assures him that being an ally of the dark is not the same as being allied with evil. Morally, Graulas is correct. According to the categorical imperative, mere contact with notorious beings and an ability to be impervious to certain negative emotions might work to your benefit as long as the actions undertaken in both cases could become a moral law and don't treat other people as means. Graulas actually encourages Seth to use his new-found powers however he likes, for good or bad, and the fact Graulas is giving moral advice shows he understands how to make right and wrong choices.

Lesson One: Demons Are Deliberate— Deliberately Evil, That Is

Keep in mind, though, that all the while Graulas is dying a slow, painful death and knows he will enter an equally slow, painful eternity. It isn't until he's at the Grim Reaper's doormat that he finally makes an open plea for help from Seth. In *Keys to the Demon Prison*, Graulas requests that should Seth retrieve the Sands of Sanctity, one of the five artifacts sealing Zzyzx, to return to the preserve and heal him with it.

This is the first time Graulas acts in a way that is less than moral, in Kant's opinion. Graulas's request isn't based in duty since he's acting out of self-preservation and desperation to avoid punishment befitting his kind. Graulas's second immoral act is his admission that he helped Seth in the past just for his own amusement, which could count as him using

Seth as a means to obtain some form of entertainment. Two strikes so far. Maybe Seth saving his life might count for something.

Sadly, when Seth restores him to health using the Sands of Sanctity, Graulas destroys Grandpa and Grandma Sorenson's house on the preserve and overturns the magical treaty, thus demolishing the categorical imperative (metaphorically speaking) in the process. It turns out that his friendship with Seth was driven by a longing to return to power, so he used Seth as a means. This also brings new, nefarious meaning to Graulas's past offers of aid. Evidently, these were not done out of a desire for his assistance to be assumed as moral law or out of a sense of moral duty. Quite the opposite, it seems.

Before he departs, Graulas accuses Seth of being too trustworthy and amicable and admits he pitted these qualities against Seth. Granted, Graulas spares Seth his life, which Kant might view as a moral act since sparing someone's life could be seen as a universal moral rule. But Graulas's reason has more to do with showing Seth who's boss as opposed to demonstrating genuine mercy and compassion.

"I am what you would call evil," Graulas asserts to Seth. "Pure, deliberate evil. I am aggressively self-serving. I take great pleasure in destruction. At times, I cause harm to get gain and at times I cause harm for the sheer enjoyment of breeding mayhem." Thus, despite Seth's demonstrations of moral behavior, Graulas never truly learns what it means to be good and is confined to his inherently evil nature.

But maybe Graulas is just one bad demonic seed. Luckily, there are more demonic hosts afoot in *Fablehaven*, such as one aging crone named Nagi Luna. Which brings us to our next lesson in demon training.

Lesson Two: The Road to Zzyzx Is Paved with Bad Intentions

Unlike Seth, the Sphinx, *Fablehaven*'s central villain, has some different life goals. In *Keys to the Demon Prison*, the Sphinx finally gains possession of the five magical artifacts that will open Zzyzx. His MO reeks of unethical behavior as the Sphinx claims deception is a key ingredient for him to achieve victory in opening the demon prison yet asserts he is behaving in the best interests of the world. Obviously, that's a load of philosophical waffle.

But the Sphinx isn't the only one making big moral blunders here. Nagi Luna, an ancient demon, repays the Sphinx's long-time friendship by making him a Shadow Charmer and agreeing to help him open Zzyzx. At first, their pairing seems like a match made in anywhere but Heaven. Nagi Luna is a dominant force who wears her bad deeds like badges of honor. She brags about how world powers have fallen and plagues have emerged by her hand. So it's safe to say her actions violate the basic premise of duty-based ethics: she acts in ways that satisfy her own thirst for destruction and people become nothing more than mere pawns.

But in a classic pass-the-buck maneuver, the Sphinx ends up admitting that opening Zzyzx was all Nagi Luna's idea. (Naturally, blame the demon.) He claims he was merely using her since their goals were united. That's a nice admission on his part, but it earns him far fewer ethical points than any of Seth's acts of kindness and heroism.

Sadly, since the Sphinx violates the categorical imperative at every turn, it's impossible for Nagi Luna to learn anything good from him. Needless to say, Nagi Luna is wickeder than Graulas, at least at first. While Graulas's offers of aid do ultimately stem from ill will rather than a sense of duty, the information still helps Seth and his family put a stop to various evils right beneath their noses. To be fair, Graulas could have kept his chapped-lipped mouth shut. But the same can't be said for Nagi Luna, who can only express her indignations at everyone's indiscretions and incompetence. When the Sphinx ends up introducing Seth to Nagi Luna in a sort of Shadow Charmer meet and greet, Seth wants nothing to do with her. Since this happens after Graulas's betrayal, it's no wonder Seth is less than eager to become her new pal.

But it turns out that Nagi Luna recognizes Graulas's mark on Seth, which irks her. She criticizes Graulas's fascination with humans and accuses him of being too concerned with their "trite philosophies." While she never explains what she means, we do know that Graulas, judging from his actions, knows a little something about human ethical systems. Though he elects to neither learn from nor participate in them, he's at least familiar with them. That's more than can be said for Nagi Luna. She offers to help Seth keep Zzyzx closed (definitely a good thing) only so it provides less competition for her (not so good). The Sphinx provides a poor moral model and Seth serves as a far better one, and perhaps it's this that Nagi Luna doesn't want to expose herself to. Graulas at least knew about duty and moral behavior but didn't necessarily act on these. But Nagi Luna seems utterly closed off to the idea of even attempting to be moral. Once a mean, old demonic hag, always a mean, old demonic hag.

Nagi Luna eventually triumphs over the Sphinx, with Graulas's help actually, and assumes control over all five artifacts. The Sphinx's toppling might qualify as a moral act to both demons' credit under the categorical imperative since it would be considered moral law to remove immoral leaders. But Nagi Luna's motivations are guided, as are Graulas's at this point, by a desire to unleash chaos upon the world. Needless to say, this really wouldn't be considered good moral law nor does it view people as ends.

Graulas and Nagi Luna eventually stand on the same side but play two very different power plays. Not only are these demons incapable of learning moral behavior, they can't even behave rightly towards their own kind. When Zzyzx is opened and an epic battle ensues on the Shoreless Isle, Nagi Luna betrays Graulas by giving him misleading information about a magical sword Seth now wields. While withholding information that may strengthen an opponent might be a moral act, Nagi Luna just wants to see Graulas defeated to please her own overinflated ego. Thus, Seth is, once again, viewed as a means rather than an end. Though the ultimate end proves disastrous for Nagi Luna, Graulas, and the rest of their devilish comrades as their old prison collapses and they're driven into a brand new hellish hidey hole for all eternity.

Pity they never learned how to be good during their time in the mortal realm.

I Can't Make You Evil Any More Than You Can Make Me Good

These words are uttered by Graulas to Seth, emphasizing how his evil nature is there to stay. Nagi Luna doesn't make any such declarations to the Sphinx, but if she could, her words probably would have been the same. It appears no matter how good or even mediocre of a moral influence these demons are exposed to, the examples just don't take.

Between both demons here, Graulas is the only one who shows early promise at becoming a moral agent despite his infamous past. He's certainly exposed to a consistently good moral example in Seth and at least grasps the difference between being good and being bad. Not everything Graulas does is evil but, in the end, he only knows how to treat Seth as a means. Thus, to him, Seth's friendship and compassion are merely commodities to be exploited, not moral traits to be admired and imitated.

As for Nagi Luna, she's a lost cause from the start and the Sphinx's poor influence doesn't help matters. Her intentions are driven, not out of sense of duty to establish her behaviors as moral laws, but a longing to unleash a season of lawlessness. Likewise, she treats the Sphinx, her sole friend (term used loosely here) as a means to her own end. Thus, while the demons of *Fablehaven* are certainly rational, the commands spelled out by Kant's categorical imperative just don't seem to impose any lessons on them.

And speaking of lessons, there is one final piece of advice when it comes to training a demon: you might be able to lead it out of Zzyzx but you can't make him (or her) good.

V

Imagined Devils

12
Use the Force, Luke(ifer)

A.G. HOLDIER

Weighing in at just over 320 pounds, the Dark Prince, Satan, left quite the impression during his first appearance in *South Park* when he burst out of a cloud of flame to get ready for his boxing match with Jesus Christ. After centuries of preparation, Lucifer was ready to challenge the much smaller Son of God to the final battle between good and evil. As Jesus himself called it, this was to be "the most crucial and serious time in all history."

Just like the Book of Revelation describes it, right? Or will Armageddon not be broadcast live from the South Park Forum for only $49.95 on pay-per-view?

Although the Bible is admittedly lacking in references to boxing gloves, like many theistic worldviews it certainly gives us images of the forces of good and evil locked in combat. Like opposing generals leading great armies of troops, God and the Devil are commonly believed to be in continual clash, each one enjoying successes and failures in their eternal, evenly matched fight. Though the details vary, many see the general layout of the spiritual landscape as a balanced scale: good versus evil, angels versus demons, God versus the Devil. Satan is the Moriarity to Jesus's Holmes, the Megatron to God's Optimus Prime. Both of these options are necessary for the literary tension to proceed; no one knows which side will ultimately win.

After all, in the larger metaphysical sense, like "up" with no "down" how could we possibly see something as "good" unless we have an "evil" thing to compare it to? Without Satan, South

111

Park has no one for Jesus to box—so why, then, would we need Jesus? Isn't the Devil a necessary complement to God?

No Match

Despite the popularity of this question, every major monotheistic tradition—Christianity, Judaism, and Islam—answers it with a profound and resounding *no*. The early Christian philosopher and theologian St. Augustine of Hippo (354–430) explicitly denounced this sort of dualistic spirituality, arguing that God, as the Supreme Being, could never genuinely be threatened by an equally powerful opposite god—in fact, the co-existence of two such entities is logically contradictory. There isn't any tension in the conflict between God and the Devil since it's metaphysically impossible for a perfect God to lose. Satan is indeed real and dangerous, but only as a derivative power insofar as God allows him to exist, says Augustine—they are far from evenly matched. So, evil isn't a powerful force to be contended with or consumed by, but is wrapped up as a by-product of the free will of God's created creatures.

But why do so many of us in the twenty-first century understand spirituality in this wrong-headed bipolar fashion, despite its being demonstrably unorthodox? If God and the Devil aren't actually evenly matched, why do we think they are? To answer this, we must look even further back and farther away than Augustine; indeed, we must consider (in the words of one scruffy-looking smuggler) a "hokey religion" from a long time ago in a galaxy far, far away.

The Ways of the Force

In the *Star Wars* universe, there's no mention of the Devil or of a god he opposes. Instead, the Jedi religion (and its counterpart, the Sith) focuses on the mystical Force: an energy field comprised of light and darkness that heroes and villains can bend to their will. In the words of Jedi Knight Obi-Wan Kenobi, "the Force is what gives a Jedi his power. It surrounds us and penetrates us. It binds the galaxy together." Individuals all fall somewhere along its spectrum, leading essentially good lives or—like the iconic villain, Darth Vader—being devilishly seduced by the power of the evil Dark Side. Like two faces of a coin, the Jedi and Sith are necessary and equal opposites if balance is to be maintained; the Light Side cannot exist without its Dark counterpart any more than a scale can be a scale with a weight pan on only one side.

This holds true even if no individual follower of either side of the Force survives to carry on the tradition. Luke Skywalker's Jedi revival would have still been theoretically possible in the absence of teachers like Kenobi and the diminutive Yoda since the Force would still have existed to be discovered and used—the training would simply have been far more difficult (and require much greater supernatural intervention). The Force, like God, the Devil, and any other spiritual object, isn't identical with the material creatures that tap into it; it *is* what it *is*—light and dark—no matter who's around at any given time to interact with it.

In many respects, the Force does appear to be divine. Not only is it morally structured in a good-versus-evil framework, but it mystically influences the events surrounding its agents' lives and supernaturally empowers them with miraculous abilities to carry out what would otherwise be called Fate. However, the most important factor in an agent's interaction with the impersonal, omnipresent Force is the Knight's own willful power of choice. As Kenobi explains to Skywalker in one of their early training sessions:

KENOBI: Remember, a Jedi can feel the Force flowing through him.

SKYWALKER: You mean it controls your actions?

KENOBI: Partially. But it also obeys your commands.

Unlike either God or the Devil, the Force has no personal identity or character; it's like a super-charged, spiritualized version of magnetism or electricity that needs a willful actor to choose how to control it.

We Are Our Choices

So, that choice becomes the crucial factor in deciding whether an individual will become a Jedi or not: Darth Vader was tempted by the opportunities offered by the Dark Side and chose to turn away from the Jedi path he had previously been following to become a Sith instead. Luke goes through a similar temptation over the course of his story, but manages to win out over Vader's lures to maintain his good nature—and, in fact, help Vader to find redemption in another willful choice at the end of *The Return of the Jedi*. The devilish Vader's corruption was freely chosen, so his redemption was likewise.

However, talk of "redemption" in *Star Wars* is, strictly speaking, wrong. To speak of Vader's corruption to the Dark Side isn't really any different than if we were to speak of his "corruption" from the Dark Side back to the Light; since both sides are fully equal, neither is "better" than the other (any more than "heads" is better than "tails" on your quarter)—they are simply different. In the absence of some over-arching standard that defines one side as morally superior to the other (such as a God that *Star Wars* is notoriously silent about), the Force is simply a morally neutral power to be used. All that matters is the role you personally choose to play in the grand narrative of the cosmos, for Jedi or for Sith.

You Bet Your Zoroaster

Here we can return to Augustine's thoughts on the matter. Augustine would agree that much about a person's moral character hinges on his or her freely-willed decisions. He would, however, strongly reject the notion that our choice is balanced between two equal options. Indeed, Augustine explicitly targeted this kind of dualistic spirituality to point out its contradiction to both monotheism and logic. Having spent nearly a decade as a member of the Manichaean movement, a Persian branch of Gnosticism that was influenced strongly by Zoroastrianism and viewed the universe as the battleground between the equally matched forces of light and darkness (sound familiar?), Augustine was well aware of what he was up against.

To think of God and the Devil as two sides of an equal scale means that you're no longer thinking monotheistically, but rather bi-theistically (as in Zoroastrian theology with its good Jedi-like god, Ahura Mazda, and its fully equal Sith-ish counterpart Angra Mainyu)—you don't have one God, but two. And neither god can truly be called omnipotent, for even if they can do everything else possible, they still don't have power over each other. No, Augustine said, if God is indeed the only

Supreme Being and Creator of everything that is not Him, then the Devil is, by necessity, less powerful than his creator, God. They are clearly not evenly matched. In order to be a true monotheist, Augustine argues that you must recognize God as the creator—and, therefore, empowerer—of the Devil.

But the next problem is obvious: if the Devil is not a necessary being, why would God choose to create the Devil? How could a good God possibly allow such an evil creature to infest and corrupt His universe?

The answer is simple: because Lucifer chose to do so. Even if there are not two equal gods to choose between, humans have the free will to choose whether to obey God's commands and follow His plans or not—and Satan, Augustine argued, likewise had this choice. Unfortunately, he chose very wrongly, but such is the danger of genuine freedom; if Vader has the ability to choose rightly, he must also be able to choose the opposite or else he has no real choice at all.

So, Augustine says, since a good God can only do and create good things, Satan must have originally been created good, but *chose* to become evil at some point after that when he rejected God. The two beings are far from complementary.

Seduced by the Dark Side

A looming question remains: if Augustine is right, what does *evil* really mean? We might speak of a moral decision as a fork in the road: should Luke walk down the good path with Obi-Wan or the evil path with Darth Vader? But this assumes that both paths are equal with each other and Augustine will have none of that. Instead, he suggests that there's really only one path, God's path, and anything else that doesn't follow that path is evil—not because it possesses a different property called *evil*, but because it possesses, in a sense, less God.

Because he recognized a good God as the source of everything else that exists—both in its initial creation and its ongoing sustenance—it wasn't a far stretch for Augustine to conclude that something about existence itself is necessarily good. Only the good God necessarily exists; the only reason anything still exists after its origin, Augustine says, is because God gives it the power to do so. So, everything that exists directly participates in the reality of the existent God.

Certainly, Augustine's God has a specific plan in mind for how He would will His created reality to proceed and He had every ability to orchestrate His universe in such a way that no one ever acts differently, but such a universe would not be populated by creatures who are free in any meaningful sense of the term. By granting some of His creatures (at the very least, angels and humans) the ability to choose to agree with Him or not, God forced each of those creatures—you and me included—into the moral dilemma of existence: we must choose whether we'll follow God or not. To choose to do so completely (or at least as much as we can, given Augustine's views on original sin) means that we'll fully experience the reality of God, the source of all existence and ultimate meaning of our own; to choose to do otherwise means that we'll *not* fully experience that reality and will lack some fundamental piece of what it means to exist. This lack—*deprivation*—is the essence of evil.

Evil as Absence

So, evil isn't the same type of thing as good; Vader isn't equal to Kenobi. To speak of evil is merely to name a void, something that lacks substantive reality and exists only as an adjective for freely willed decisions of created creatures who act contrary to the will of God. Evil, strictly speaking, doesn't exist, anymore than cold or darkness exists; just as those are both defined by *absences* of either heat or light, evil is simply the absence of God.

If the mental picture for the Force is a scale held in perfect balance, then the metaphor for Augustinian theology is the gymnasium climbing rope: the self-sufficient God is at the top, supporting everything else below Him in their existence at varying degrees of moral participation in His plan for reality. Because Satan exists, of course, he's on the rope, sustained by God, but at the very bottom-most point.

The Force Is Strong with This One

This picture of genuine monotheism is a far cry from the spiritual dualism that's found in the stories that entertain us, like *Star Wars*. The way monotheism sees it, God and the Devil can't be evenly matched; any tension present in the narratives of our lives centers on our decisions, not their actions.

But stories need tension. Luke needs to struggle against Vader just as much as Harry Potter must fight Lord Voldemort or the Fellowship must set out against the forces of Sauron. In each case, the archetypal battle between good and evil is typified by two camps of relatively equal power: Hogwarts versus Death Eaters, Rivendell versus Mordor, Jedi versus Sith. Such a structure makes for fantastic stories filled with legendary battles fought by iconic characters. But we should be careful not to conclude that the real world has to be that way.

For an author, creating a conflict between two forces—one obviously righteous and one clearly malevolent—is a useful device to rely on and, to a certain extent, we can find parallels between such tales and monotheistic philosophy. However, we mustn't forget Augustine's point that God is in a category of His own. As the Creator of everything else—including His so-called adversary, Satan—God is never in a position of genuine danger like Princess Leia or Frodo Baggins. Indeed, biblical conflict centers around the ultimate destiny of human souls caught between spiritual forces, *not* the final destiny of those spiritual forces themselves. Will we choose to fulfill our destiny as God has laid it out for us, or will we be tempted into choosing otherwise and missing out on all that we could possibly experience?

A Mordred-ful Model

While it's hard to find a perfect example of Augustine's conception of the Devil in pop culture, instead of *Harry Potter*, *Lord of the Rings*, or *Star Wars*, I can see a shadow of the idea in the old European legends of King Arthur and the Knights of the Round Table. If you recall the tale of Arthur's downfall, betrayed by the lecherous Lancelot, the King was attacked by his own son, Mordred, at Camlann. After a mighty battle, Mordred lies dead and Arthur must be spirited away to the isle of Avalon to recover from his terrible wounds; there the Once and Future King awaits to reclaim his kingdom and lead his people once more.

Here, just as in Augustinian theology, we have a devilish character who was originally innocent (Mordred), but who eventually grew to resent and rebel against the powerful ruler who created him (Arthur). The only reason Mordred had power is because of the King whom he sought to dethrone, but was never genuinely capable of replacing. Here we have a fair picture of the Devil's relationship with God. Any fight between these two forces is like swatting a fly with a Buick.

The Force Will Be with You . . . Always

This is not to say that we can't draw comparisons to the work of Rowling, Tolkien, or even George Lucas—we simply must be careful about the connections that we try to make. Anyone who uses the Force as their mental picture for understanding God's relationship with the Devil is as wrong as those who think that Greedo shot first.

As Augustine has helped us to see, the Devil is inferior to God, far from equal to his Creator, but wholly and freely opposed to Him. By allowing His creatures the ability to make free choices, God was required to allow us to sometimes make wrong decisions. Whenever we do this, we fail to live up to His perfect standard (or, we fail to reach the top of the climbing rope) and are forced to experience a diluted version of His reality; this freely chosen deprivation is evil and the Devil is simply one particular creature who has routinely and intentionally positioned himself as far from his Creator as possible. Neither evil nor Satan exist necessarily nor are in any way equal to God.

The Dark Side can't ever win since it's only diminished Goodness and doesn't actually exist on its own. Ultimately, any boxing match between Satan and Jesus is pointless, no matter how excited the people of South Park were to see it. Augustine makes it quite clear: there's no doubt over who's really "the undisputed ruler of your spiritual kingdom."

13
Our Demonic World

JONATHON O'DONNELL

Demons are readily available enemies. They're opponents of the heroes in fantasy novels from Patrick Rothfuss's *Kingkiller Chronicles* to Cassandra Clare's *The Mortal Instruments*, in television series like *Supernatural*, and in videogames such as *Diablo* and *Dragon Age*.

These demon personalities are sometimes nuanced (though more often not) and frequently have their own motives and their own positions in the works' setting and history. However, in all of these works, demons are an enemy that the audience can easily accept: to those of us living in the historically Christian West, the very word 'demon' carries certain connotations of evil, or at least of danger. By using that word, authors are able to use those connotations in a way that frees them from longwinded descriptions or explanations. Such demons might be violent and grotesque or subtle and seductive, corrupting or destroying.

Occasionally, a demon might break ranks and join the side of the good, but they are at best anti-heroes, frequently with a questionable moral code or wrestling with the inherent darkness of their nature. More often such characters will be part-demon, products of licit or illicit unions between a full demon and a human who are then forced to wage an internal war against some kind of genetic darkness.

The 2013 videogame *DmC: Devil May Cry*—a Western re-imagining of the existing Japanese franchise *Devil May Cry* by Cambridge-based developer Ninja Theory—is no exception. The game's narrative is bombastic and ridiculous, frequently

veering between parody and a critique of modern social ills so
ham-fisted one is left confused as to whether it is intentional
parody or simply lacking in elementary insight. Set in Limbo
City, the game stars Dante, a rebellious half-demon half-angel
'nephilim' who lives in a trailer and spends his days clubbing,
drinking and having one-night stands. This lifestyle is tragi-
cally brought to a close when his trailer-park paradise is
tracked down by demons in the employ of the demon king,
Mundus.

At this point, the narrative gradually reveals that the reality we humans know is a facade. Our world is ruled by demons
who manipulate an oblivious humanity through their control of
industries like the media, banking, and junk food. The social
commentary employed in this leaves little to imagination.
Mundus is known to the human world by the pseudonym Kyle
Rider, a prominent international banker whose office is littered
with photos of himself posed with various heads of state and
other political or religious leaders. The demon-run Raptor
News Network clearly parodies that of the American conserva-
tive Fox News Network in both rhetoric and appearance, with
its anchorman Bob Barbas being a thinly veiled expy of Bill
O'Reilly. The rebel group that Dante finally joins, The Order, is
an underground hacktivist organization, whose white-haired
leader Vergil (Dante's long-lost twin brother) wears a mask
strikingly reminiscent of the *V for Vendetta* masks infamously
used by hacking collective Anonymous. At the end of the story,
Dante and Vergil succeed in the mother of all WikiLeaks,
revealing the truth of this demonic cover-up to humanity at
large, and the game's ending plays out to a sequence of instant
messages, photographs and impromptu news articles as people
realize the truth of their enslavement and begin to fight back.

Limbo City

Rather than just through narrative, however, *Devil May Cry*
also portrays the interplay of illusion and reality, truth and
deception, through aesthetics and gameplay, specifically in its
use of the realm of Limbo. The realm of Limbo is portrayed as
the demonic reality behind the facade of the human Limbo
City, which is itself a thinly-veiled illusion designed to make
humans conform. Limbo is the world as it truly is, and in it the

demons who control the world are stripped of their human disguises, buildings twist and deform, CCTV cameras transform into unblinking eye-stalks, a television station becomes a prison for damned souls, and vending machines become organic monstrosities, the soft-drinks they dispense being their hallucinogenic body fluids. Ads and signs also alter to display 'true', hidden meanings: those advertising popular soft-drink 'Virility', for example, change to read 'Obesity' and 'Stupidity' (notice the level of subtlety here).

In one part of the game, Dante enters into the Raptor News Network itself to confront Bob Barbas's true form and the screen adopts the appearance of greyscale CCTV footage being broadcast on the news. Dante's battle is then given a commentary by Barbas in which his struggle is recast as the actions of an irrational, mentally disturbed vandal and terrorist. The game doesn't just wear its ideological heart on its sleeve, it then proceeds to rub said sleeve in your face several times in case you missed it.

There are few nuances here, and the overall message of anarchic rebellion against corrupt and corrupting powers is cut and dried. However, because of its gratuitous story and its conscious efforts to ape the spirit of the times in which it was produced, the game can shed light on some interesting representations of demons and the Devil in today's West, as well as their relation to notions of truth that are no longer tied closely to the religious heritage of demons themselves. The game portrays a struggle to reveal deception, but it is a deception with little room for traditional religious ideas of truth and is instead rooted in a more contingent and human-centered understanding of reality—though it has to be conceded that the representations that point to these more interesting concepts are probably mostly inadvertent.

From Absence to Counterfeit

Devil May Cry's demons fall into two categories, which in a sense are actually opposed to one another. On the one hand, the demons are the ones who have cast a glamor over our reality, allowing them to manipulate us in accordance with their evil whims and quest for dominance (the ultimate purpose of which, if there is one, is never revealed). On the other hand, the reality that they hide is itself demonic: a distorted world in which ordinary human laws and power are rendered meaningless. Angels never appear (aside from the figure of Dante's mother in his backstory) and the odd reference to them implies that they occupy the same twisted reality as the demons they oppose, that of Limbo.

As far as the narrative lets on, there's no ultimate reality beyond Limbo itself, and at the end of the tale humanity at large is given the power to see into Limbo directly and thereby see the hidden, ultimately demonic, truth of the world they thought they knew. This is quite unusual, and curiously makes *Devil May Cry*'s demons both the hider and the hidden, both those who try to obscure the true nature of reality and the true nature of the reality that is obscured. While at first glance the story might appear to replicate more traditional notions of demons or the Devil as a corrupting force that perverts civilization, the game's narrative complicates this. Let's see why.

Slavering Mindless Beast?

For a large portion of Christian history, the Devil was viewed mainly as a defeated power. While he was, technically, 'god of this world', Jesus's triumph over death in the Resurrection had ultimately condemned Satan to inevitable loss. His role as 'god of this world' was, in a sense, a title that highlighted his own powerlessness, because the seat of true power, of the true God, resided in Heaven. 'God of this world' was really no god at all. This powerlessness of the Devil can be seen in various texts, and is most clearly represented in his depiction in Dante's Inferno, from which the heroes of *Devil May Cry* take their names.

In the *Inferno*, written in the fourteenth century, Satan is a slavering, mindless beast, trapped in a frozen lake at the foot of a crater made when he fell from Heaven. He tries to free himself, but the beating of his wings merely hardens the ice that holds him. He is no real threat, merely an obstacle. The narrator Dante (not our Dante) and his guide Vergil (again, not our Vergil), simply climb down his body to pass beyond Hell into Purgatory. This passive, defeated image of demonic power extended into other aspects of society. Even as late as the twelfth century there are accounts of priests ritually summoning demons for information! Such practices, while frowned on, were not seen as heretical or dangerous: after all, demons were subordinate creatures who could pose no active threat to Christianity or God's divine plan. They were to be used, not feared.

This probably seems quite bizarre to a lot of modern readers. The Satan we know from popular culture is a seducer and schemer, debonair and alluring in his evil, and while ultimately out-thwarted by good is nonetheless a force to be reckoned with. Our current ideas of Satan owe more to John Milton's seventeenth-century epic poem *Paradise Lost* than they do to the *Inferno*. In this work, Satan is an active force striving to overthrow the forces of good and light, who succeeds through deceit in causing humanity's fall. This is the Devil we know: the calculated evil of *The Omen*'s Damien Thorne and *The Devil's Advocate*'s deliberately named John Milton, portrayed by Al Pacino.

One reason a passive, defeated Devil seems alien today is the way the Devil and his demons were viewed in Christian Europe shifted radically between the fourteenth and seventeenth centuries. This occurred in response to the rise of heretical movements (themselves arising in response to the devastation wrought by the Black Death), who sought to break away from the Catholic Church in pursuit of other forms of Christianity. The popularity of such movements not only needed an active response by the Church in the form of militant crusades but a more passive response in the reconsideration of doctrines. The result was a reimagining of the Devil as an active force of corruption, working to disrupt the unity of Christendom and subvert God's plan for history.

But Christianity now had a problem: the Devil was a fallen angel, a creation of God gone woefully astray rather than an independent evil power, as existed in some older religions. Since God was omnipotent, true power, specifically the power of creation, was His alone. As such, the Devil was deprived of the ability to create, or at least to create something lasting or 'true', but was now also required to be able to manipulate the human world in potentially threatening ways. This logic led to the idea that devilish powers could influence the world through a corruption of Christian sacraments and practices. This is where the legend of the infamous Black Mass originates, in which priests would perform the Eucharist on an altar made of a naked woman and services would end in mass orgies presided over by Satan in the form of a black cat or goat. While mostly a result of overactive imaginations, the Black Mass embodied a concept of a new and active Satanic power. The demonic ability to manipulate, seduce and corrupt was for the first time more than an act that damned foolish individual humans, but was able to create change through its distortions of existing institutions, beliefs, and rituals.

This transformation in how demons are seen to operate, and the growing scope of their power, had a number of consequences regarding their relationship with truth. In Christianity evil does not come from an independent source such as an evil co-equal deity, but neither does it spring fully from God as in older forms of Judaism where God creates both good and evil. The Devil is a fallen angel, cast down from Heaven for trying (and failing) to usurp God's throne. Evil is not a negative force that simply exists, but is the result of a willful turning away from Good, and is therefore an absence or lack of that Good.

The Devil's passivity in the *Inferno* is one form of this absence. Paralyzed and unthinking, the old Satan could only slobber and rage at his downfall. The new Satan, while still doomed to failure (since he fights against an omnipotent power), could actively attempt to challenge his fate. In doing so the absence of good and truth, which he had previously embodied is transformed into something more akin to a counterfeit of those qualities. For the first time Satan had some measure of individuality and of autonomy in his evil.

The difference between being simply false and being a counterfeit is important to note here. While a counterfeit is false, it is something false that appears like something true. A counterfeit is dangerous precisely because it can be mistaken for something real and genuine. This was the main danger of the new, active Satan and the heretical movements with which he was associated. Since he now had the power to draw active power through the corruption of existing beliefs and practices, a time could potentially arise in which such counterfeits of truth eclipsed the truth itself, rendering humanity little more than puppets of a Satanic system. Indeed, this is often the scenario envisioned and preached against by apocalyptic movements today, who condemn what they see as the Satanic influences of modern society turning people away from God. This is also the scenario described in the narrative of *Devil May Cry*, albeit with telling differences.

Just Humans and Demons

In *Devil May Cry*, the idea of demons as corruptors and usurpers of existing systems of power is most clearly portrayed through the game's representation of mass media, where The Order's hacktivist collective and the demon-run Raptor News Network war over the interpretation of reality and truth. The demonic reality is a lie, but it is a lie that all but the enlightened see as the truth. It is a counterfeit truth. The idea is also played with in regards to other real-world institutions the game shows demons controlling: food, finance, government, even foster care.

These are systems that must be claimed by the heroes, although they are secular rather than religious (religion, perhaps surprisingly, plays no role in the game's narrative). *Devil May Cry*'s Black Mass is conducted not in desecrated holy grounds but in corporate offices and television studios. As the game progresses, Dante and his allies in The Order strike at these institutions one by one, taking them from Mundus's control. However, this act of usurpation is itself something of a subversion. Prior to the final battle, Mundus attempts to dissuade Dante from his course by telling him that without his control the order that governs human civilization would collapse into anarchy, reverting to a primitive state of being. While on one level this is just the villain's standard line, attempting to persuade the hero that his tyranny is necessary, it more subtly implies that the systems that govern human civilization are demonic in origin. Dante and Vergil's struggle is not a struggle to reclaim corrupted institutions from demonic hands but to claim those institutions for humanity for the first time. Indeed, as Limbo City's facade unravels, the reality hidden beneath the surface is merely the demonic realm of limbo unveiled for ordinary humanity to see.

There is no mention of any God in *Devil May Cry* and the angels are little more than background flavor. There are just humans and the demons who control them, and who may really be the true architects of 'human' civilization. The game is about a rebellion against an evil society, but not one aimed at reclaiming a lost innocence or pristine past, or God's forgotten plan for the world. The image of the Devil as one who twists symbols and institutions for his unholy purposes is turned on its head in *Devil May Cry*—instead humanity must themselves 'corrupt' the symbols and institutions of a demonically-run civilization, twisting their power and influence in unintended ways to bring about change.

The demonic society depicted in *Devil May Cry* is a deception, a lie or counterfeit, and the only truth there is to find. Or at least the only truth that remains to be found, which is another question. Even if the angels embodied a higher truth, they are gone. And in the absence of any higher truths, what remains for a humanity freed from the chains of slavery except to manufacture their own? Such a conclusion is in keeping with its main narrative, which shares little with the religions from which the primary antagonists derive, instead drawing on ideas of secularity and individualism and a fear of conformity, authoritarianism and government control.

It's a very modern story, with a modern take on truth. When you pull back the veil of deception, what lies behind is not the eternal truth of a divine plan but something contingent, anarchic, and little different in form from the lies it has overthrown. 'Mundus' is the Latin word for 'world', probably an allusion to the classic unholy trinity of the World, the Flesh, and the Devil that led humanity away from God. The difference in *Devil May Cry* is that when the World is vanquished the path that opens up is not the path to God but just to another world, albeit one slightly freer than the one before it. Maybe.

14
The Elvish Devil

RAY BOSSERT

How might your perception of demons change if you weren't human? What would the Devil mean to you if you were, say, an elf from Middle-earth? Would demons evoke the same fears? Would the Devil have different powers that he could exert over you? Or would you have different powers you could exert over him?

These are implicit questions at the heart of Tolkien's *The Silmarillion*, a sort of Elvish Bible, drawn from a fictional manuscript originally composed *by* elves. In this book, the Devil-figure is named Melkor (the elves give him the nickname Morgoth). He is one of many Ainur (something like angels), created by the evidently omnipotent Eru (Iluvatar to the elves).

When Melkor descends to Middle-earth, he has free reign, causing earthquakes and volcanoes like a primordial fire-god. Perhaps even more troubling, Melkor is also free to genetically engineer the dreaded orcs, breeding them from kidnapped elves. This is the part of the book that always makes my skin crawl (well, this and the giant cosmic spiders). Orcs, those demonic-looking monsters with bad teeth and cockney accents, aren't really demons at all. From a strictly taxonomical basis, orcs are a species of elf—those otherwise beautiful, graceful creatures that stepped out of advertisements for hair products.

Melkor's transformation of the elves is called his "vilest" act, and much of the book reads like an attempt to understand why a creator-god capable of making such fabulous creatures as elves would allow Melkor to turn them against their wills into such loathsome things as orcs. Thus, *The Silmarillion* is about understanding evil as *elves* understand it.

Elvish Ideology

As the medieval philosopher Boethius (around 480–525) explains, we never really understand something according to *its* own, inherent nature; rather, we can only perceive things in terms of *our* own nature. We can't really comprehend what the Devil is, but we can understand what the Devil is *to us*, or, at least, we can understand the Devil in terms of human characteristics. We imagine Devils tempting us, tricking us, or even possessing our bodies, all to lead human souls to Hell.

But every element of *The Silmarillion*'s tales—from the creation narrative to predictions of the apocalypse—is colored by an *elvish* ideology. Elves understand the Devil in terms of elvish characteristics or what it means to be an elf. Because the main feature of Tolkien's elves is that they're artists, they perceive the cosmos in terms of art. Therefore, they perceive evil in terms of art as well. For elves, goodness is art that conveys wisdom and beauty, while evil is art (also called magic and technology) that dominates and distorts. For humans, the Devil is the tempter, the one who perverts reason and leads men to make poor choices that lead to damnation. For elves, Melkor is a bad artist who destroys beauty and corrupts artistic skill; his ill deeds have aesthetic effects rather than spiritual ones.

Tolkien Takes a Page out of Medieval Philosophy

Even though it's rooted specifically in aesthetics, the elvish understanding of evil overlaps with a very human medieval theology. Art requires design, and design requires a plan. The elvish faith that the universe follows an artist's plan resonates with a medieval belief in Providence, especially in light of Boethius's *Consolation of Philosophy* (around A.D. 524). Boethius was a Christian patrician who served as an official under Theoderic, king of the Ostrogoths, until Theodoric imprisoned and executed him for treason. Boethius wrote the *Consolation* in prison while awaiting his execution. He was a lofty-minded soul confined to live in a bleak, harsh age of brutality and barbarism. In this regard, one might imagine Boethius like some kind of elf living in a world overrun by vicious orcs and their cruel overlord.

Boethius was Tolkien's kind of a guy, and he was also a go-to source for medieval thinkers pondering the problem of evil. At first, the *Consolation* might seem an odd choice to talk about the Devil, since Boethius doesn't consider the Devil directly. But Boethius does investigate the question of evil. The *Consolation* asks why an omnipotent, all-knowing, loving God would allow evil to go unpunished and innocents to suffer. It's a dialogue between a forlorn, despairing Boethius and a personified Philosophy.

Boethius fears that random Fortune (not the Devil) rules the world, but Philosophy offers solace by using Socratic reasoning to explain the nature of good, evil, and Divine Providence. It is Boethius's description of Providence that Tolkien seems to have in mind when the elves rationalize how Iluvatar could permit a Melkor to even exist.

Describing Providence, Boethius famously juxtaposes free will against God's foreknowledge (medieval philosophers were very anxious that God's ability to see the future might prevent them from making their own choices). He argues that we see people making choices all the time, but that doesn't necessarily mean we influenced their choice; likewise, God (who transcends time) sees what people will freely choose without locking them into it. Boethius further argues that seeing our future choices allows God to anticipate them and set up the cosmos in ways that minimize damage or nudge us in the right direction.

Arts and Crafts with Iluvatar and Melkor

Tolkien, writing mythology, *shows* us precisely this Providence in the elves' creation myth: a story in which the world is made through music that incorporates the improvisations of many performers with the designs of a single composer. Iluvatar will tolerate Melkor's evil towards the elves because, in the end, it actually provides raw materials for well-crafted art.

Melkor's first evil deed occurs in a breakout solo performance during this celestial jam session. When Iluvatar commands his Ainur to play music for him, Melkor seizes the opportunity to improvise an original theme song "to increase the power and glory of the part assigned to himself." Here,

Melkor, who "had been given the greatest gifts of power and knowledge," sounds like a fairly standard Luciferean character—the mightiest of the angels who becomes overproud. Iluvatar has the Ainur play three times and does not finally stop Melkor until his antics become aesthetically repugnant. The Ainur were free to improvise; their free will is preserved, and their improvisations are incorporated into the overall theme—just as Boethius writes that God's foreknowledge embraces our choices.

During the third performance, Iluvatar's theme takes a deep, somber turn, but Melkor interrupts with a catchy, repetitive, and self-aggrandizing ditty. Tolkien, perhaps with a pun in mind, suggests that Melkor makes bad art—the original Devil music.

Bad art is that which doesn't express something greater, doesn't lift an audience to lofty desires. Instead, bad art expresses base, personal desires, or merely shows off. It's the difference between classical music and a commercial jingle. But, as Boethius will realize through his philosophy, it is impossible to really make anything independent of the Creator. Iluvatar informs his rebellious musician that he anticipated all of the changes, that even the best parts that Melkor improvised were still inspired by Iluvatar as the source of creation, and that the changes have not ruined Iluvatar's plan. Iluvatar also explains that the music had a secondary effect: it created the world (which Melkor wanted to create). In this way, Iluvatar already knows all that is to come; plus, he knows secret parts of the future creation that the Ainur don't know yet. And so, Tolkien invites the reader to imagine that nothing that happens in Middle-earth, no matter how heinous or evil or perverse, can ultimately destroy Iluvatar's artwork.

Melkor errs in seeking music as a means of gaining power rather than expressing truth or beauty, yet this is not quite how Melkor falls. He is impatient that the material world hasn't been created yet, so he thought he'd hurry the process along. Melkor wants to be a *maker*. This goal isn't bad—and, indeed, Iluvatar planned to do precisely what Melkor wanted done. The problem is that Melkor cannot actually make anything; as a creature (a created thing himself), he can only be an artist, never a true Creator.

Melkor, You're Doing It Wrong

Melkor's frustration can also be expressed in Boethius's philosophy. At one point, Boethius argues that all desire tends towards a good. Even material things like wealth, fame, and pleasure are good in themselves. Evil, for Boethius, derives from *how* we try to acquire what is good. He compares two men trying to reach the same goal: one follows a natural method and one uses an unnatural method. According to Boethius, the unnatural method will only ever approximate the goal; it will produce something that resembles the desired object, but it will be missing an important component, and therefore fail to satisfy.

Boethius is, of course, speaking about humans, not supernatural entities like Ainur, but the principle applies. In the beginning, Melkor's desires are for something good. As mentioned before, being a creator is typically a positive thing in Tolkien's imagination. Indeed, Iluvatar is himself a creator. However, Melkor can make nothing "that had life of its own, nor the semblance of life." He can only be what Tolkien calls a *sub-creator*—an artist.

For Tolkien, Iluvatar alone can create through natural means—it's his nature to make life from nothing. An artist might be highly skilled, but no artist ever caused a thing to exist without using pre-existing materials. At best, the artist takes elements of created matter and rearranges them to resemble something else, like mountains, or happy trees, or Italian cars, or giant space robots. Sub-creation is itself a grand and noble goal for Tolkien: the good sub-creator refines beauty and preserves wisdom. As Tolkien writes in his "Essay on Fairy Stories," true art is an attempt to enchant, to share emotion and express truth—it's what makes his vision of fantasy powerful and meaningful rather than just escapist titillation. Still, unnatural artists can pervert art's techniques into an exertion of power and domination. Tolkien argues this is the difference between how he uses the terms *art* and *magic*: the former is when tools are used for beauty, the latter is when tools are used for control.

Orcs

Discussion of sub-creation brings us back to the origin of orcs. Melkor despairs that he can only ever be a sub-creator rather than a creator. He isn't content with the good he's capable of: he desires the good of being the Primary Creator. He can never have this, though—so, like the bad man in Boethius, he takes a method "contrary to nature" and merely "approximates" his goal. Melkor, like Satan, is the "great ape"—a mimic of what he would be, and yet he fails at being a successful imitation. He sub-creates horrible things rather than beautiful ones: "that dark time Melkor bred many other monsters of divers shapes and kinds that long troubled the world" . . . like dragons or dinosaurs. Among them, the elves "by slow arts of cruelty were corrupted and enslaved; and thus did Melkor breed the hideous race of Orcs in envy and mockery of the Elves." Orcs aren't really a new thing, but they are as close as Melkor can muster.

Although he wishes to be a sole creator, Melkor doesn't breed a race of artists (artists would be potential rivals). He still manages to mold orcs in his own image, though, since they are instruments of domination and power. At Melkor's command, they destroy the very beauty that he deprived them of experiencing. The orcs, then, are Devilish philistines. They not only lack art, they are enemies of art. And yet that destruction becomes a source of a deeper, more somber beauty in the *text*. Iluvatar allows Melkor to destroy the artist elves because it makes a more beautiful story. It creates a sense of tragedy and enables the weaving of an epic tale. The elves are sacrificed on an altar of genre where Melkor unwittingly serves as antagonistic high priest. Iluvatar seems aware that he's in a story, and that the best stories need bad things to happen in them. Good art has its dark strokes as well as its light ones. The elves answer the problem of evil by imagining Melkor as a kind of cheap, corporate maker of bad art, and Iluvatar as a kind of deified Andy Warhol who takes bad art and transforms it into something edgy and new.

Children of Iluvatar

At first, it might seem unfair that elves can be sacrificed against their will for the sake of a story. At least in the narrative of Genesis, the serpent has to convince humans to disobey a direct order from God. The poor elves whom Melkor deceives and kidnaps haven't even met Iluvatar or the Valar (the Ainur who live in Middle-earth). It doesn't seem very sporting. It's a bit as if the serpent convinced Adam and Eve to eat the apple before they were told not to—but God banished them from Eden anyway.

Although both elves and humans are described as Children of Iluvatar, the relationship between Creator and creation is vastly different for the two races, so the relationship between Devil and elf is different as well. Melkor has leeway over these elves that would be nightmarish to imagine for humans—a Devil that could just snatch whole populations away and transform them into a race of hideous slaves is a terrifying prospect. It steals away the notions of free will. If orcs, like Lady Gaga, are just "born that way," who can expect them to behave differently? Furthermore, if their behavior is generally evil—raping, looting, and pillaging the homes of elves and people—what hope could they ever have of salvation?

No Elves Go to Heaven

Unless, of course, elves never had hope of salvation to begin with. And what's a devil to do with a creature that can't be damned? When an elf is killed, their spirit goes to a place called "the Halls of Mandos"—possibly forever. Sometimes elves can be reincarnated, but this isn't standard protocol, and residence in the Halls of Mandos isn't a particularly desirable fate. Worse yet, elvish lore suggests that the world will eventually end and be recreated, but that there's no guarantee that elves have a place in the new world. Elves are part of the world in a way that humans aren't—and though wiser and in some ways more powerful beings, they are more subject to the influences of the world. Orcs are not demons, nor are elves angels (although Tolkien writes they are "more like in nature to the Ainur" than men). Their spiritual nature is much more united to physical nature (perhaps this is why an elf, not a man, wounds Melkor in battle).

Boethius wouldn't offer elves much consolation on this point. He writes that eternity mustn't be thought of as infinite time, but as a state outside of time. Therefore, physical creatures can't really experience eternity because their physical natures bind them to time (the measurement of physical change). The elves seem to realize this. Despite their enormously long lives, elves are tied to time because they are tied to the physicality of Middle-earth; they aren't designed for true eternity. As Tolkien writes in his essay "On Fairy Stories," faerie aren't meant for Heaven or Hell; theirs is a third road.

The point is, this elvish ontology helps explain the Melkor's behavior. Elves aren't merely artists; they're material for art itself. Using them to make bad art can be vile, but it doesn't necessarily defeat their inherent purpose for being. In a meta-fictional way, elves very much exist only to make stories for humans.

What's at Stake?

The stakes in the battle between humans and the Devil are eternal life and a place in Heaven. The stakes in the battle between elves and Melkor are how long you get to keep your fancy fortress in the posh section of Middle-earth—something that will inevitably fall to the ravages of entropy anyway. This should bring some comfort to the real-world human reader of the story as we are, in a fashion, more valuable than elves. Despite their long, glamorous lives, the elves refer to human death as "the Gift of Iluvatar." Human death isn't a punishment, but a providential intervention to spare us the effects of Melkor's influence on the world. Ultimately, Tolkien isn't really writing about elves or the Devil—he's writing about us.

To argue that an elvish myth on evil ends up being a story about the nature of man might sound like a kind of anthropocentrism, but it again returns us to Boethius's medieval worldview. Boethius holds that humans are the greatest beings of physical creation—so long as they remember they were made to be so; Boethius also argues they become lower than animals when they forget their nature. Healthy self-esteem is the key to happiness.

Tolkien invites us to better understand ourselves by imagining what we aren't. Had Melkor turned humans into orcs, then evil could erase our free will. But human freedom is necessary for *both* Tolkien and Boethius because humans face final judgment; we choose Heaven or Hell. We can be judged only if we are responsible for our actions; we can only be responsible if our choice is free. Elves face no final judgment, so they enjoy freedom far more precariously. Our freedom is necessary for the long-term plan; elvish freedom is not. Melkor might exert immense physical power, but he can only mess with things that don't upset the final goal.

The Mythical MacGuffin

Early in *The Silmarillion*, Melkor is imprisoned by the Valar for his misdeeds to other creatures. However, the Valar eventually release Melkor when he seems to have reformed. Obviously, Melkor's reformation is short lived, and we discover evil and art are related in a second profound way. After certain elvish tribes are brought to Valinor (the home of the Valar), an elf named Feanor creates the silmarils—jewels that capture liquid light from enchanted trees. Melkor burns with desire for the silmarils more fiercely than a geek waiting in line for a Comic-Con exclusive collectible. Melkor desires art. That's a healthy enough desire since a goal of art is to produce desirable objects.

But, as Boethius writes, obsession with private property is the first influence that destroys the relative peace of primitive human society. Most dramatic conflict, whether in fiction or in real life, derives from different people wanting the same objects. In the case of *The Silmarillion*, those objects are pieces of art—the titular silmarils. Melkor doesn't just appreciate art; he becomes an obsessed collector, literally hell-bent on claiming the silmarils. His desire to own overwhelms his desire to produce: consumerism spoils the artist. After stealing the silmarils, Melkor wears them in a crown (bringing to mind Boethius's warning that we make an "obvious mistake" when we think decorations make us beautiful when our souls are ugly). His possession of the jewels leads Feanor's tribe to swear an oath to reclaim them, and the elvish epic becomes a struggle of elf against Devil not for eternal life, but over the control of art in Middle-earth.

Even after the Valar finally imprison Melkor, the war for art continues on with Melkor's protégé, the demonic Sauron, also known as the Lord of the Rings. Sauron is like Melkor in that they are both originally from the Ainur (although Sauron is a lower-ranking spirit), and therefore more or less fallen angels. Unlike Melkor, Sauron is not only the obsessed collector, he is also the producer and even arguably the material of the art he most desires—he forged the One Ring from his own essence. It's a bit narcissistic. And the rings themselves are also unlike the silmarils (whose only purpose was to be pretty); Sauron constructs rings of power not beauty. In the hands of a devil, art is perversely used as a means to dominate rather than elevate. It is the bad art that Tolkien calls magic. In the *Lord of the Rings* trilogy, Sauron's ring can only be used in a devilish way—and, thus, anyone who would use it becomes devilish.

Going in Circles

In Tolkien's fiction, the Devil becomes a tangible, material figure. Although he begins as a supernatural entity, he is, in a way, incarnate, and adopts a physical form that seems to calcify the longer he dwells in Middle-earth. While this physical manifestation allows him certain super-human strength over lesser creatures, it also brings weaknesses—such as his injury at the hands of the elf Fingolfin, and, later in the story, his capacity to be stunned by a seductive sleeping spell cast by the elf Luthien.

Melkor's evil makes him less than he was, and Boethius's Philosophy describes evil as having precisely just such an enervating effect on its practitioners. Wickedness, as Philosophy explains, is its own punishment because it strips humanity away from the criminal; wickedness literally turns humans into beasts—an image that resonates with the transformation of elves into orcs.

Furthermore, Boethius suggests that evil—the attempt to rebel against God's authority—ironically makes you more subject to external forces. Toward the end of his treatise, Boethius's Philosophy depicts Providence in an analogy: a spinning disc with God at its center. The more you move away from the center of the disc, the further you find yourself being dragged around as the disc spins. In his attempt to flee Iluvatar's influence, Melkor might be said to experience precisely this kind of motion. Whereas he had once been free to improvise in the celestial choir of Iluvatar, the worldly Melkor must consider a myriad of real world factors that limit his actions. Away from Iluvatar, he must anticipate the influence of the Valar on his long term plans, the military strength of various elvish armies, the effect of political alliances between elves and men, not to mention resource acquisition and management for his own forces. Melkor's rebellion has, in fact, made him far less free than he was under Iluvatar. His quest to dominate Middle-earth forces him to react to the wills of inferior beings.

From an elvish perspective, the Devil is not merely a power that exerts itself over lesser creatures, he is an individual with personal character traits that leave him vulnerable to being tempted, baited, frightened, and even captured. Thus, Tolkien shows how this Devil's limitations leave him well within the confines of Providence.

VI

C.S. Lewis's Satan

15
The Illogical Road to Hell

MICHAEL VERSTEEG AND ADAM BARKMAN

When someone mentions the Devil, what's the first image that pops into your head? A demonic king who rules over a valley of fire? Or maybe even one of your relatives at Thanksgiving dinner? Most people would answer that they imagine something along the lines of a man colored in red who has the legs of a goat, a long tail, horns, a goatee, and carries around a pitchfork.

Although this picture of the Devil may seem either childish or terrifying to some, the popular Christian novelist and Oxford professor, C.S. Lewis (1898–1963), imagines the Devil in quite a different fashion, somewhat more perilous than a sunburnt faun from Narnia. According to Lewis, the Devil is not a material creature that attacks in plain sight; he is a cunning, spiritual being who seeks to manipulate and capture the human mind, stealing us away from our heavenly home. It is his ultimate desire to steer human beings, similar to cattle, into the gates of Hell itself, so that we may dwell with the damned as "food" for the demonic host. At this point you might just think to yourself, "The sunburnt faun doesn't sound so bad anymore now does it?"

By manipulating the human mind and thereby persuading us to follow him, the Devil seeks to claim us as his own. If this is so, how exactly does he go about doing this? Lewis suggests that the Devil manipulates the human mind, not by clear and sound argumentation and reasoning, but rather the opposite— through unreason, cloudy-mindedness, and bad logic. The Devil's tactic can be understood as *irrational* persuasion, in which he promotes fallacious, or faulty reasoning to steer the human mind towards his own goals. This depiction of the devil is made clear in Lewis's satirical work *The Screwtape Letters* (1942), in which he imagines a written correspondence between the two demons Wormwood, an aspiring young tormentor, and his uncle Screwtape, an experienced demon in close contact with the Devil himself. In a series of letters Screwtape provides advice to his nephew regarding Wormwood's "patient," noting the various ways by which to manipulate the human mind through the subversion or inhibition of human *reason*.

Irrational Thinking

According to Screwtape, argument is too unpredictable. Engaging a human's reason would be fighting on "the Enemy's" or God's own ground since, according to Lewis, reason is an aid to Heaven. Thus, rather than arguing their way into the human mind, Screwtape suggests that evading human reason is a much more productive route. By doing so, these devils are able to promote irrational thinking within the human mind, making a human person susceptible to fallacious reasoning. As a result, false conclusions can be produced and ideas become unnoticeably twisted and construed without a person knowing it.

Although Screwtape and Wormwood are not themselves the Devil, their tactics and techniques found in *The Screwtape Letters* exemplify the same manipulative character of the Devil that Lewis wants to convey: a deceitful and cunning spirit, who uses bad reasoning and poor logic to steer us according to his own purposes. He is the Great Deceiver, the Master of Irrationality, drawing us away from Heaven and from God by supplementing our minds with poor reasoning.

Now, if fallacious logic and bad reasoning are the ways by which the Devil tries to influence us, what exactly does sound logic and good reasoning look like?

Logically Bedeviled

Logic is the tool by which philosophers, or any rational-minded person for that matter, engage in argumentation. Similar to the laws of arithmetic within mathematics, there also exist within the discipline of logic certain laws for problem-solving and critical thinking. These laws include those such as the *Law of Non-Contradiction* or *Modus Ponens*.

These laws provide us with guidelines to form arguments while also enabling us to differentiate between good and bad reasoning. If an argument employs correct and logical reasoning, then such an argument will follow these laws and guidelines and can be taken as a good argument. If an argument follows incorrect and illogical reasoning, then it will end up violating these laws, committing what is known as a *logical fallacy*, defined simply as an error of thinking. Examples of logical fallacies may include the *Genetic Fallacy, Ad Hominem, Post Hoc Ergo Propter Hoc*, and the *Straw-Man Fallacy*. Such logical fallacies emerge when logic is carelessly applied or ignored completely, producing bad arguments and poor reasoning. Logic is the standard of how we are able to assess good and bad arguments; it is how we are able to recognize both sound and faulty reasoning.

Lewis points out that the Devil wants nothing more than to divorce the human mind from proper logical thought. If our minds are not guarded by reason and logic, we then become susceptible to all kids of irrational argumentation, easily manipulated by the Devil's fallacious logic. In *The Screwtape Letters* the devils Screwtape and Wormwood recognize this fact, and try to exploit it. In his first letter to Wormwood, Screwtape informs his nephew that it is better to avoid or undermine human reason altogether rather than to engage it and put forth arguments in trying to influence the human mind. To see just how these devils go about their devious business let's look at some of the advice that this aged devil has for his nephew.

Demonic Inception

Screwtape suggests that one of the best ways to incapacitate human reason is to blind or suppress it with unclear and hazy ideas. As Screwtape says, "Keep his mind off the plain antithesis between True and False. Nice shadowy expressions—'It was a phase'—'I've been through all that'—and don't forget the blessed word 'Adolescent.'" The proposed idea here is to evade the obvious question of whether or not something is true or false by putting labels upon a certain belief; in this instance,

Christianity. Thus, instead of considering whether or not something is true or likely true, the goal here is to focus a person's mind on a specific "term," in the hopes that the very consideration of truth itself will go unaddressed within their thinking. This method, according to Screwtape, uses what he calls *jargon,* or "practical propaganda."

Wormwood's patient, we are told, is undergoing a "dry patch," or a "trough," in which he is experiencing emotional instability towards his newly adopted Christian faith. Screwtape suggests that in order to exploit the patient's emotional state Wormwood ought to fill the patient's mind with jargon, suggesting to him that his newfound Christian faith is but a "religious phase" which he'll just lose interest in. What Screwtape intends here is to focus the patient's mind exclusively on the jargon term "religious phase," rather than on the question of the veracity of Christianity. This, however, diverts the patient from the main issue at hand: is his Christian faith, wavering or otherwise, true?

By diverting the patient's attention from this main issue, Screwtape and Wormwood have influenced Wormwood's patient to commit the logical fallacy known as the *Red Herring,* or the *Beside-the-Point* fallacy. This fallacy is committed when a given statement or premise misleads or distracts one's attention from the main issue at hand. Although a person may experience disinterest towards a specific belief, such a fact is wholly independent of whether or not the belief in question is true! By simply labeling Christianity a "religious phase," the patient is unconsciously drawn away from the question of whether or not Christianity is true. And if he is not careful, such a question will continue to go unaddressed and, in the hopes of Screwtape and Wormwood, the patient may simply dismiss Christianity on the basis of its being called "a religious phase." In a clever way, this fallacious logic leads one away from even considering the invaluable question of whether or not something is true. But, logically speaking, what exactly happens if the patient does dismiss Christianity as false *on the basis* of his losing interest in it?

Non-Sequitur

From a logical standpoint, for the patient to conclude "Christianity is false" based on the premise "I am losing interest in Christianity" is a good example of the logical fallacy known as *Non-Sequitur,* meaning "it does not follow." This fallacy is committed when a specific conclusion is not warranted from the argument's premises. The basic premise in this case, "I am losing interest in Christianity," is entirely disconnected from the conclusion "Christianity is false," and would therefore be considered an invalid argument. Now, if Screwtape *were* trying to use reason or argumentation within the mind of the patient, this fallacy would be easily recognized for what it is: an error of thinking. But that is exactly why Screwtape wants to *avoid* reason and argument in the first place! He recognizes that he would be committing a non-sequitur if he tried to use reason to persuade the patient to conclude, in this instance, that Christianity is false. Thus, he is quite right in saying, "There is no conceivable way of getting *by reason* from the proposition 'I am losing interest in this' to the proposition 'This is false.' But, as I said before, it is jargon, not reason, you must rely on." Since reason would only inhibit Screwtape's intentions, he must rely on fallacious logic to do the job.

So, if clear thinking and valid reasoning would show the Devil to be a deceiving fraud, it makes sense that the Devil would rely upon the antithesis of reason—unreason—as the method by which he tries to influence the human mind. Indeed, according to Lewis, if we're guided by reason we would logically arrive at the Pearly Gates, since reason can, from Lewis's perspective, bring us to the doorstep of Heaven (of course to *enter* in other things are required!).

Influencing a human person to reason poorly and make an illogical conclusion would certainly serve the Devil's purposes in leading us further into his embrace and further from "the Enemy." By diverting us from the "plain antithesis between True and False" and leading us to produce false conclusions, the Devil makes us think what he wants us to, guiding us on the "gentle slope" towards Hell. And if the Devil can derail or circumvent human reason altogether, as Screwtape attempts with his so-called jargon, the mind becomes susceptible to ill-reasoned arguments and manipulation.

Educated Ignorance

Reason, according to Lewis, is not only our best defense against the Devil's schemes, it's also a tool given to us to help us on the road to Heaven. Thus, the last thing the Devil wants is for us to arrive at the truth on solid rational grounds. If the Devil can stump our rationality, he will do so in a subtle and unnoticeable way. And in this next case it seems the Devil can even make irrationality be perceived as "educated" and "learned."

In one of his letters to Wormwood, Screwtape refers to something that he calls "The Historical Point of View." This refers to a specific perspective in regard to history that views statements from the past with unmitigated suspect and criticism. The "learned man," according to Screwtape, doesn't ask whether or not any statement made by an ancient author is true or false; rather, he only asks who influenced the author, or about the general history of that time period, or the significance of such a historical statement. Those who lived in the past are seen as unsophisticated or unenlightened since, after all, what could pre-modern and ignorant medieval or ancient authors possibly know, right? According to Screwtape, here are the ramifications of such an idea:

> To regard the ancient writer as a possible source of knowledge—to anticipate that what he said could possibly modify your thoughts or your behavior—this would be rejected as unutterably simple-minded. And since we cannot deceive the whole human race all the time, it is most important thus to cut every generation off from all others; for where learning makes a free commerce between the ages there is always the danger that the characteristic errors of one may be corrected by the characteristic truths of another. But thanks be to Our Father and the Historical Point of View, great scholars are now as little nourished by the past as the most ignorant mechanic who holds that 'history is bunk.'

According to this view of history, any claims or statements made in the past are simply dismissed based upon their temporal position within history itself. As was the case with Screwtape's red-herring jargon, the consideration of truth or falsity of such historical claims or statements is simply unaddressed. Such historical statements are just dismissed at face value on the basis of their existing within the past. And the goal, according to Screwtape, is to "cut every generation off from every other," preventing truths which lie within history from correcting the errors of the present. This apparently "educated" and "learned" perspective on the past is, however, deeply fallacious. In fact, Lewis himself was partly responsible for coining the name of this specific logical fallacy—the fallacy of *Chronological Snobbery*.

You Snob, You

Chronological Snobbery consists of the "uncritical acceptance of the intellectual climate common to our own age and the assumption that whatever has gone out of date is on that account discredited." The assumption is that the modern historian is in some way supremely "privileged" compared to those who lived in prior centuries. Now, just because something was stated or believed to be true in the past, such a fact does not therefore entail that the statement or belief itself is on that basis false. It could very well be that views from the past are, in fact, false. But truth or falsity is based on argument and evidence, not upon a thing's temporal displacement. For example: the Ptolemaic model of the galaxy has indeed been shown to be inaccurate. But such a fact is based on evidence from modern cosmology, not upon the premise "this model of the galaxy goes back to ancient Greece." The question of when or where a statement may have been said has no weight or consequence upon the truth or falsity of that belief. And to suggest otherwise is to commit the fallacy of Chronological Snobbery, as Screwtape would want us to do, preventing us from learning from the past.

In order to come to the conclusion of whether or not something is true, such a task involves rational discourse and looking at the statement or belief itself. You can't rule out a statement or claim immediately based upon its position in time. But truth, from the Devil's perspective, is something which he must steer us clear of. Proper rational discourse is exactly what the Devil wants to *prevent*. Thus, the fallacy of Chronological Snobbery is used by the Devil, according to Lewis, to keep us from the truth. If one falls for this fallacious view of the past, it is easy to conclude such things as "those medieval Christian scholars were full of fluff," or even "the Bible is *just* an ancient document—it's of no great significance anymore." This fallacious perspective of history precludes any possibility of one's finding truth or knowledge within the past. And from the Devil's perspective, such a view would lead one to possibly preclude any possibility of truth being found in "primitive" religion—such as Christianity—in which case, his manipulation has succeeded.

The Circle of Hell

The Devil has many tricks up his sleeve—either by inhibiting reason itself or convincing us we are rational or "learned" when we are not. He persists in confusing our minds, and in this case, causing our heads to spin.

Wormwood's patient has become an increasingly humble man and Screwtape wants to exploit this new development. Screwtape suggests that Wormwood draw the patient's attention to the fact itself that he has become humble, claiming that, "all virtues are less formidable to us once the man is aware that he has them." When the man is feeling lowly or down-in-the-dumps, Wormwood is told to sneak the idea into his mind that the patient, being in the frame of mind he is in, is being humble. And according to Screwtape, at the onset of this realization the patient will almost immediately gain a sense of pride at his own humility, thinking to himself "By Jove! I'm being humble.'" Once this has occurred, Screwtape instructs that if the patient becomes aware of his pride and tries to smother it, Wormwood ought to lead the patient to feel proud of his very attempt of suppressing his pride, making him think again of how humble he really is! But again, pride at his own humility will consequently appear and the patient will once again try to suppress his pride. At this point, Wormwood would once again make him feel proud for recognizing his pride. In this situation, the patient's mind would be filled with a cycle of phasing between pride and humility, which could last indefinitely. Here's a step-by-step sequence of the patient's train of thought to demonstrate exactly what is going on:

1. **(H) Humble**

2. **(P) Proud of his own humility**

3. **(H) Humble again by recognizing and trying to suppress his pride**

4. **(P) Proud of suppressing his pride**

5. (H) Humble again by recognizing and trying to suppress one's pride

6. (P) Proud of suppressing one's pride

7. Etc.

In this situation the patient's train of thought becomes trapped within a potentially unending regression. This is possibly an example of a *Logical Paradox*, or more accurately, an *Infinite Regress*, wherein a causal relationship is transmitted through an indefinite series of sets. The causal relationship in question revolves around the natures of humility and pride, which are diametrically opposed to one another. Humility excludes pride, and vice versa. And in this situation the patient's sense of humility is causally linked to his becoming proud, which in turn is linked to his becoming humble again since one cannot be both humble and proud at the same time. It becomes a continual shift between being humble and proud, a potentially never-ending cycle.

Logically speaking, this causal relationship could continue to cycle for an infinite amount of time. However, the idea here for Screwtape is simply, once again, to confuse or subvert the patient's reason. An infinite regress, in this case, would override the patient's reason since it causes him to think in a circle. It would confuse and inhibit reason, since one cannot rationally argue out of an infinite regression. And the Devil, wanting the human mind to be divorced from human rationality, is eager to employ any tactic, such as this, which would inhibit one's ability to think in a coherent manner.

Highway to Hell

These are some of the logical fallacies that Screwtape and Wormwood practice in *The Screwtape Letters*, and all are examples of what happens when logic and proper reason—the children of *Logos* Himself—do not guide the human mind. Such fallacies exemplify the manipulative technique that the Devil himself would employ in trying to influence the human mind. Red-Herring, Non-Sequitur, Chronological Snobbery, and Infinite Regress—all are examples of the way in which the Devil attempts to steer us according to his own purposes.

It's not through reason that the Devil persuades us, for reason, according to Lewis, is an aid on the road to Heaven. The Devil must rely rather upon unreason, irrational thinking, and fallacious logic to manipulate the human mind. And if reason is the road to Heaven, than unreason could be said to be the highway to Hell.

16
Either Demons Exist or God Doesn't

Thomas Ward

It can be enlightening talk about how the *idea* or *character* of the Devil in movies, novels, and other works of art gives us this or that insight into human nature or our place in the world. But let's cut to the chase: does the Devil really exist?

Most thinking people nowadays would say *no*. If pressed, they might explain that the Devil and other demons are a superstition from a bygone age, they're incompatible with a scientific understanding of the world, they're mere inventions of wicked priests who sought to scare people into submission, they're mental makeshifts, projections of subjective human terrors onto the world of nature, and so on.

But C.S. Lewis—of *The Chronicles of Narnia* fame—said that the Devil and other demons do exist, and he gave a philosophical argument for his view in his book called *The Problem of Pain* (1940). Lewis was an academic, literary critic, medievalist, novelist, poet, as well as a lay theologian, and Christian apologist. We need the Devil and other demons, he thinks, to explain how certain kinds of evil can exist in this World alongside an all-knowing, all-powerful, all-good God, as envisioned by Christians, Jews, and Muslims. Or to put it more bluntly: if you believe in God and want to be a reasonable person, you've got to believe in the Devil, too. It's a *damned* good argument given certain assumptions which aren't crazy.

Non-Crazy Notions about God

These non-crazy assumptions boil down to two basic views: first, God exists; second, there is no evil for which God is morally responsible. To say that God exists is to say that there is a being that is ultimately responsible for the existence of the universe and everything in it. Since He has made everything, we can assume that he has an extremely high degree of Power, so high in fact that He can do anything that can be done in our universe. For all practical purposes, He is *All-Powerful*. Also, since He invented everything that He made (what else could have invented it?), we can assume that he has an enormous intelligence; so He's *All-Knowing*. And since He has no need of anything and yet does good things for people all the time (like bring them into existence), we say that God is extremely Good or, to fit the pattern, that He's *All-Good*.

Because God is All-Knowing he always knows what is good to do. Because God is All-Powerful he always can do what He knows to be good to do. And because God is All-Good he always wants to do what is good. So it seems to follow that God couldn't possibly be morally responsible for any evil. For surely to act in a way such that you're morally responsible for evil is to fail to do good. But God can't fail to do good—He knows what's good, can do what's good, and wants to do what's good. That's just what it's like to be God.

Lots of reasonable people accept this view about God and lots don't. We're not going to settle who's right in a few pages— or even try to. This is why I'm saying that this view about God is *not-crazy* rather than *true* or *false*. If you believe in God but *not* in the Devil or demons, you might develop a new belief by the end of this chapter. If you believe neither in God nor demons, then just roll with me for the sake of argument; probably you'll come to a better understanding of what believers believe in, or ought to believe in, and a better understanding is always a good thing.

The Problem of Evil

Lewis's argument for demons begins with reflection on the so-called *problem of evil*, which is almost surely the best reason for not believing in God. It tries to show that people who believe all that stuff about God, in particular that He's All-Powerful and All-Good, have unwittingly committed themselves to believing contradictory propositions, and no reasonable person wants to be caught doing that. Think about it: if God is All-Powerful then it seems to follow that God can prevent any evil from happening; and if God is All-Good it seems to follow that He wants to prevent any evil from happening. But evil happens all the time. Something's gotta give.

It's hard to see how we're going to deny that there's evil in the world. So it looks like what's gotta give is something about God: either He isn't All-Good, or He isn't All-Powerful, or He's neither, or He doesn't exist at all.

Everyone I know who has taken the trouble to think about the problem of evil has come to feel its force, no matter what they believe about God. But many people have thought that the problem doesn't pose quite as serious a threat to the reasonableness of belief in God as it seems to at first glance. They point to various possible reasons why God might have allowed evil to occur. For example, evil seems to be necessary for some really great human qualities to emerge, such as courage, mercy, and forgiveness. These really add to the overall goodness and nobility of the person who has them. And people with qualities like these really do add to the goodness and nobility of the universe as a whole. So maybe God allowed there to be evil so these qualities could have a place in the world. Others have suggested different reasons why God might allow there to be evil. But the most common suggestion by far is what has come to be called the *free will defense*.

You Made You Do It

A Christian philosopher-saint named Augustine of Hippo (354–430) usually gets the credit for the free will defense. Here's the basic idea: God has made a world that contains free agents—people like you and me—and we can use our freedom for good or for evil. When you cheat on your taxes or squash a spider you're freely doing evil and it's your fault, not God's. When you give your coins to the Salvation Army or mow your neighbor's strip of lawn that's adjacent to yours, you're freely doing good and you get the credit. Maybe there are demons and angels on our shoulders, but they can't make us do anything; we're free to do what we want.

Sure, God knew, or at least had a pretty good idea, that his free agents would misuse their freedom and do all the very naughty things we've done over the centuries. But He made us free agents anyway. Why? Because you've got to be free to be able to love, and God judges that love is a very great good. Without freedom we couldn't love each other and we couldn't love God. If you think hard enough about what makes a world good, you'll see pretty quickly that the best sort of world is not merely a world without evil. It's easy to imagine a world with no evil that's actually pretty boring: suppose that instead of making our world God made a different world which contained exactly one thing—a yellow rubber ducky. This world would have no evil in it, because the rubber ducky can't do any evil and there's nothing else in the world to do evil to the rubber ducky. But this world is nothing really to write home about.

On the other hand, a world like ours which contains a great deal of love, even though it comes with a boatload of evil, is a world that is at worst very interesting and at best very good indeed.

So, yes, there is evil, and yes, God is All-Powerful and therefore could prevent all evil; but God is All-Good, and the way He has chosen to express this goodness in our world is *not* to will the non-existence of evil but instead to create free agents who have the ability both to love and to hate, to do good and to do evil. And there's nothing inconsistent about these claims. So it looks like we can be realistic about the evil in the world and still hold on to a traditional conception of God as All-Powerful and All-Good.

The Baby Bat

The free will defense says that God's not to blame for the evil in the world—*we* are. And maybe this really does get God off the hook for lots of evil: all the evil things, in fact, that come about as a result of the free decisions of human beings. But surely this doesn't cover all the evil there is. Not every drought or flood or hurricane or tornado can be blamed on human-induced climate change. My wrath has never to my knowledge caused an earthquake. And what man, woman, or child is there under heaven who could be blamed for what happened to the baby bat?

The baby bat haunts my dreams. A philosopher named John Perry told this story about a cave with bats hanging from the roof, as bats do, with an enormous mound of guano (that means *bat poo*) on the floor. Cockroaches live in and feed on the guano. One time this baby bat lost its grip (its baby bat claws were tiny and weak) and fell down to the mound. It broke its little baby bat wing, so it couldn't fly back up to the roof to mommy and daddy bat. And, it turns out, cockroaches don't always eat just bat poo; they'll take baby bat when they can get it. So as the baby bat sank down into the guano the cockroaches made a meal of it.

Then there's the deer in the forest. This story comes from another philosopher, William Rowe. Think of Bambi, but instead of having his mom killed by a hunter, he is caught in a lightning-caused forest fire. He tries to run to safety, but he's badly burned. Finally he makes it to a clearing and escapes the fire, but it's too late—he's mortally wounded. He dies slowly, in agony from his burns and panting with thirst.

Evil like this, evil that doesn't seem to be caused by human beings, is sometimes called *natural evil* because, it seems, it's just a part of nature, a part of the way the world is set up. Lightning, fire, and flesh just do their thing, and too bad for Bambi. Gravity, guano, and cockroaches do their thing, and the baby bat is *S.O.L.* And things get worse when we think about natural evils that happen *to* human beings, which we won't do now because that would just make us even more depressed.

The free will defense is no use here, it seems. Evils that humans do with their freedom might be tolerable in a world with the great good of love, but what good is achieved in a world with natural evil?

Demons to the Rescue

This is where the Devil and demons save the day—philosophically, I mean. Since humans aren't morally responsible for natural evils, we're left with three alternatives: God is morally responsible for natural evils, nothing is, or something else is. We can rule out the first alternative right away because it's the contradiction of one of our basic presuppositions—God's not morally responsible for any evil. The whole point of a solution to the problem of evil is to show that God really is who His followers say He is: All-Good and All-Powerful. So it's really just about those last two alternatives: either nothing is morally responsible for natural evils, or something else is.

But *something's* gotta be morally responsible for these evils given our presuppositions. These say that at the Back of All Things there is an All-Good *Person*; this means that what goes on in this world has come about, either in whole or in part, due to *decisions* made by this divine Person. It follows from this that nothing happens by chance; for all that happens, someone has decided that it should happen. The bad things we humans perpetrate are in part due to God's decision to keep us in existence and sustain the regular order of nature. But the *morally relevant* part of these bad actions gets pinned on human decisions. By definition we don't have humans to blame for natural evils, so every aspect of a natural evil, including the morally relevant part, has got to be assigned to some non-human decisions. Not to God's, by hypothesis. So to something else's.

The *something else* here has got to have a certain kind of nature. It's got to be non-human and non-divine. It's got to be personal, that is, it's got to have intelligence and a will and be capable of making decisions and acting. Oh, and since the something else (or the *somethings* else) must be the perpetrator(s) of all natural evil, they've got to be at least a little bit wicked. Or maybe a lot wicked, once you start thinking more about that baby bat. And It or They must have superhuman powers, since they can do a lot more than make a baby bat fall from the roof: they can cause earthquakes and terrible storms, they can direct an asteroid to earth or cause a solar flare big enough to shut down our smartphones for a couple of days. That's serious power. And for all we can tell they must be spirits rather than animals, since we have no notion of an unseen animal that could cause an earthquake or a solar flare. So here's what we have on our hands: a super-human, non-divine, personal, malevolent spirit. And that's about as good a definition of *Devil* as you're ever going to find.

Here's the payoff: all the evil things in the world not caused by human actions are caused by diabolical actions. The demons are free just like we are, and they were made free for the same reasons we were: to love each other and to love God. This means that the demons weren't made to be demons; originally they were good spirits, like guardian angels, Gabriel, St. Michael and all that crew, but unlike that crew they did very bad things and thereby became demons.

The Devil Didn't Make You Do It

One of the bad things that demons do, apparently, is to try to entice or trick us humans into going along with their wicked ways. In *Genesis*, in the Bible, a serpent dupes Eve into eating the forbidden fruit and so begins the long story of bad things people do to one another, what we call, euphemistically, *history*. St. Peter said in one of his letters that the Devil prowls around like a lion and seeks the ruin of souls.

C.S. Lewis takes up this theme with gusto in several books. In *The Magician's Nephew* (1955)—one of the *Chronicles* books— there is a devilish witch, Jadis, who magically invades the newly made world of Narnia and tries (but fails) to get the little boy Digory to eat that world's version of the forbidden fruit. In *Perelandra* (1943) the demon-possessed physicist, Weston, tries (but fails) to get the Green Lady of Venus to do the one thing her god has forbidden her to do: to sleep on "the fixed land" rather than the floating islands that make up the majority of her planet's habitable terrain. And that junior demon, Wormwood, in *The Screwtape Letters* (1942) seemingly spends his whole life trying to sway his assigned human to the ways of darkness, frequently writing to his uncle, Screwtape, seeking advice.

But remember: Lewis thinks that we humans have free will. So we don't need demons whispering in our ears to do damnable deeds; we're very good at them on our own. And this means that we don't need demons to explain how we humans went bad. Instead, Lewis thinks, we just need them to explain how our world has what we call natural evil. Messing with human beings is a kind of sideshow for the demons. Their chief cosmological role is to make sure that Mother Nature remains red in tooth and claw.

The postulation of demons stretches the free will defense to cover the whole class of natural evils—which therefore turn out to be no more or less natural than the evils that we humans cause. So the free will defense can be made to account for all evils whatsoever. We and the demons are to blame, not God. Problem of evil solved.

Not as Crazy as It Sounds

This isn't as crazy as it sounds. Many reasonable people believe in God, but the problem of evil presents a serious challenge to the reasonableness of belief in God, so believers need a good response to this problem. If God turns out to be morally responsible for evil, any evil at all, then He's not who believers believe in—either he's not morally perfect, or he's weak, or both, or maybe He doesn't exist after all. So believers have got to find a way to show that God isn't morally responsible for evil.

Human beings can only account for some evil. Animals and other non-intelligent things (like trees and stones) are incapable of moral responsibility. But something has got to be responsible. So we conclude to the existence of a special kind of personal being—the Devil and demons—in order to account for the evil humans can't account for.

You might be thinking that an argument for demons is just the sort of philosophy that a writer of fantasy stories would invent. Lewis's argument for demons, maybe, is just the product of an overactive imagination. Well, maybe it's the product of an overactive imagination, but it's not *just* this; it's a reasonable inference from far less controversial claims.

If you think that some version of the free will defense is the only explanation of the existence of evil that is compatible with the idea that God is All-Good and All-Powerful and has created everything there is; and *if* you think that human beings can't account for all evils, *then* you've got to admit that either this idea of God is fatally flawed or there are creatures other than human beings endowed with free will who do evil.

It comes down to this: either demons exist or God doesn't. In Lewis's mind, atheism is far less plausible than belief in demons.

VII

Rock-a-bye
Beelzebub

17
Man, the Devil Rocks!

ERIC SWAN

Oh, to be alive in 1966! The Beach Boys, The Rolling Stones, The Beatles, and Motown Records—this was a golden age in music. I wouldn't be born for eight more years but I can practically hear "Wild Thing," one of the year's most popular songs, blasting out the window of some teenager's bedroom down the block.

True, once your records stopped spinning, there was much to contend with: the War in Vietnam, the draft, race riots, the advent of the miniskirt . . . Indeed, 1966 was a dynamic time, and in the next few years, and decades, social norms and systems would be challenged in ways that would swing between liberating and . . . downright disturbing.

Anyway, the innocence and homogeneity of the 1950s was over, and society could not stand in the way of the coming revolution.

Somewhere, the Devil was brewing coffee after a long slumber.

Just as it does today, in 1966, pop music fueled and reflected the transformations taking place in the minds of America's youth, and society at large. It had been nearly ten years since Elvis provoked America with his sexually suggestive gyrations, so "Devil with a Blue Dress"—a good starting point for Devil songs, the subject of this chapter—was hardly scandalous for such progressive times. In fact, this tune performed by Mitch Ryder and the Detroit Wheels reached #4 on the Billboard Hot 100, so if anything, it was rather well received. (The song was actually written by Shorty Long and William "Mickey" Stevenson, and released as a single in 1964.) The lyrics are very forgettable and modest in their portrait of a flashy female, but the rhythm and chorus—which are generally the most memorable parts of a song—are catchy as Hell. Mom and Dad probably loved this song; it transcended ages and demographics with its fusion with the hit by Little Richard, "Good Golly, Miss Molly," arguably one of the greatest rock'n'roll songs of all time.

The Pelvis

Before I go any further, I should tell you that this song was the earliest song with "Devil" in the title that I could think of prior to writing this chapter. I was surprised to discover that three years earlier there had been another song with "Devil" in the title, and that too was well received, reaching #3 on the U.S. Billboard charts. You might guess, and you would be correct, that "Devil in Disguise"—the first devil song in pop music—was made famous by none other than Elvis "The Pelvis" Presley. In this song's chorus, Elvis laments: "You look like an angel / Walk like an angel / Talk like an angel/ But I got wise / You're the Devil in disguise / Oh yes, you are / The Devil in disguise." We learn a little more through the lines "You fooled me with your kisses / You cheated and you schemed / Heaven knows how you lied to me / You're not the way you seemed."

While I would argue that "Devil with a Blue Dress" is much more memorable and infectious, the two songs have one major thing in common: they personify the Devil and liken "it" to a seductive and reckless woman. Sounds a bit misogynistic, right? Nonetheless, judging by the success of these songs, listeners accepted this characterization, and however unflattering it was to compare a woman to the Devil, it was also understandable.

How so? First, most lead singers in the early days of rock-'n'roll were men, and thus any song about love and attraction naturally featured a woman as the "other." Second, in those instances when a man was trying to express in song how a woman broke his heart, such as through an act of betrayal, one way was to literally demonize her—call her a Devil. The Devil has connoted deception and treachery since the writing of the Book of Genesis and by invoking this term musicians could quickly connect with their listeners.

As songwriting became more sophisticated over the next few years (in the wake of groundbreaking lyrics by Bob Dylan, no doubt, who profoundly impacted the Beatles, the Stones, the Grateful Dead, and everyone else), the way the Devil would be portrayed in pop songs became much more variable. This is when things get interesting. In more or less chronological order, the following pages will be devoted to the study of the most significant Devil songs from the late sixties to the mid-nineties, and what these songs suggest about the nature of the Devil, Man, and the relationship between the two.

Please Allow Me to Introduce Myself

If you don't know that phrase, you need to stop reading this chapter and go buy (or I should say, download) the Rolling Stones' "Sympathy for the Devil," or preferably, all of *Beggars Banquet* (1968). That way, you can familiarize yourself with other gems like "No Expectations" and "Street Fighting Man" once you're through decoding this masterpiece. If you need to know one Devil Song, it's this one. Why? Where shall I start? Besides the catchy chord progression and overall groove, it's wide and deep in terms of historical references, and audacious in its examination of the Devil's role in shaping human destiny. It's unabashedly confrontational, timely and timeless, and wholly original. However scary it may sound, it makes you think— even question your nature. This is Mick Jagger and the boys at their finest, and *Rolling Stone* magazine ranks it #32 in their list of "The 500 Greatest Songs of All Time."

Sung from the first-person perspective of the Devil, it sounds at first as if the Devil is a living and breathing person. The Devil tells us he's no mere mortal though, or in his words, "I've been around for a long, long year / Stole many a man's soul and sealed his fate / I was 'round when Jesus Christ had his moment of doubt and pain." In a boastful and unapologetic manner, the Devil reveals his complicity in atrocities across the ages, including mass murder spanning unspecified religious wars, the Russian Revolution, World War II, and finally the assassinations of the Kennedy brothers. What I find to be most fascinating is how the Devil is presented as personal ("I rode a tank, held a General's rank / when the Blitzkrieg raged, and the bodies stank"), and also *transpersonal*. In other words, the Devil isn't just one person, but countless individuals who have engaged in destructive and immoral acts at both specific points in time, and across time. The Devil seems to be Humanity itself, or at least part of our humanity.

One of the song's most memorable lines, "I shouted out, Who killed the Kennedys? / When after all it was you and me" supports this possibility. However antagonizing it may sound, whether we fired the fatal shot, hired the hitman (or hit*men*), deceived the public, or engaged in fanatical worship of a flawed leader, we had some role in their demise. How is that? One explanation is a broader notion that the Devil exists within all humans, perhaps as a "primal force" that drives people to destroy one another, be it through direct violence or something more insidious, like the quest for power—or even the obsession with those who hold power.

At the height of the cultural revolution and disorder of the 1960s, this tune must have sounded chilling—made even worse by the searing guitar licks of Keith Richards and those "*ooo-who-who*" wails which seem to celebrate the Devil. Naturally, some people were repelled by the violent and anti-establishment lyrics. Others were galvanized. It depended on the listener's willingness to open his mind and acknowledge the destruction taking place in the name of God, Country, Democracy, Freedom—or whatever words people were using to justify their actions. I'm pretty sure this song would not have flown in December of 1963; but in 1968, just a short time after Senator and Presidential candidate Robert Kennedy was killed, it would have been hard to disagree with the sense that the Devil was not in the details—Hell, he was everywhere, manifesting through the actions of living and breathing people, including but not limited to Lee Harvey Oswald and Sirhan Sirhan.

A Friend of the Devil Is a Friend of Mine

Students of rock'n'roll history know that the Grateful Dead almost played the Altamont Speedway Free Festival in 1969, where the Hippie/Woodstock Dream and one poor guy named Meredith Hunter were killed, and the Stones were forevermore saddled with the baggage of being labeled "trouble," if not downright "evil." For those who don't know, basically the Grateful Dead went to the concert site, saw the *bad craziness* (as Hunter S. Thompson might call it) unfolding, and refused to play or participate—the peaceniks that they were. Hunter got into a skirmish with one of the Hells Angels (who were the security for the concert), and was stabbed to death by another member of the Hells Angels when he pulled out a gun and rushed the stage where the Stones were playing.

Although they weren't as vilified nor held accountable as the Stones were, who were performing as Hunter was being stabbed, the Grateful Dead were chastised by concertgoers and the press for their inaction on this fateful day. Within a year's time, they expressed an alternative form of sympathy for the Devil, and it's worth mentioning here because, it too is a famous Devil song, it presents a more forgiving portrait of the Devil and Man in the aftermath of "Sympathy" and Altamont, it's a logical transition between the Devil songs of the 1960s and 1970s, and I love the Grateful Dead.

"Friend of the Devil" from the folk-rock gem *American Beauty* (1970) describes one man's encounters with the Devil, in which "he" first loans and then vanishes with a twenty-dollar bill that the narrator really needs as he flees from The Law. Played on acoustic guitars, this song-story speaks of a kinship with the Devil despite the Devil's trickery. The chorus in the song is, "I set out running but I take my time / A friend of the Devil is a friend of mine / If I get home before daylight / I just might get some sleep tonight." The upbeat arrangement and benevolent nature of the lead vocalist Jerry Garcia (RIP) help ensure that the song doesn't get misinterpreted as pro-Satan in the aftermath of "Sympathy for the Devil" and the Altamont debacle. Nevertheless, how are we to understand a friendship with the Devil?

In my view, the friendship revolves around forgiveness and grace. The narrator knows he's made some mistakes but in that he's no different from anyone, perhaps even the Devil, who after all, just took back what he lent the narrator. An honest tale of being scorned and trying to find reprieve, I see this song as more pro-redemption than pro-Evil. It's an expression of a kinship with other outcasts, even criminals. It's worth wondering if Robert Hunter, the Grateful Dead's chief lyricist, wrote this song as a peace bridge to the Rolling Stones; as if to say, *I understand what you meant by "Every cop's a criminal / and all the sinners saints" and I agree that we're all flawed, in fact, it's our nature. A friend of the Devil is a friend of mine. Let's accept and love each other and move on.* To this day, this is one of the Dead's most enduring songs, and it's been covered by other non-Satanists Lyle Lovett, Tom Petty and the Heartbreakers, and Counting Crows.

Devil Went Down to Georgia

If you know two songs with the word "Devil" in the title, chances are this is one of them. Written and recorded by the Charlie Daniels Band in 1979, it reached #3 on the Billboard Top 100 list at the peak of its popularity. How does a country-and-bluegrass-style song scorch the competition in an era of disco and Jimmy Carter? Because the song has superb craftsmanship, a dramatic story driving it to conclusion, and one hell of a catchy title. Sure, "My Sharona" and "Da Ya Think I'm Sexy?" are great songs from 1979 too (no comment, please), guaranteed to get you out on the dance floor, but they can't hold a candle in terms of lyrical and musical complexity to "Devil Went Down To Georgia."

For the unaware, the lyrics describe the Devil as a very real entity who goes to Georgia in hopes of stealing a soul. Apparently, he's behind on his quota and needs to make a quick score. What better, unsuspecting victim than a country boy and fiddler named "Johnny"? Presumably, Johnny would be interested in a better instrument—a gold one, no less—if he can outperform the Devil, which is a ludicrous possibility given the Devil's secret proficiency with the bow, and the arrogance that comes with supernatural powers underneath his facade.

In this song, the Devil is represented as someone or something that can be defeated. And by a kid no less! One can imagine how this song (read: sermon) went over in the South: very, very well. I suspect it was natural for the band, which consisted of Southerners and religious men by origin, to share with the greater listening community this tale of triumph over the Devil. It mirrored a life they probably knew well. Along the way to fame, I have no doubt that various "Devils" or temptations came across their path, but by focusing on the music and not on vice they vindicated themselves and good country-folk like Johnny who "outclassed" the Devil. In sum, people really identified with this song—lyrically, musically, and spiritually—and not just in the South. It offered encouragement to all and to this day, it's still in circulation.

Runnin' with the Devil

Some people would rather party with the Devil than triumph over him. They're more concerned with their own pleasure and survival than the needs of others. Enter Van Halen and the 1980s, a period of self-centeredness and excess as society faced the possibility of nuclear war and apocalypse. Hopefully, reader, you are a Van Halen fan, and therefore own a copy of *Van Halen I* (1978), their debut. By virtue of this, you know the first track—"Runnin' with the Devil"—which simply must be included in a chapter about Devil songs; it too made the US Billboard Hot 100 list. Like any Van Halen composition, it doesn't take a genius to understand this song. The boys are describing a young adult male traveling a path of self-destruction like so many others in the decadent scene characterizing many American cities circa the late 1970s. "I live my life like there's no tomorrow / and all I've got I've had to steal." This person has "no love to call real" or "anybody waiting at home" and is "living at a pace that kills."

In this song, the Devil is invoked to connote aimlessness and depravity. By "running with the Devil," you were surviving, but very much at risk of dying young—a lifestyle that sounded alluring to the disenfranchised, disillusioned, and hard rock fans everywhere. This song and Van Halen in general, seemed to celebrate anti-social debauchery and thus opened the door for bands like Mötley Crüe, who would soon become famous for their own Devil song—"Shout at the Devil" (1983). Some might say that Van Halen was just extending the "heavy metal" sound and building upon the pro-Satan image made famous by Black Sabbath in the earlier part of the 1970s; and that was a rejection to the peaceful vibes promoted by the hippies. We need to remember that music is a conversation, a cycle of listening and talking. Fortunately, there's always someone waiting to join in the dialogue and say something new.

I've Got a Devil's Haircut in My Mind

In the mid-1990s, Beck was no loser. After exploding out of nowhere like a psychedelic hip-hop poet with his signature tune "Loser," he went on to win big with a string of hits, such as "Where It's At," "The New Pollution," and the track of interest to us here—"Devil's Haircut" (1996). Let's be honest, that song, like so many others in Beck's catalog of genre-defying music, does not lend itself to easy interpretation, but it's infectious and memorable as Hell. All it takes is one listen and you'll be repeating the chorus: "I've got a devil's haircut in my mind!" While I can't claim to know what a devil's haircut actually looks like, judging by the nasty guitar riff driving the song, I believe it says something along the lines of *Back off, I've got more important things to think about than my hair style.*

Above all, this song conveys an *attitude*; an attitude that stems from an honest and discouraging sense that "Everywhere I look there's a devil waiting" and "something's wrong 'cause my mind is fading." Beck's dystopian portrait of the world we've created for ourselves by the mid-1990s reflects a sentiment shared by religious and secular people alike, and that is: everything's going to Hell. Indeed, at the end of the twentieth century, the world around us has become increasingly abused and fractured, so much so that it's even "trippy," which Beck expresses through his unique lyrics (such as "Heads are hanging from the garbage man trees"). Even if it's oblique, Beck tells us you have to have a certain mental toughness just to cope with it all and that's what a "Devil's Haircut" represents, at least to me. Less confrontationally than the Stones in 1968 and a punk rocker's mohawk in 1979, a "Devil's Haircut" announces *It's a brave new world. Do what you need to survive.* This validated the perspective of many, especially "Gen-Xers," and it's a view that's alive to this day.

Where the Devil Do We Go from Here?

At the dawn of the twenty-first century, we're left wondering about the future of the Devil song. Who will come along next and say something original about this fascinating figure or force we call "The Devil"? Will we be able to put our electronics down long enough to even care?

18

We Sold Our Souls for Rock'n'Roll

STEVE NEUMANN

I'm a golden god!

—ROBERT PLANT, Los Angeles, 1975

It was March of 1975 and Led Zeppelin was the biggest rock-'n'roll band in the world. Robert Plant was being interviewed by music journalist Stephen Davis in Los Angeles at the Continental Hyatt House—appropriately dubbed the Continental Riot House—when he bounded out to his balcony, revealing with open arms and tousled mane his divine nature to the masses below.

Led Zeppelin had it all. Thanks to their pugilistic manager, they had signed a ridiculously lucrative deal with Atlantic Records at the start of their career before they were even heard, went home each night with ninety percent of ticket sales, and broke attendance records with every tour even though they eschewed TV performances and didn't even put out singles. They rented entire floors of swanky hotels, where wriggling throngs of nubile, doe-eyed groupies would claw and clamor for access to their hippie-haired heroes. It seemed like the band was supernaturally blessed. As Robert Plant told a young Cameron Crowe later that same year, "The music's gelled amazingly well. Everyone loved *Physical Graffiti*. It's like we're on an incredible winning streak."

But there were sinister whispers. It was rumored that band mastermind Jimmy Page, an admitted admirer of infamous occultist Aleister Crowley, had sold his soul to the Devil in exchange for bulletproof success. It was further alleged that their iconic song "Stairway to Heaven" contained a hidden message, that you could hear the homage "here's to my sweet Satan" when the song was played backwards. And, sure enough, Led Zeppelin's dazzling climb to stratospheric stardom appeared to be paid for with catastrophic suffering: in August of 1975, Robert Plant and his wife were nearly killed when their car careened off a cliff while vacationing in Greece; while away on tour in America in 1977, Plant's only son died suddenly from a stomach infection; and in 1980, the band lost both its drummer and its soul when John Bonham died after a bender of heavy drinking. The Devil apparently got his due.

The Devil's Interval

Have you ever listened to a piece of music and felt vaguely uneasy yet strangely attracted to it? If so, then you were likely seduced by the tritone of the Devil's interval! In music, the Devil's interval is often employed to create a spooky or tense feeling. It's been used in compositions as diverse as Wagner's *Götterdämmerung* and the theme song of *The Simpsons*. The ominously named Black Sabbath, which started out as a blues-based rock band, became masters of the Devil's interval. When they formed, they were intrigued by the way people would line up outside movie theaters to be scared out of their wits by horror flicks. They wanted to recreate this feeling in their music. At a time when most rock groups, including Led Zeppelin, were singing about peace and love and flower power, Black Sabbath would blaze a dark path through rock'n'roll's forest, forging the molten blues into heavy metal.

This diabolical formula would propel Black Sabbath to superstardom. To date, they've sold seventy million records worldwide and fifteen million in the United States alone. But Ozzy and the band would experience their share of tribulation, too. Whereas Robert Plant proclaimed himself the Golden God, Ozzy Osbourne would come to be known as the Prince of Darkness by his fans—and his detractors. This menacing moniker is not without some justification, given Osbourne's personal history. In addition to Sabbath's overtly demonic persona—their first compilation album released in 1975 was called *We Sold Our Soul for Rock'n'Roll*—Ozzy claimed that there was a lot of "insanity" in his family, and that he had made several attempts at suicide at the tender age of fourteen "just to see what it would feel like." And because of his incessant, over-the-top drug and alcohol abuse, Ozzy was kicked out of Black Sabbath in 1979.

Playing Devil's Advocate

Is it mere coincidence that many of the English rock groups of the 1960s, such as Led Zeppelin and Black Sabbath, cut their teeth on the tunes of American black blues musicians of the 1920s? What was the connection between London and Mississippi? What was the connection between musical talent and His Malevolent Magnificence? Allow me to play Devil's advocate for a moment.

Jimmy Page and Robert Plant were veritable connoisseurs of the blues, being particularly interested in the musical and personal exploits of trailblazing bluesman Robert Johnson. Johnson, so the story goes, wanted to play the guitar more than anything else in the world; but there was one problem—he sucked. So he went down to the crossroads of Clarksdale, Mississippi at midnight and met the Devil himself. The Lord of the Underworld made Johnson the King of the Delta by granting him the ability to play guitar like a prodigy in exchange for his soul. Sound familiar?

Consider Jimmy Page again. Though he was a successful session guitarist before forming Led Zeppelin in 1968, contributing to such established bands as the Who and the Kinks, he nevertheless had an inscrutable charisma and peculiar prowess both behind the mixing board as well as under the psychedelic limelight. In the studio, he was a bona fide alchemist, squeezing the best from each instrument—including Plant's industrial-strength voice—transmuting all that lead material into the glittering gold of Led Zeppelin. On the stage, Page elicited sounds from his 1959 Gibson Les Paul Standard that would've made even Jimi Hendrix cry Mary, had he lived to see it. Although Jimmy Page seems to have survived his alleged deal with the Devil relatively unscathed, Robert Johnson was fated to be a founding member of The Twenty-Seven Club—those musicians who never lived to see their twenty-eighth birthday. Think of the aforementioned Jimi Hendrix, Janis Joplin, Jim Morrison and, more recently, Kurt Cobain and Amy Winehouse.

Between the Devil and the Deep Blue Sea

The moral of the myth of selling one's soul to the Devil in exchange for success is that with great happiness comes great suffering. It's simply the price you pay. There ain't no free lunches. If you can remember back to your economics class, it's similar to the concept of "opportunity cost." In almost every area of our lives, in order to get something we really want, we have to give up or forgo something *else* we really want. Life's a bitch that way.

This inevitable cycle of joy and sorrow, pleasure and pain, has occupied human thought and art for millennia. The polarizing German philosopher Friedrich Nietzsche (1844–1900) had a lot to say about both happiness *and* suffering, and his penchant for theatrical polemics is strangely akin to the showmanship of many a rock star, not unlike our Golden God and Prince of Darkness. As far back as 1882, Nietzsche claimed that in order to "jubilate up to the heavens" a person had to endure "depression unto death." Though it may sound like Nietzsche was somewhat of a Negative Nancy, the book this sentiment comes from bears the title *The Gay Science*, where "gay" means "joyful" or "cheerful," and strongly implies the desire to dance and laugh. Nietzsche's name for this paradoxical state of affairs where you wholeheartedly accept both the good and the bad that life (or is it the Devil?) throws at you was "amor fati." It's Latin for "love of fate." Nietzsche tied the love of fate to what he called the "eternal recurrence of all things," and introduced it with that quasi-literary flourish favored by philosophers, the thought experiment. In *The Gay Science*, he asked his readers what they would think if a demon came to them in the middle of the night with the following scenario:

> This life as you now live it and have lived it, you will have to live once more and innumerable times more; and there will be nothing new in it, but every pain and every joy and every thought and sigh and everything unutterably small or great in your life will have to return to you, all in the same succession and sequence—even this spider and this moonlight between the trees, and even this moment and I myself. The eternal hourglass of existence is turned upside down again and again, and you with it, speck of dust!

What would be your reaction? Do you love your life *so much* that you would want it to eternally recur? Sure, it's easy to say that any of us would gladly have the eternal repetition of our favorite vacation, our first kiss, the births of our children, and our achievements at work. But would you be willing to *sell your soul* for those things? Even if you had your own tropical island, and your first kiss was with Channing Tatum or Gwyneth Paltrow, and you discovered the cure for cancer—would you still be willing to endure the absolute worst moments of your life over and over again? What if, in spite of these amazing experiences, you lost your legs in the Boston Marathon bombing? Or your children died when their jumbo jet crash-landed on that San Francisco runway, just when you thought they were safe and sound?

The Devil's Not as Black as He's Painted

Nietzsche goes on to ask if you would "throw yourself down and gnash your teeth and curse the demon who spoke thus," or if you would say that the demon was "a god and never have I heard anything more divine!" He sets this up as such an emotionally sharp contrast because, if you *really* think about it, you're just not going to have a lukewarm response to the question. It's like contemplating a Zen koan, those mindfucking little riddles that eventually force you to transcend your normal habits of thought.

We'd prefer to tell the demon that we only want the good bits of our lives to repeat eternally, or that we'd like to be aware of the fact that our lives are repeating—not unlike Bill Murray's character in *Groundhog Day*—which would give us a chance to change things going forward. But that's not what Nietzsche had in mind. He wants to know how well disposed toward your life you would have to be to declare such a scenario *divine*. Divine! But if fate necessarily entails a certain amount of inescapable anguish, then how can you possibly *love* it? How can you love something that is so repulsive? That's the koan.

Nietzsche himself was no stranger to suffering. While not a member of the Twenty-Seven Club, he died a humiliating death at a mere fifty-five years of age, and suffered from debilitating migraines, incapacitating gastrointestinal distress and unpredictable vision. Nor did he enjoy much recognition in his own lifetime, either—certainly nowhere near the likes of our Heavy Metal Heroes—but he considered himself to be happy nonetheless. In fact, he considered himself to have achieved the brass ring of amor fati. He believed that there were basically two options, two approaches to handling the problem of suffering inherent in loving fate: the first one is an ascetic approach, where life is viewed as either a mistake or a punishment that must be put right by denying oneself worldly pleasures. If you opt for as little pleasure as possible, so the thinking goes, you'll get as little suffering as possible. Nietzsche epitomized the second approach: the affirmation of life in spite of suffering.

After Robert Plant lost his only son, he withdrew from the life he knew and "tinkered on the village piano and grew so obese drinking beer" that nobody knew who he was. Ozzy Osbourne, after being fired from Black Sabbath, was so fed up with rock stardom that he locked himself away in a hotel room for three months, getting drunk and stoned every day. But the demon's koan of amor fati doesn't give us the option of drowning our sorrows in drink or drugs—that's just self-deception at best and cowardice at worst. And mere resignation to fate is, almost by definition, neither love nor hate. So that doesn't solve our dilemma either. I suppose you could develop a "scientific" view of life, where you are able to intellectually understand how everything is interconnected like a chain, and therefore see that if you affirm even one tremendous moment of your life, you *technically* affirm *every* moment. But love, as any rock star worth his salt will tell you, isn't rational like that. You may understand why the world works the way it does, but you can't live in light of that knowledge.

At this point you might be asking yourself what's so great about loving fate. I mean, what's wrong with trying to orchestrate your life in such a way that you end up with more pleasure than pain, or more happiness than sadness? Well, nothing. But Nietzsche insisted that amor fati is the very *formula* for greatness. Why? Because if you can allow the expression of your most powerful passions because you're strong enough to control them, then you will experience a joy that is different from the joy of simple pleasures. Loving fate requires just that kind of strength. If you're not strong enough, you might end up like Black Sabbath's "Iron Man," who took revenge on humanity when they mocked his time-traveling prophecy. No one wants to be *that* guy.

Golden God, Prince of Darkness, and the Antichrist

I've read and listened to more interviews with Robert Plant than you can shake a pitchfork at. I don't know if it's his personality or a certain British coyness, but it's hard to tell whether or not he believes all his fame and success was worth it. After all, he almost joined the Twenty-Seven Club in 1975. He lost a child in 1977. He got divorced. Friends abandoned him. Critics excoriated him. But despite some questionable artistic tangents in the 1980s, he has nevertheless enjoyed a considerable amount of success since his Zeppelin days. The past decade alone has brought him critical acclaim for his collaboration with Alison Krauss on their album *Raising Sand*, being made a Commander of the Order of the British Empire, and being honored as part of Led Zeppelin by President Obama at the Kennedy Center in 2012.

And Ozzy Osbourne, who, only three years after his termination from Black Sabbath lost his guitarist Randy Rhoads when his tour plane crashed while buzzing his tour bus, has long been a favorite target of the Religious Right. This is mostly because of alcohol-induced antics like biting the head off a dove at a Columbia Records executives meeting, and utilizing song and album titles like "Mr. Crowley," "Speak of the Devil," and "The Ultimate Sin." And drug and alcohol addiction has hounded him throughout his solo career, forcing him in 1986 to finally check in to the Betty Ford Clinic in attempt to get the old monkeys off his back. But Ozzy nevertheless won a Grammy in 1994 for his solo work. And in 2005 both he as a solo act and Black Sabbath were inducted into the UK Hall of Fame. And that's just for his music. Ozzy would go on to achieve even wider appeal and fame with his reality TV show *The Osbournes*, which included his family.

Nietzsche—or the Antichrist, as philosopher Walter Kaufmann christened him, because he thought of himself as standing at the beginning of an anti-Christian epoch—had an approach to amor fati and the eternal recurrence of all things that was more self-conscious than either the Golden God or the Prince of Darkness. One of the last books he wrote, *Ecce Homo*, is "Nietzsche's own interpretation of his development, his works, and his significance," according to Kaufmann. In this somewhat indulgent autobiography, Nietzsche talks about more than just his work. He goes on at length about his ailments and his attitude toward them. He believed that suffering not only made him stronger, but was a stimulus for life, for actually living *more*. He talked about "the will to life rejoicing over its own inexhaustibility." For Nietzsche, living more meant creating new things and new possibilities of life, and it's the very act of creation that confers value on what's created. It's a little like God creating human beings: we're only valuable because God created us, and we're only loved because we're valuable.

"We Are Each Our Own Devil . . .

. . . and we make this world our Hell," said playwright Oscar Wilde. And it's hard to disagree with him. Ozzy made his own bed with drugs and booze, as did Zeppelin's drummer John Bonham, who literally died in his own bed after a Herculean drinking spree. It's easier for us to accept our suffering when our own reckless actions cause it. If we willingly sell our soul to the Devil, we can't really complain when the Devil gets his due. Bon Scott of AC/DC, Steve Clark of Def Leppard—pretty much anyone from Mötley Crüe—the list of self-inflicted misery goes on and on. What's harder to swallow is when life seems out to get us *despite* our best intentions.

Even if we're able to commit ourselves to the love of fate, there's no guarantee that we'll achieve it. And even if we do achieve it, there's no guarantee that we can sustain it. But whether we make our own Hell or not, it's only by continually creating ourselves anew that we can redeem the Devil of fate.

Plant seems to strike the right note when he says in the song "Houses of the Holy" from *Physical Graffiti*:

So your world is spinnin' faster
Are you dizzy when you stop?
Let the music be your Master
Will you heed the Master's call?

19

Satanic Metal—So Bad It's Good

NICK JONES

Can worshipping the Devil and doing evil in His name ever be a good thing? Yes. When it comes to Satanic heavy metal music, there's one sense in which it can. Satanic metal can sometimes be good artistically in virtue of its immoral features, especially when it's produced by musicians who are actual Satanists, as opposed to those who are just pretending.

The Devil—who's got all the best tunes—has always enjoyed a high profile in the history of rock'n'roll, and no more so than in the heavy metal scene. From early bands like KISS dressing up as super-scary demons, to fans making funny little Devil's horns symbols with their hands, to members of black metal bands burning down churches and murdering each other all in Satan's name, the Devil's murky shadow is cast over the entire genre.

I'm interested in the more extreme uses that the Devil is put to by some heavy metal musicians. As well as the church burnings and the murders, there are plenty of bands who glorify and revere Satan in their lyrics, who urge their audiences to commit crimes in His cause, or whose music blasphemes against God and the Church. In short, I'm interested in Satanic metal.

It's Just Noise, Isn't It?

Like many sub-genres of heavy metal music, there's a boring and pedantic row about how exactly Satanic metal should be characterized. A simple working definition will do: Satanic metal is heavy metal music that expresses the Satanism, either

177

real or pretend, of the bands whose music it is. That said, it will actually be useful to note some of the other common traits of the music that's put in this particular pigeonhole.

Satanic metal is usually taken to be a form of extreme metal—heavy metal that's especially intense or brutal, whether on account of a very high tempo, guitars turned up quite loud, or vocals that are guttural or shrieked, often to the point of sounding inhuman or unintelligible. And as Keith Kahn-Harris points out in his 2007 book *Extreme Metal: Music and Culture on the Edge,* one of the main features of extreme metal is that it involves *transgression*—a breaking of the rules or boundaries.

This transgression can take various forms. Musically, extreme metal is transgressive when it pushes the boundaries in terms of its tempo or heavy sound and so on. And lyrically too, extreme metal can be transgressive with lyrics that are obscene or offensive in various ways. With Satanic metal, this lyrical transgression can take the form of blasphemy. Indeed, Steve Asheim, the drummer in the Satanic metal band Deicide, has claimed that the whole point of Satanic music is to blaspheme.

And within the extreme metal genre, it at least used to be the case that Satanic metal was equated with black metal—a form of extreme metal with extra dark lyrics and typically shrieked vocals. Nowadays though, while a good deal of black metal does take the form of Satanic metal, there are other kinds of black metal such as Nazi metal which needn't be anything to do with Satanism, and there have been Satanic metal bands like Akercocke who don't obviously fall into the black metal category.

Satan's Little Helpers

Some Satanic metal musicians are genuine Satanists. Others aren't. But it's not always easy to work out which ones are, and the whole question of what it is to be a genuine Satanist is a tricky one. There are different forms of Satanism, Satanism means different things to different people, and different people use the trappings of Satanism for different purposes. Even so, there are three broad levels of commitment to Satanism that Satanic metal musicians can have.

The lowest level of commitment that they can have is to pretend that they are Satanists, and there are various reasons for doing this. Some bands claim to worship the Devil simply to shock, or to look very cool, or to gain a reputation for being anti-Establishment. Others want to explore their own fascination with religion or with the occult, or to revel in the whole Satanic aesthetic. And then there are musicians who promote Satanism as a means to achieve a tremendously important political goal, such as voicing their opposition to the Church or to organized religion more broadly.

In the next place there are Satanic metal musicians who aren't pretending, but whose Satanism is 'non-theistic'. Non-theistic Satanists don't actually believe in the existence of the Devil, and their Satanism doesn't amount to a religious belief. A good example would be the kind of Satanism practised by Anton LaVey and the Church of Satan that he established in California in the 1960s. LaVey's Satanism, while it uses much of the imagery and many of the rituals traditionally associated with Devil worship, doesn't invoke the existence of Satan as a real being. Rather, it's a certain philosophy of life that champions individualism, pleasure-seeking, and going against the Establishment. There have been lots of Satanic metal bands who are genuinely committed to something like Satanism of this kind, and who use Satanic imagery and themes in their music, but who don't actually believe in the existence of the Devil as He's traditionally conceived.

Finally, there are the genuine 'theistic' Satanists. Theistic Satanism involves belief in and worship of an entity—the Devil—who is in some sense or other God's enemy, who is a force for evil in the world, or at least for something other than what God commands, and who really does exist. There are quite a few Satanic metal musicians who have explicitly stated their commitment to this kind of Satanism, and it's this Satan, who they take to really exist, that these musicians invoke when they are insulting God, or when they are inciting their audiences to break the law, or when they themselves commit crimes in promoting their Satanic image.

As an aside, the most notorious case of crimes committed in the name of the Devil by Satanic metal musicians involved the murders and church burnings that I touched on earlier, in Norway in the early 1990s. Varg Vikernes, a.k.a. Count

Grishnackh, the sole member of Norwegian black metal band Burzum, was convicted in 1994 on three counts of church burning, as well as for the murder of Øystein Aarseth, a.k.a. Euronymous, the singer with fellow Norwegian black metal band Mayhem, and consequently served nearly fifteen years in prison.

The Evil that Men Do

Let's focus on the kind of devilish things Satanic metal musicians get up to when they are going about their business. Whether it's masturbating into the Communion sherry on one of their album covers, effing and jeffing about God in their lyrics, or buggering a Goat of Mendes live on stage, there's little these people will stop short of. And let's assume for the sake of argument that doing each of these things is morally wrong. What implications does this have for the artistic worth of their output?

Some people reckon that if an artwork involves the artist or the audience doing immoral things, then this spoils the artwork's artistic value. An overused example that's appealed to here is the 1935 movie *Triumph of the Will*, which is often claimed to suffer artistically, despite its superb cinematography, because it glorifies Nazism.

Others have it that any moral judgments that we make about an artwork should have nothing at all to do with our evaluation of its artistic worth. Here the thought is that the fact that *Triumph of the Will* immorally glorifies Nazism doesn't take anything away from or add anything to that movie's artistic value. The moral judgements and the artistic judgements we make should be kept entirely separate.

Another view again is that if an artwork involves the artist or the audience behaving immorally, then this can in fact sometimes improve the artistic value of that artwork. I think that this is the case with some Satanic metal. Sometimes the immoral features of Satanic metal can count in its favor, artistically-speaking.

In arguing this, I'm not saying that it's a *morally* good thing for Satanic metal bands to film themselves defecating all over the hymn books in their local church for one of their music videos and the likes—I'm assuming that these kinds of acts are immoral. I'm just saying that when Satanic metal bands commit immoral acts in their work, that can sometimes count in favor of their work's artistic value.

Good Satanic Metal?

So how might behaving immorally count in favor of the artistic worth of a piece of Satanic metal? To answer that question, we need to think about what makes for *good* Satanic metal—and by 'good' here, I mean good in the artistic sense. This will depend on what the band in question is trying to achieve with its music, which in turn will depend to a significant extent on what the aims of art in general are, and on what the aims of heavy metal music, extreme metal, and Satanic metal are. Once we know those aims, we'll be able to decide which Satanic metal acts achieve them, and which don't. In other words, we'll have the yardsticks against which good Satanic metal can be measured.

There are lots of different features that make for good Satanic metal. Trying to list them all would be like trying to list all of the features of a smash hit pop song. Instead, I'm going to mention just three of them. Each one is an artistic aim of Satanic metal that can be successfully achieved by Satanic metal musicians behaving atrociously. And in each case it's those who are actual Satanists who will be best placed to successfully achieve the aim in question, and to produce Satanic metal that's better artistically as a result.

Rock'n'Roll Rebels

The first aim is one manifestation of the transgression that's a main feature of extreme metal, and it's an aim that Satanic metal shares with the wider genres of heavy metal, rock music, and indeed rock'n'roll itself; namely, *rebellion*. Rebellion has always been at the heart of the aesthetic of rock'n'roll, and of its noisier, heavier descendants. Rock'n'roll bands and musicians have often been painted as rebels, and the spirit of rebellion is something that they've tried desperately hard to embody in both their lifestyles and their music. As a result, rock'n'roll music, heavy metal and Satanic metal that successfully captures this rebellious spirit can be critically acclaimed, at least in this respect.

Satanic metal musicians can sometimes successfully achieve the artistic aim of rebellion by immoral means, for example by sacrificing their children to Moloch as a publicity stunt, flouting what God commands at *Leviticus 18:21*. Indeed, the very act of behaving immorally can itself be intentionally rebellious whatever form it takes, where the moral rules that we're required to abide by are deliberately transgressed and broken.

The Ultimate Rebel

It's perfectly possible for Satanic metal artists who are genuine non-theistic Satanists, or who are just pretending to be Satanists, to successfully rebel with their acts. But it's those Satanic metal musicians who are genuine theistic Satanists who are capable of rebelling to the greatest degree. After all, Satan is the ultimate rebel, with his naughty disobedience of God and consequent fall from grace. While pretend Satanists and non-theistic Satanists might well rebel to the extent that they are sticking two fingers up at the Establishment or to shock and offend, the rebellion that theistic Satanists are attempting is something rather more grand. By acknowledging the real existence of the Devil, and by revering Him and following Him in His rebellion against God, they are attempting the biggest form of rebellion that there is. That's why Satanic metal musicians who are genuine theistic Satanists are in prime position to successfully achieve the artistic aim of rebellion in their work by immoral means.

Performing Unspeakable Blasphemies on the Host

Blasphemy is the second artistic aim of Satanic metal that I want to bring in. If Steve Asheim is right, or even if blasphemy is just *one* of the points of Satanic music, then Satanic metal that blasphemes nicely will have this counting in its favor when it comes to judging its artistic worth. And since we're assuming that blasphemy is immoral, we have another of Satanic metal's artistic aims which can be successfully achieved when bands do wicked things.

Calling God Rude Names

Again, Satanic metal musicians who are pretending to be Satanists can say blasphemous things, and they can potentially blaspheme well. And so can genuine non-theistic Satanists. But in each case there's a sense in which they don't really mean it. Calling Jesus a twazzock just for the shock value, or in order to provide a cutting social criticism of the Church as an institution, is to use blasphemy instrumentally, as a way to achieve a further independent goal. To truly blaspheme though is to really mean what you say, to be committed to the existence of the God you're blaspheming against, and of the Devil in whose name you're blaspheming. And if it's more clearly immoral to blaspheme when you really mean it, then it's those Satanic metal musicians who are genuine theistic Satanists who are most able to successfully achieve the artistic aim of blasphemy, and to behave immorally in doing so.

Walking the Walk

A third artistic aim whose successful achievement makes for good Satanic metal is one whose successful achievement makes for good art in general, and that's *authenticity*—being true in your work to who you are and what you know. Authenticity is very often thought to be an artistic virtue, with many people taking a dim view of artists who 'talk the talk' but don't 'walk the walk'. Think of the 'rock'n'roll rebel' who's in fact entirely clean-living, or the comfortably middle-class gangsta rapper who writes lyrics glorifying life in the ghetto but who has no knowledge of what life in the ghetto is like, or the self-styled working-class punk band who claim to remain true to their roots despite 'selling out'. Satanic metal artists can be authentic, but not all of them are.

Satanists Keeping It Real

So which Satanic metal musicians are the authentic ones? It's pretty obvious that those who are just pretending to be Satanists aren't 'walking the walk'. Whatever artistic merits their work might have, authenticity in their Satanism isn't going to be one of them, by definition.

Meanwhile, some Satanic metal musicians who are genuine non-theistic Satanists can possess a degree of authenticity, if they're fully committed to the philosophy of life that their kind of Satanism amounts to. Take those who coerce young women in their apartment block to give birth to the Devil's spawn for an MTV fly-on-the-wall documentary. That can be a means of promoting an anti-Establishmentarianism that they wholeheartedly believe in, for example.

But for people who like their Satanism to be of the *full fat* variety, it's going to be Satanic metal artists who are genuine theistic Satanists who can lay the greatest claim to authenticity here—those musicians who actually believe in the existence of the entity in whose name they carry out their unsavoury shenanigans, and who get up to these things in the service of a Dark Lord that they really do worship. Such Satanists may well be immoral, and they may or may not get to spend all eternity in Hell sitting in a vat of boiling hot custard, but at least they're 'keeping it real'. And in doing so they show that the artistic aim of authenticity can also be successfully achieved by Satanic metal musicians who behave immorally in producing their art.

Clearly It Would Be Better if There Were More Satanists

So there are various ways in which Satanic metal can benefit artistically on account of the quite appalling things that musicians get up to in the course of their work, some of which frankly beggar belief. When it comes to the artistic worth of Satanic metal, worshipping the Devil and doing evil in His name can be a good thing. In fact, as far as the artistic value of Satanic metal is concerned, the more Satanists there are the better. *Ave Satanas!*

The only problem is, it turns out that there aren't any Satanic metal musicians who are genuine theistic Satanists after all. Yes, there are plenty who have claimed to be. But once we've ruled out those who insist that they are Satanists but who don't actually believe in His Infernal Majesty, those who mistakenly think that Aleister Crowley or Anton LaVey believed in the Devil, and those whose genuine theistic Satanism was just a phase they were going through, we find that the cupboard is bare. There are no Satanists in the cupboard. What we need are more people like Charles Gray's character Mocata from the movie *The Devil Rides Out*. People whose eyes you must beware. And who can shred a mean guitar.

VIII

Our Satanic
Social System

20
What the Devil's on TV Tonight?

LIZ STILLWAGGON SWAN

A few years ago, while getting a pedicure, I admitted to my nail technician that I'd recently become obsessed with the TV crime drama, *Criminal Minds*. I also told her that I'd noticed a creeping sense of anxiety in myself after a few months of regularly taking in all those stories about the Devil in human form inflicting pain and misery on people in every way imaginable (and unimaginable).

Given my background in psychology, it didn't surprise me that the show had lured me in and made me an avid fan of its amazing cast of characters who expertly get inside the head of dangerous criminals in order to anticipate their next move and prevent them from inflicting further harm on society. What did surprise and even disturb me was that, despite my generally positive and upbeat nature (some might disagree), I'd become fascinated with the show's horrific stories about devilish deeds like murder, rape, and kidnapping, and furthermore, that I thought of the show as excellent entertainment.

Why *did* I enjoy watching these macabre and dreadful stories about how awful human beings can be to one another? My nail technician, also a fan of the show, agreed that the show was dark and dreadful, but revealed that she felt more aware of the world around her from watching it, better able to protect herself, a single mother, and her daughter from potential Devils lurking in the shadows of real life. You might be skeptical about her assumption that people like those depicted in *Criminal Minds* and other TV crime dramas like it actually exist out there in the real world. But I recently took a few forensic anthropology classes (at my university) in which we studied many true criminal cases where people were killed and disposed of in unspeakable ways.

The Devil is alive and well and very busy out there in the real world. I now think that my nail tech was on to something. TV crime dramas allow the viewing audience to come to know intimately the Devil in human form, and to experience the associated fear and dread—for better and for worse—all from the safety and comfort of our living room couch.

Are We All Sickos?

TV crime dramas are among the most popular shows on TV today. *CSI* (short for "crime scene investigation") claims a global viewing audience of almost seventy-five million, and has five times been named the most watched TV show in the world. A profound question about human nature is why the TV-viewing audience (present author included!) is so drawn to the scary, brutal, and often disturbing stories depicted in TV crime dramas (like, for example, when people and sometimes young children disappear on *Without a Trace*). *CSI* showcases the crime scene investigators, usually a sub-division of the local police unit that is first on the scene when a dead body is discovered. The show details the scientific methods used in collecting and analyzing the evidence associated with the crime scene. However, because it's TV, the crime scenes and the stories behind them are especially dramatic, violent, and gruesome.

The criminal investigators on popular TV crime dramas, such as *Criminal Minds, Without a Trace,* and *CSI,* get up close and personal with the Devil in human form in their everyday work. They experience first-hand the devilish things humans do to one another in the name of love, greed, jealousy, and corruption—all characteristics of the devilish side of humanity. As first responders on the scene, these characters (and their genuine counterpart in real life) ideally encounter the crime scene undisturbed and have the responsibility of collecting all the physical evidence that may be relevant to the case if it winds up in a criminal courtroom.

Some viewers are no doubt interested in the science depicted on the show—DNA profiling, fingerprint analysis, hair and fiber examination, estimation of time and manner of death—but it's safe to say that the main draw of these shows is the stories themselves. Why are we so drawn to these dreadful tales about the so-called "Devil inside" that makes some human beings do horrific things to other human beings? Are we all sickos? Maybe.

The Devil Shadow

Psychologist Carl Jung (1875–1961) developed the notion of the *shadow archetype*, which was that part of someone's personality that was obscured from view and would occasionally surface just enough for us to catch a glimpse of it. The shadow is largely hidden from view and is mostly negative in nature since we tend to be more aware of our positive traits and unaware, or at least less aware, of our faults and devilish tendencies.

Jung explained that the shadow was one character of the collective unconscious—the long and deep history we share not only with our parents and our direct ancestors, but with all of humanity. Each person's individual shadow can be understood as a single layer of the much larger and darker shadow cast by all of humanity. Crime dramas that depict examples of the full-blown expression of the shadow archetype speak to all of us because they tap into that very deep and dark core of all humanity. While we're consciously fearful of, and repulsed by, the devilish tales told on these shows, they succeed in affecting the collective unconscious by casting a shadow dark enough even to eclipse our own personal shadow.

Carl Jung's insight into the shadow of humanity that applies to all of us helps to explain the morbid curiosity and attraction these shows have for us. It at least explains the fact that the stories appeal to the dark side of each one of us (or at least, that they have this powerful potential; not everyone loves TV crime dramas, just most of the world's population). Crime shows are also the adult equivalent of all the mystery, fantasy, sci-fi, paranormal and supernatural stuff that most of us loved to indulge in as kids. I remember being thrilled by ghost stories, horror movies, and sci-fi TV shows like *V* (the original one from the mid-1980s, for those of you old enough to remember it!). And although our choices for entertainment change as we mature (or at least get older), our fundamental human obsession with the dark side of humanity and the scary unknowns of the universe remains.

But, you might say, mystery is one thing. Human misery (as depicted on these popular crime shows) is quite another. So we still need to consider the question of why we widely and without a second thought consider these morbid stories entertaining. It's one thing to be fascinated by them, but to consider these all-too-real stories of murder, rape, and kidnapping *entertainment?* What is wrong with us? Truth be told, watching others suffer fear and agony has a long history in the entertainment industry—dating back to ancient Greece.

Couch Catharsis

Aristotle wrote about the notion of *catharsis*—the idea that it is, in a sense, healthy to watch tragedy unfold on the stage (or on the TV screen, as the case may be) because it allows us to experience the negative emotions and effects associated with tragedy from a safe distance and without any negative consequences. Furthermore, Aristotle believed that if we experienced tragedy vicariously through the actors in the passion play, we would be less likely to act out horrific tragedies in real life. Based on this theory, it's possible that modern-day TV crime dramas fulfill this cathartic role for their millions of avid fans. It could be that watching these powerful stories of personal tragedy and horror on TV allows us to experience the conflict between Devil and humanity from the safety of our comfy family room couch. But does watching these crime dramas make us any less likely to commit violent crimes in real life? It's hard to say.

Take, for example, the current controversy raging over the violent videogame industry. A few decades ago, it was a cliché to blame heavy metal music for dysfunctional, depressed teenagers and even for teen suicide. Today, the finger is pointed at violent videogames and how they corrupt a young mind's ability to distinguish between fantasy and reality. There have been some high profile cases recently in the media wherein violent video games almost certainly played a part, most dramatically the 2012 Newtown, Connecticut, massacre of twenty school children and six staff members (plus the shooter's mother and the shooter himself) executed by an avid gamer who some suspect used videogames to 'train' for his shooting spree. If a causal link can be identified between playing videogames and enacting violent behavior, then it seems Aristotle's theory of how catharsis works would fail in this case. But videogames are so interactive these days that they might not count as an example of the 'visual arts' Aristotle had in mind, wherein one simply watches, but doesn't interact or intervene in the drama.

But the theory certainly does apply to the genre of TV crime dramas, which depict a confrontation between the Devil and humanity that can be explored through the characters on the show. Fiction allows for countless possibilities of how one might react to the conflict between human and Devil or, more generally, between good and evil. A clear contrast can be seen, for example, in criminal investigators who reject the shadow archetype (like the character Garcia on *Criminal Minds*) and those who intellectualize it (like Dr. Brennan on *Bones*). Some viewers will identify with Garcia in feeling repulsed by the horrible things people can do to one another, and thus feel vindicated that someone else feels the same way, and responded just as they would have. Other viewers may identify with Bones (the character) in accepting that evil exists in the world and just wanting to discover the truth, to solve the mystery. In essence, these TV characters fulfill the same role as theater actors in ancient Greece in that they allow the viewing audience to vicariously identify with different possible ways of dealing with the real evil that exists in the world through creative fiction and drama. They provide an avenue by which we can be titillated by Devil stories, and yet be safe.

The CSI Effect

TV crime dramas comprise a very successful entertainment industry that informs and misinforms the viewing audience about the role that forensic science plays in helping investigators solve crimes. The so-called "CSI effect" refers to the fact that people who are involved in criminal court cases, mostly jury members, can be very misinformed about how forensic science works and the role it plays in the legal process, from their familiarity with TV crime dramas like *CSI*. For example, jury members these days are generally aware of DNA analysis, at least from TV, but unclear on how it works and what it's used for.

It's becoming more common for jurors to demand DNA evidence in a criminal court case even when it's irrelevant to solving the case. Take, for instance, a murder trial where jurors have to determine whether a certain suspect (the defendant in the trial) is guilty or not. If the defendant admits to having been at the crime scene, say, a girlfriend's apartment, then a sample of his DNA that is from the crime scene is not helpful to the case because it only demonstrates that the defendant was (at some point) at the crime scene, which he's already openly admitted. DNA is only useful in cases where the defendant denies having been in location X yet his DNA is found there (for example in blood spatter scraped from the wall). A DNA sample does not identify a single human being (since there is so much overlap in DNA from person to person) but it does narrow down the likelihood of the DNA sample having come from a particular person—the suspect in a criminal case—to one in a billion or more, which is plenty to go on, especially in conjunction with other types of evidence relevant to the case.

The CSI effect also refers to the jury members' unrealistic expectations about how fingerprint samples and DNA samples are processed. On *CSI,* for example, investigators get DNA results within a few hours, and use fancy computer programs to match fingerprints and identify criminals. In real life, however, DNA profiling takes months or even years due to the huge backlog of samples awaiting processing in labs all over the US (in large part due to the CSI effect—more jurors in more criminal court cases demanding DNA samples even when they're not going to be useful to the case!). Fingerprint comparison is, perhaps not surprisingly at this point, very different in real life than it is on TV. In true police work, fingerprint comparison is time-consuming work done by human experts, aided by computers.

Anthony E. Zuiker, creator of *CSI*, was asked for a comment on the CSI effect, and replied that although the science depicted in the show is real, the show isn't intended to be educational—it's meant to be entertainment, and clearly succeeds on that front. He claims no responsibility for the side-effects of the wild popularity of his show, nor should he. TV and Hollywood are entertainment engines, fundamentally, even though people may learn something from them along the way (especially from networks intended to be educational, such as the Discovery channel). But this raises the question of why forensic science is portrayed in such a warped way on TV.

Beating the Devil at His Own Tricks

One possible explanation for why forensic science is warped in TV crime dramas is that the nitty gritty of what crime scene investigators do on a daily basis can be tedious, frustrating, and often without resolution—which wouldn't make for good entertainment. Forensic science is manipulated on fictional TV crime dramas in order to serve the needs of the viewing audience.

Criminologist Evan Durnal explained in an *Economist* article published in April 2010 that the CSI effect is the result of "a longing to believe that desirable, clever, and morally unimpeachable individuals are fighting to clear the names of the innocent and put the bad guys behind bars."

Durnal is right. We do long to believe, and even *need* to believe, that law enforcement, science, and the law are all on our side, working to prevent the Devil from unleashing too much misery on society. We feel safer knowing that real-life sickos such as serial killers Ted Bundy, Jeffrey Dahmer, and John Wayne Gacy were all eventually apprehended and punished for devilish behavior. There's a deep-seated human need to experience resolution, to see things put right and, most fundamentally, to know that we are safe from the shadow and safe from the Devil. And in the intense, fast-paced, and gripping typical TV crime drama, we're getting a satisfying resolution to an awful human tragedy all in forty-three minutes (minus commercial time). It's like crack for crime mystery addicts.

Not only are these shows deeply satisfying in resonating with the Jungian shadow archetype of the Devil side of humanity, but they also fulfill the cathartic need of the human community to see the bad guys intercepted and punished for their devilish deeds—their seizure and public retribution allows us to breathe a collective sigh of relief knowing we are in a better and safer world now. Only something that touched us deeply on psychological and philosophical levels could become such a global obsession.

Another popular TV crime drama, *Cold Case Files,* is a case in point. This show highlights stories of kidnapping and murder that have been "cold" (unsolved) for a long time. The episodes generally conclude with a long-awaited answer to an unsolved mystery, wherein, for instance, a grown man who was kidnapped as a boy finally returns home to see his aged mother who never gave up hope that he'd one day return. This show in particular plays on the human need for resolution, for an answer to the mystery. It serves a cathartic purpose of giving us hope through other people's stories of triumph over evil, of reward after a long wait, of beating the Devil at his own tricks.

21
Souls for Sale

JEFF EWING

Selling your soul to the Devil in exchange for a longer life, wealth, beauty, power, or skill has long been a theme in books, movies, and even music. Souls have been sold for knowledge and pleasure (Faust), eternal youth (Dorian Gray), the ability to play the guitar (Tommy Johnson in *O Brother, Where Art Thou?*) or the harmonica (Willie "Blind Dog Fulton Smoke House" Brown in the 1986 movie, *Crossroads*), or for rock'n'roll itself (the way Black Sabbath did on their 1975 greatest hits album, *We Sold Our Soul for Rock'n'Roll*).

The selling of a soul as an object of exchange for nearly anything, as a sort of fictitious commodity with nearly universal exchange value, makes it perhaps the most unique of all possible commodities (and as such, contracts for the sales of souls are the most unique of all possible contracts). One theorist in particular, Karl Marx (1818–1883), elaborately analyzed contracts, exchange, and "the commodity" itself, along with all the hidden implications of commodities and the exchange process. Let's see what Marx has to tell us about the "political economy" of the Faustian bargain with the Devil, and try to uncover what it truly is to sell your soul.

Malice and *Malleus Maleficarum*

While the term *devil* is sometimes used to refer to minor, lesser demons, in Western religions the term refers to Satan, the fallen angel who led a rebellion against God and was banished from Heaven. In Christian theology, a banished Satan is the prince of the other fallen angels, who attempts to coax humanity into sinning against God, where they'll be sent to Hell, presumably tortured indefinitely. Satan's encouragement of people to sin is part of his overall war against God, where he plans to overthrow Heaven and God's rule. The war against Heaven and God's forces ultimately culminates in Armageddon, the final battle between good and evil, and the Apocalypse, the end of the World (preceding the birth of a new one).

The Devil doesn't have the omniscience, omnipotence, and omnipresence of God, nor does he have the power of creation— he prepares to wage a war against God via a number of tactical measures, including demonic possession, temptation, straightforward conversion of individuals towards an evil life, and (you guessed it) either encouraging or accepting human trades of souls for worldly pleasures.

An early depiction of sales for souls is found in the *Malleus Maleficarum* (1487), which lists supposed instances of pacts with the Devil, though perhaps the earliest and most influential example is the story of Doctor Faustus, immortalized in both Christopher Marlowe's *Doctor Faustus* (1604) and Johann Wolfgang von Goethe's *Faust* (1808), each inspired by the legend surrounding the German alchemist, astrologer, and magician Dr. Johann Georg Faust. Little verifiable fact is known about Dr. Faust, but he probably was born in the late 1400s, and died in 1540 or 1541. Numerous magical and alchemical abilities had been associated with Faust, and those powers had widely been attributed to a pact with the Devil.

The Quintessential Salesman

In even earlier Christian theological tradition (dating back perhaps as early as the sixth century), Theophilus of Adana is held to be a cleric who sells his soul and is redeemed by the Virgin Mary. These stories typically involve an individual seeking worldly success, pleasure, knowledge, power, or even love, and they barter with a demon or the Devil for the success of their goal (sometimes until a natural death, sometimes for a particularly defined amount of time) in exchange for their eternal soul.

Sometimes they get exactly what they bargained for—and are sometimes satisfied at the time, other times find their side of the bargain wanting—and other times they are tricked, granted what they wished for but then the unspoken terms of their side of the bargain change around them. The *Twilight Zone* episode "Escape Clause" has this theme, where a hypochondriac sells his soul for immortality, only to be eventually faced with the possibility of spending life in prison.

The essence of these stories is the sale of an eternal soul to the Devil for a worldly gain of some kind, and this theme has permeated Western culture ever since, in art forms as diverse as music (the Charlie Daniels Band's "The Devil Went Down to Georgia," where the Devil bets the fiddle player Johnny a golden fiddle if Johnny beats him in a fiddling contest), movies (*Rosemary's Baby*, where Rosemary's husband Guy contracts with a coven that Rosemary will unwillingly give birth to the Antichrist in return for Guy's successful acting career), television (many episodes of *The Twilight Zone*), videogames, and numerous works of literature (including of course *Faust*, and implied in *The Picture of Dorian Gray*).

X Marx the Spot

A long-standing staple of media in the West, the concept of selling your soul in exchange for some worldly end—often secured with a written contract for exchange—attempts to transform the human soul into a commodity for sale on the spiritual market. Karl Marx, the radical German philosopher, economist, and revolutionary, wrote Volume I of his great work *Das Kapital* (Capital) in 1867 and grounded this key work in an analysis of the commodity and exchange relationships under capitalism.

Marx wrote a number of influential works throughout his lifetime, but his most distinct contribution to the study of the political economy of capitalism comes in the form of his magnum opus, *Das Kapital*. Marx starts Volume I with an analysis of "the commodity," which is an object that is exchanged (bought and sold) in a market. Understanding commodities is important to understand capitalism. All commodities, Marx argues, have two kinds of value—their *use value* (how useful a thing is, what desires or needs it can fulfill) and their *value* (how much labor went into their production). This latter concept is complex to understand (the labor content of a good, its *value*, is represented by its *exchange value*, how much it should exchange for on the market, and *exchange value* is modified by a number of other factors to translate into a monetary *price*, what a good costs in an actual transaction), but you can roughly summarize Marx's point by describing all commodities under capitalism as objects that have both real uses and, simultaneously, various prices that determine how much you can get in return for it in a market. Marx also clearly points out that an object (or service) has to have *use value* to have *exchange value* (because if labor somehow produces something that no one has any use for, that labor will have no value at all).

C Is for Capitalism

Capitalism is distinct from most other economic systems in the sense that production, the transformation by human labor of resources and other goods, occurs primarily for the sale of those objects on the market. In prior Western economic systems, production of goods predominantly occurred for reasons other than sale, and a proportion of those goods were forcibly "tribute" to the owners of resources and tools used in production (landlords under feudalism, slaveholders under slavery).

While capitalism is distinct for being the only economic system in which most production occurs for sale on the market, it's also distinct for being a system in which the means by which people produce (resources, tools) are privately owned by particular individuals, the capitalists. Capitalists also are certainly willing to sell resources and goods which have been cultivated or produced for reasons *other* than sale on the market, but the fact that the majority of production is intended for sale is the distinctive factor.

Marx also assumes that all exchange occurs between goods that have equal exchange value (that is, Marx assumes no one gets cheated). While this is not always true and people may be cheated in fact quite often, Marx's economic analysis starts from best-case-scenario assumptions about capitalism and how it works—no one gets cheated, no one is coerced, the playing field between capitalists is competitive—to show the necessary consequences of capitalist production in the best of all possible worlds. Workers agree to sell their labor-power (their capacity to labor) in exchange for wages, with which they can meet their needs on the market by buying goods and services. Marx assumes that their pay must on balance enable them to meet their needs (or else why would they agree to work for someone else's benefit?), and thus the value of their yearly labor power sold on the market is roughly equal to the value of the goods and services they need to survive the year at a socially determined average level of acceptability (that is, they get paid enough to survive and live a life at an acceptable quality), and in households with dependents this wage level covers the ability for dependents to survive as well (including children and stay-at-home spouses).

Capitalists attempt, via a variety of measures, to get workers to work *in actuality* to produce value beyond their wage level, a condition Marx refers to as *exploitation* (where one works for more than what one gets in return) and capitalists take home excess over what they've paid workers in the form of *surplus value* (or, in monetary form, profits). Thus, while workers agree to contract their capacity to labor in exchange for the income they need to meet their needs, capitalists try to maximize the commodities workers produce beyond that point in order to gain profits from production—workers make more value than they get paid for, and capitalists reap the rewards.

What Can I Get for This Soul?

In fiction, movies, music, and other media, characters have sold their souls for a number of various goals, such as immortality in our aforementioned *Twilight Zone* episode, a successful acting career in *Rosemary's Baby*, money in Washington Irving's "The Devil and Tom Walker," or even redemption (upon sending other souls Hell's way) in the 1981 movie *The Devil and Max Devlin*.

In the *Faust* mythos, Faust exchanges his soul with Mephistopheles for knowledge and power. In *Doctor Faustus*, Marlowe contracts with Lucifer (the Devil) through the demon Mephistopheles, selling his soul to Lucifer in exchange for twenty-four years of his every wish being served by Mephistopheles's hand. The final night before the contract is up finds Faust begging for mercy, but to no avail. Goethe's *Faust* begins with Mephistopheles betting God that he can turn one of God's loyal followers (Faust) away from God. Faust, an alchemist and scholar, despairs over the limits of his knowledge, and is approached by Mephistopheles with a wager that the Devil can provide Faust the transcendence he seeks and Mephistopheles will be Faust's servant on Earth. The stakes of the wager are that, if Mephistopheles succeeds and Faust finds a moment he wants to live forever, Faust must serve him forever in Hell. While there are differences in the details of the two versions of *Faust*, both find Faust wagering his soul in exchange for knowledge and worldly gain, using his soul as an object of exchange.

In Oscar Wilde's *The Picture of Dorian Gray*, Dorian Gray is a culturally literate and wealthy young man of extraordinary physical attractiveness. Basil Hallward, a painter creating a portrait of Dorian, introduces him to a friend, Lord Henry, who makes Dorian upset with a speech about how quickly youth and beauty fade. Worried about the loss of these, Dorian's most notable traits, Dorian curses the portrait, which he fears will someday remind him of his lost youth and beauty. Dorian pledges his soul under the condition that the painting bears the weight of time and life, thus allowing him to stay forever young and beautiful. Over time, Dorian devotes himself to hedonistic pleasure and debauchery, and with each self-serving or other-harming action he notes his portrait (in his possession) becoming more hideous. Dorian Gray makes no direct deal with the Devil, but 'wagers' his soul for beauty following Lord Henry's prompt, and continues a life of increasing 'sin', hedonism, selfishness, and debauchery under Lord Henry's prompting, and thus Lord Henry serves the same function in *Dorian Gray* as the Devil does in direct adaptations of the Faustian legend.

In *O Brother, Where Art Thou?* the convicts Ulysses Everett McGill, Pete Hogwallop, and Delmar O'Donnell are three escaped convicts in 1930s Mississippi, trying to find Everett's hidden stolen treasure. Of the number of odd situations and strange characters they encounter on their journey, one of which is their encounter with the guitarist Tommy Johnson (modeled after the real-life blues musician Tommy Johnson) who sold his soul to the devil for the ability to play the guitar (a claim made by the real Tommy). Later, Tommy is found to be almost a victim of a lynching by the Ku Klux Klan until our convicts intervene. For Tommy, his soul was used as an object of exchange for skill in playing the guitar (and apparently he never pulled a 'Devil Went Down to Georgia' and challenged the devil to keep his soul). Tommy Johnson shows yet another potential object of exchange for a human soul—guitar skill (thus widening the range of potential worldly gains from knowledge, power, and wealth, to presumably the whole range of potential skills, like the ability to make sushi, speak Italian, master the Etch-a-Sketch, or perform terrific card tricks). All these examples exhibit the diversity of 'things' you can trade a soul for—knowledge, power, skills, beauty. . . trading souls is the Amazon.com of bartering—you can get anything for them, and all you have to do is be willing to spend eternity in Hell, or otherwise serve the demon who served you (or whatever else the specific terms of agreement end up to be).

Marx and the Commodified Soul

Marx was a materialist—he didn't think there was truth to metaphysical, religious, or spiritual claims. Thus, Marx would argue that there is no soul to be traded or a "Devil" to trade it to—but let's just forget that for a moment, shall we? Assuming there is a soul and a Devil to trade it to, what kind of tradable entity or object might the soul be? The soul can be traded for *anything*—it is a true universal commodity. In this respect, it resembles the traditional function of gold, the commodity historically linked with money, which functions as the universal measure of the value of other commodities. Gold has long been the universal commodity—like the human soul on the metaphysical level, but the soul does one better—it can grant one gold, but one cannot trade gold for one's soul (old-Catholic indulgences notwithstanding!). But why the one-sided trade-ability?

Gold is the universal commodity on the Earthly plane, but souls have effectively one buyer—the Devil (or sometimes his minions on his behalf). The trade in souls is perhaps the only *perfect* buyer's monopoly. One often recognized insight of political economy of any stripe—right-wing, centrist, left-wing, or Marxist—is that the degree of monopoly of buyers or sellers gives them nearly unlimited power to demand prices, so long as the good's sale or purchase is important. Since the Devil, according to fiction and movies, can effectively grant *anything*, the use value of what he has to offer is nearly limitless (according to fiction he can grant worldly power, nearly infinite knowledge, almost ageless invulnerability à la Dorian Gray, and so forth), and the good he asks in return is something everyone has according to Western theology.

Capitalism runs differently from the rules of the Devil in one respect—capitalist commodities are sold for monetary profit, and thus production occurs for what is called *effective demand* rather than demand itself—for capitalism it doesn't matter what you want or need, unless you have the money to pay for it, which you might not have. If you do not have the money, your need does not get met, even if it kills you.

The Devil, on the other hand, asks only the tradable commodity everyone has from the time they are born—their soul. And since everyone has effective demand (what they need to trade to the Devil) and the Devil can grant nearly any desire (except for true salvation, access to Heaven, et cetera, . . . obviously!) and has a complete monopoly over the provision of worldly desires via the trade of a soul (while Western theology holds that God will provide, God will not presumably provide *all* things, and does not trade in souls), the Devil has the *market* power to ask the highest price—the soul—if the person trading it wants something badly enough to pay.

As a commodity, the soul has important use value—it is the source of immortality (survives death), made in the image of God, and one's choices in life impact the final use value of the soul. This relates to Marx's development of the labor theory of value—labor creates or develops use values in goods (natural objects come ready-made with use value, but it takes human labor to make nature useful for needs, even if that labor is as simple as picking an apple from a tree). Your labor then ultimately determines the use value of your soul (even if that use value starts out supposedly pure) in a similar way to how labor determines the use-value of other resources and goods. Simultaneously, the soul has nearly unlimited exchange value. You could perhaps classify the soul has having a similar status to 'nature'—the use-value precedes but is modified by human labor, and its development and generation occur for reasons other than commodity exchange and profit. The person who sells their soul loses its use-value in favor of its exchange value, and the Devil enlarges his Hellish kingdom.

Souletarian Revolution?

As we've seen, from the pseudo-immortality of Dorian Gray, the knowledge and power of Faust, the guitar-playing skill of Tommy Johnson, the acting success of Rosemary's husband in *Rosemary's Baby,* or the immortality of *Twilight Zone*'s "Escape Clause" can all be purchased at the cost of a human soul. The soul is not produced to be a commodity—in Western theology God does not generate souls as objects for sale to the Devil—but nonetheless, while having almost universal exchange-value (much like a more powerful, spiritual version of gold) souls traditionally have only one buyer—the Devil. This monopoly status grants the Devil the ability to extract the ultimate deal, the permanent human soul, in exchange for all of these worldly gains, setting up the drama behind all person-sells-soul-for-random-stuff plot-lines. The soul fits loosely within the Marxian labor theory of value tradition, in that the use-value of the soul (its possibility of admittance to Heaven or Hell) is impacted by human activity, much like natural resources or other goods.

By this analysis, it is more possible to sell a soul to the Devil (in Western theology) and get your needs met than it is (for many people) to get needs met through capitalism. This is because *unlike* the market for souls, capitalism only provides based on *effective demand*, and if you can't pay, you can't survive if your only resource is within the market. The Devil asks a high price, a person's immortal soul, but the human soul is a resource *everyone* has (so all demand is 'effective demand'). The height of the price isn't that different from Marx's materialist account of capitalism (if Marx's atheism and materialism are right, the ultimate price is not the final abode of a human soul, but the natural and material death of a human body), as capitalist exchange tendencies allow many individuals the world over to die from lack of their needs being met, many poor and working class people pay the highest price under capitalism. Nonetheless, the sale of your soul to the Devil, the soul as the ultimate object of exchange (but where the individual pays the ultimate price) is a staple of Western literature—and one that makes clearest sense when looked at with Marx's critique of political economy.

22
Bill Hicks and Satan

ROGER HUNT

Before succumbing to pancreatic cancer in 1994 at the age of thirty-two, Bill Hicks was an American comedian active throughout the 1980s and early 1990s, performing on Rodney Dangerfield's *Young Comedians' Special*, *Late Night with David Letterman*, HBO, and other famous places. His unique blend of reason and humor vaulted him to such fame that he's now considered to be one of the most influential comedians ever, at least according to British audiences (they rank him as the fourth best of all time). His reputation in the US, however, is . . . well, not really existent. I bet you never even heard of this guy till now, right? There's no good explanation why, but perhaps it's because his stand-up routine consistently vilifies almost every aspect of America including its politics, religious ideals, and culture.

At the heart of his comedy, which is more a humorous critique rather than observation or clever punch-lining, is a conception of Satan explored through a dialogue, rather than any kind of explicit philosophical treatise. His style is reminiscent of the ancient Greek philosopher Socrates, who roamed from city to city interacting with citizens, politicians, and sophists, or self-proclaimed teachers of rhetoric, pointing out ignorance, hypocrisy, and the suppression of knowledge through a very curious form of questioning, which ultimately left the questionee either enlightened, utterly confused, unsure of himself, or haphazardly dismissing him. Ironically enough, Hicks suffered a similar fate to Socrates, who died of hemlock poisoning while incarcerated for corrupting the youth, by succumbing to a rapidly spreading pancreatic cancer. One can't help but imagine that it was either those in the social spotlight poisoning him because they were upset at his caricature, God striking him down, or perhaps even the Devil intervening to stop Hicks's disclosure of the satanic procedures.

Boy George at a Klan Rally

Hicks's comedy is an exploration of the Devil's methodology. On my read, it is a three-point plan. Suppress knowledge to create an ignorant population that will consume hypocritical products. Suppression, ignorance, and hypocrisy seem like pretty good watchwords for an ambitious Satan. Satan does this to hide the real truth from us, a truth that Hicks exposes at the end of each set:

> Wouldn't you like to see a positive LSD story on the news? To base your decision on information rather than scare tactics and superstition? Perhaps? Wouldn't that be interesting? Just for once? 'Today, a young man on acid realized that all matter is merely energy condensed to a slow vibration—that we are all one consciousness experiencing itself subjectively. There is no such thing as death, life is only a dream, and we are the imagination of ourselves . . . Here's Tom with the weather.'

Hicks's stand-up has little patience for those who turn a blind eye to what he considers monumental follies of reason. He grew up in Texas, where his family was Southern Baptist and part of the evangelical Christian movement, and Hicks used this experience to bolster his stand-up, while also vilifying them as ignorant red-necks who spend little time thinking about moral, philosophical, or other worldly issues outside the context of their rural lives. He attributed this stereotypical apathy to basic ignorance. Hicks understood rural America as not only unable to understand, but also unwilling even to explore the rest of the world.

He presents a scene familiar to all of us who have visited the southeast—a morning at the Waffle House:

> You know I've noticed a certain anti-intellectualism going around this country ever since around 1980, coincidentally enough. I was in

Nashville . . . and I went to a Waffle House and I'm sitting there and I'm eating and reading a book. . . . This waitress comes over to me (mocks chewing gum) 'What you readin' for?' Wow, goddamnit, you stumped me. . . . I guess I read for a lot of reasons—the main one is so I don't end up being a fuckin' waffle waitress . . . Then this trucker in the booth next to me gets up, stands over me, and says [*mocks Southern drawl*] 'Well, looks like we got ourselves a readah.' What the fuck's goin' on? It's like I walked into a Klan rally in a Boy George costume or something. Am I stepping out of some intellectual closet here? I read. There. I said it. I feel better.

Satan is the Devil in the details. Hicks's comedy works because it turns common symbols on their heads. In this case, there is a vague reference to the story of Adam and Eve, in which a snake, representing Satan, feeds Eve an apple, making her aware of her nakedness, causing shame, and creating what we might call the human condition. In that story, knowledge ruined everything. However for Hicks, knowledge is the pathway to freedom from the forces that seek to repress our humanity. In this bit, we have a woman sincerely curious, albeit somewhat skeptical of Hicks's choice to read. But as soon as she's able to get more information, in comes the man, "Looks like we got ourselves a readah," effectively protecting this woman from the knowledge which may be her salvation from a job at the Waffle House. The Devil, in this case, is not the snake that offers an apple from the tree of knowledge, but the force which actively suppresses the search for knowledge.

Out in the Bush

Hicks also finds satanic suppressive techniques coming from the government. Two eras of American politics particularly tickle his fancy: the JFK assassination and the Gulf War. Both events raise questions not only about the events themselves, but more importantly about how leaders in America react to serious and emotionally jaunting events. Whether or not the government is justified in limiting the amount of information available to the public, *that* they have to limit it at all leads Bill to suspect the heavy hand of Satan.

Here's Bill on George H.W. Bush, whom he believes to be one of grandest hypocrites of our time:

People often ask me where I stand politically. It's not that I disagree with Bush's economic policy or his foreign policy, it's that I believe he was a child of Satan sent here to destroy the planet Earth. Little to the left.

To this point, he examines America's role in Iraq prior to our military offensive called Desert Storm launched in the early 1990s. At that time, there were constant reports on Iraq's military operations:

I love it when Bush gets up there and says, "We live in a dangerous world." Yeah, because of you, you fucker. . . . You know we armed Iraq . . . During the Persian Gulf war, those intelligence reports would come out: 'Iraq: incredible weapons—incredible weapons'. 'How do you know that?' 'Uh, well, . . . we looked at the receipts . . . We're going in for God and country and democracy and here's a fetus and he's a Hitler. Whatever you fucking need, let's go!

The end of this bit is most important to his theory on Satan. He's worried about our government leaders distracting us from the truth as if we can't handle it, which in many cases may be true, but again, that we live in such a world is a crying shame for him. He reiterates this point discussing the Kennedy assassination:

People tell me, 'Bill, let it go. The Kennedy assassination was years ago. It was just the assassination of a President and the hijacking of our government by a totalitarian regime—who cares? Just let it go.' I say, 'All right then. That whole Jesus thing? *Let it go!* It was two thousand years ago! Who cares?' Go back to bed, America. Your government has figured out how it all transpired. Go back to bed, America. Your government is in control again. Here's *American Gladiators*. Watch this, shut up . . . Watch these pituitary retards bang their fucking skulls together and congratulate you on living in the land of freedom. Here you go, America! You are free to do as we tell you!

This bit doesn't criticize the conclusions of the Warren Commission, the government investigation of the Kennedy assassination, though Bill does have some thoughts including his description of visiting Dealey Plaza, where Kennedy was shot. Rather, this bit points out how our leaders feel it is necessary to either suppress information or distract us with mundane entertainment—YouTube an episode of *American Gladiators*—or more likely some other politically concocted scandal. However, again, that this happens is not necessarily the problem. Instead, Hicks worries that these tactics create a world where people are not entrusted with information they want. And in a world where people can't have information they want for whatever reason, they won't be able to make informed reasonable decisions.

Fucking Freebird

Now, one could of course argue that people could not make reasonable informed decisions anyway, thus we should limit the information we distribute to them. However, remember Hicks's basic premise about the universe, "We are all one consciousness." If one group of people starts to limit access to information to others, they've not only affected those people's minds, but also their own. This seems to create a kind of feedback loop, which produces exactly the world Hicks is criticizing. A world where he feels the need to point out the following after someone in Chicago at a 1989 show kept yelling "Freebird"—after the Lynyrd Skynyrd song of the same name—which was (and still is) something that people will often scream out at a concert as a kind of joke, usually before the encore:

> Please quit yelling that. It's not funny, it's not clever; it's stupid, it's repetitive, why the fuck would you continue to yell that? I'm serious . . . What is the culmination of yelling that? You see, we are here at the same point again where you, the fucking *peon* masses, can once again ruin anyone who tries to do anything because you don't know how to do it on your own! That's where we're fucking at! Once again the useless wastes of fucking *flesh* that has ruined everything good in this goddamn world! That's where we're at. Hitler *had the right idea! he was just an underachiever!* Kill 'em all, Adolf! . . . Start over! The experiment didn't work! Rain forty days, please fucking rain to wash these turds off my fucking life! Wash these human wastes of flesh and bone off this planet! I pray to you, God, to *kill these fucking people!*

Someone then yells out "Freebird" one more time, and Hicks responds:

Freebird. And in the beginning there was the word, *Freebird*. And Freebird would be yelled throughout the centuries. Freebird—the mantra of the moron.

Fucking with Our Heads?

Satan's goal is to mislead humanity. To bring us to a place of false consciousness, obsessed with desire, and utterly confused about the divine word. But of course, most of those "morons" yelling 'Freebird!' probably believe in God (ninety-five percent or so in America), and claim to worship and live in line with the rules and teachings of the Bible or some other religious text. However, if we accept Hicks's premise, then what does this say about believing in God? Well, it seems that a group of confused, obsessed, and uninformed people who claim to believe in God, may not realize what they actually believe in. That is, how aware of God's actual plan are we? What do we really understand about it, and how might our actions on Earth be understood in terms of that? I imagine Hicks would argue that we have completely misinterpreted what God wanted, and instead believe in a God who is actually the creation of Satan. Here are two bits that speak to us misunderstanding and mischaracterizing God:

> Why is marijuana against the law? It grows naturally on our planet, serves a thousand different functions, all of them positive. To make marijuana against the law is like saying that God made a mistake. Like on the seventh day God looked down, 'There it is. My Creation, perfect and holy in all ways. Now I can rest.' [*Gives shocked expression*] 'Oh my *Me*! I left fuckin' pot *everywhere* . . . But if I leave pot everywhere, that's gonna give people the impression they're supposed to . . . *use it*. Now I have to create *Republicans* . . .' 'and God wept,' I believe is the next part of that story.

> Whenever I encounter fundamentalist Christians who believe the world is six thousand years old, I always ask them: dinosaurs. One guy said to me: God put dinosaur fossils here to test our faith!' . . . I think God put *you* here to test *my* faith, dude. Does that bother anybody else, the idea that God might be *fucking with our heads*? I have trouble sleeping with that knowledge. Some prankster God runnin' around . . . [*pantomimes digging*] . . . We'll see who believes in me now. I am the Prankster God. I am *killing* me!

That is, in what kind of world are we portraying God as someone who "fucks with our heads"? This deeply worries Hicks, as
he notes, and it does so because it's likely that we aren't
focused on God, but rather some kind of trickery by Satan
enlisting us to believe in the wrong God.

Sucking Satan's Cock

Now that Satan has created a population which doesn't seek
knowledge, hates readahs, and is utterly confused about who or
what God is, he can now distribute his product. Unfortunately,
the Devil's product serves very little social benefit. Instead
according to Hicks, Satan doesn't much care about what he
sells as long as the person selling it has performed the proper
sexual favors to him. Satan endows the power to control the
public to those who perform fellatio. Unfortunately, there is not
much for me to quote here since these bits are just Hicks growling on stage in sexual bliss as he mimes receiving oral sex from
the likes of Vanilla Ice and Mark "Marky Mark" Wahlberg,
while grumbling, "Suck Satan's cock . . ." Essentially anything
without artistic merit and created simply to sell product captures Hicks's definition of a world controlled by Satan.

Here is Hicks on Rick Astley:

> Rick Astley? Have you seen this banal incubus at work? Boy, if this
> guy isn't heralding Satan's imminent approach to Earth, huh. 'Don't
> ever wanna make you cry / never wanna make you sigh / never gonna
> break your heart' Oh, I wouldn't worry about that without a dick,
> buddy. You got a corn nut! . . . You're not even a guy! . . . These aren't
> even people man! It's a CIA plot to make you think malls are good!
> Don't ya see? (Imitates stereotypical American in a robotic manner)
> 'But Bill, malls are good! Malls allow us to shop 365 days of the year
> at a 72-degree heat. That must be good.'

Hilarious, but also off-putting. Rick Astley made tons of
money on that one single, and actually released another
album in 2012. In what universe is the song that spurred the
now famous "Rick-Rolled" phenomenon ever of a caliber to
warrant someone a comfortable lifestyle? Not to pick on Rick,
of course, since Bill believes most all pop-stars "suck Satan's
cock":

We rock against drugs, 'cause that's what George Bush would want. We're rock stars who sell Pepsi-cola products. We're rock stars who sell Taco Bell products. Ball-less, soulless, spiritless little corporate fucking puppets, suckers of Satan's cock each and every one of them.

The marketing profession really gets him going:

By the way, if anyone here is in advertising or marketing, kill yourself. You're the ruiner of all things good. You are Satan's spawn, filling the world with bile and garbage . . . kill yourself.

Spawn of Satan

What's so clever and ultimately scary about Satan is that he never executes any plan on his own, but rather enlists "spawn," as Bill likes to say, to execute it. Even scarier perhaps is that Satan's plan is nothing more than a ploy to get as many blow jobs as possible. This means that people are sucking Satan's cock to earn the power to execute their own human plans, which are possibly more destructive than anything Satan could ever imagine on his own. It's the human capacity for aggression, hatred, and destruction that Satan wants to unleash upon the world. Perhaps Bill's genius is that he utilizes all of these aggressive and hyper-sexual themes in his act as a *demon*-stration (get it?) of all that is wrong with the world. That is, if you think Bill is too raunchy or out there or un-PC or corruptive, just take a fucking look around you, man!

23
Devil with a Blue Dress

CYNTHIA M. JONES, SANDRA HANSMANN,
AND ANNE STACHURA

W omen have often been blamed for the sins of mankind. But women aren't usually considered smart enough to actually *be* the Devil. They're typically portrayed as the less-than-optimally-clever handmaidens of the Devil, like temptresses, succubae, and witches.

Leaving aside a few movies—like *Devil* and *Bedazzled*—which literally depict the Devil as female, most traditional references are to a masculine Devil. Instead of actually being seen as the Devil, women are generally portrayed as the weak and easily manipulated tools of the Devil or the conduit of evil and temptation that lead men to their doom. Even classics such as the 1935 movie *The Devil Is a Woman* only mean this figuratively—the woman depicted in this movie is evil *like* the devil, she's wicked and malevolent and should be viewed with suspicion by men as she'll always be conniving to manipulate men to get what she wants.

Similar examples from mythology and history are easily found, like succubae who suck the souls from unsuspecting men caught in the web of their apparent feminine beauty, or entities like the Sirens from Greek mythology who lured sailors to their death with their enticing songs. But where did this unfortunate link between the Devil and women originate, you might wonder? (And if you do wonder this, you clearly haven't read the Bible recently.)

Beginning with Eve

There is some debate among historical and theological scholars regarding the Genesis story of the fall from grace, where Eve convinces Adam to eat the fruit from the forbidden tree after Eve is tempted by the Devil. Some scholars, for example, argue that Adam was present when Eve was tempted by Satan, while others argue Adam wasn't there, but only showed up after the fact to be presented with the fruit by his trusted wife.

Whether or not he was present for the conversation between the Devil and Eve does matter, from a moral culpability standpoint, because if he was privy to the conversation, then he seems to be responsible to a greater extent, given that he knew what the Devil said to Eve. The one thing that's rather clear, however, is that it was the weak-willed and easily manipulated Eve whom the Devil approached and who convinced Adam to eat. So Eve's responsible for giving in to the temptation, resulting in expulsion from the Garden of Eden and all the original sin stuff that followed.

According to some religions, this sin is passed down to all humanity and requires purging right after the birth of every child, or at least requires the recognition of fault or weakness on the part of all human beings, because of Eve. Anyone who buys into the Bible at all will have some conception of Eve as the temptress who messed everything up for the rest of us, especially good old Adam.

Secondary or Manipulative

The Genesis creation story also tells us that Adam was created first in the image of God and that Eve was formed from an unimportant bone taken from Adam's body, so he wouldn't be lonely. Woman thus originates in the Judeo-Christian mythology as secondary and inconsequential, and as a playmate for the man who was created in God's image.

The link between the first woman and great evil isn't the only one found in Judeo-Christian traditions and writings. Another link between women and demons can be found in the varying myths of Lilith who is sometimes shown devouring children, sometimes explained as the first wife of Adam (created from the same earth as Adam and refusing to be subservient to him), but almost always depicted as a demon of sorts. Other biblical examples of manipulative and evil women include Delilah, Salome, Lot's wife and daughters, and of course Jezebel.

This isn't to say that there aren't lots of evil men in the Bible, or to deny that men are depicted as bad and linked to the Devil. However, given that men historically have controlled all of the power, this "demonizing" of women, who will always be conspiring to steal men's souls as the weak-willed tools of the Devil, is one way in which this patriarchal power is perpetuated and justified.

The Perpetual Other

In *The Second Sex* (1949) Simone de Beauvoir discusses the history of the second-class status of women, quoting famous lines from the likes of Aristotle, who argued that women are defined by their lack of positive qualities and who described the "natural defectiveness" of the "female nature," and St. Thomas Aquinas, who argued that men are more complete in both soul and body. Beauvoir describes the academic history of men reflecting upon the inferiority of women as helping to maintain the inferior standing of women and to keep women relegated to the status of "incidental" beings.

Beauvoir goes on to discuss the undeniable sexism present in the history of psychology, wherein theorists like Sigmund Freud held that even a woman's orgasms are inferior to those of men. For many centuries, hysteria was thought to be caused by the movement of a woman's uterus throughout her body (the English word *hysteria* is derived from the Greek ὑστέρα, *hystera*, meaning "uterus") as it was considered a psychological disturbance particular to women, and pregnancy was often prescribed as a cure. In the twentieth century, theorists in psychology who came after Beauvoir had similarly sexist things to say, like Lawrence Kohlberg who held that females are typically at a much lower stage of moral development than their male counterparts. Kohlberg's studies formed the basis of what feminist ethicists like Carol Gilligan in her work, *In a Different Voice* (1982), reacted against.

Contemporary psychologists, who are working from less-sexist assumptions, note that women place blame and take credit in very different ways than their male counterparts, which is not surprising. A good example can be found in research on women in situations of domestic violence who often blame themselves for the violence inflicted upon them. (Of course society does a great job of blaming the victims of domestic violence and sexual assault as well.) Further, women internally attribute moral lapses—they blame themselves—while men externally attribute moral lapses—they blame external entities like the Devil, or women! Conversely, women are less likely to self-credit their successes than men. In other words, the average woman credits others for her successes and blames herself for failures, while the average man does the opposite. These psychological differences shouldn't be surprising, given what we know about the history of viewing women as evil and inferior.

Witchy Women

The sixteenth- and seventeenth-century witch-hunts in Europe and North America comprise an oft-discussed chapter in the history of female-vilifying oppression. For some time, it had been argued that Christian religions (Catholicism in particular) were solely responsible for the "trials" and killings of many thousands of women after branding them as witches and in league with the Devil. There is recent debate regarding the depth of the role these patriarchal churches played in the witch-hunts, but there is little doubt that the Catholic and Protestant churches fueled the fervor and played on people's fears of the unknown to assist in these hunts that killed many thousands of women (and some men) in Europe in rather gruesome ways, whilst linking them to the Devil. One feminist blogger claims the Catholic Church is now accusing women of being radical feminists instead of witches, which we suppose is a step up.

In addition to women as witches, history and mythology present wonderful examples of women linked to the Devil or demons, like Baba Yaga, La Malinche, Black Annis, Lamia, and the scores of scary witchy women from the Grimm fairy tales, to name but a few. Feminist theorists tell us that the three female roles found throughout history are the virgin, the maiden, and the crone. Many traditional stories demonstrate the acceptable female roles of virgin and maiden/mother, while the third part, the old woman or crone, is given evil qualities.

There aren't counterparts for men in such fairy tales. Old men aren't the scary mistresses of the Devil, after all.

Sex Goddesses

Many of the demon-women legends share some aspects, such as the "motherly-figure-gone-awry" notion. These stories of demon women are all cautionary tales of sorts in that they tell both women and men that moving outside of societal norms or the expectations of the "allowable" roles for women will lead to certain doom. Essentially, all of these characters in folklore are archetypes—a way of understanding a complex societal phenomenon in a highly simplified but ultimately recognizable representation. An excellent literary example can be found in *The Scarlet Letter* (1850) wherein Hester Prynne is vilified for sex outside of marriage. Of course it's far easier to blame women for such misdeeds as they are the ones that bear the marks of such infidelities when they become pregnant.

Sexuality is at the heart of the Othering of women, according to feminist theorists. Women's sexuality defined the gender for most of human history. The contemporary debate amongst feminist theorists over the moral permissibility of pornography, given that the majority of pornography involves the subjugation of women in some way, is an excellent example of the differences in sexuality between the sexes. Even in many contemporary societies, women are discouraged or even prevented (through excision, in some places) from enjoying sex or from reaching climax.

Returning for a moment to the Eve mythology and comparing it to other historical and mythological depictions of evil women, sexuality typically plays a role. The story of La Malinche is in many ways very similar to the Eve story, as seduction and betrayal stories like these involve common themes. La Malinche was Hernán Cortés's interpreter and lover, and she is portrayed as the great betrayer of her people for her role in the Spanish conquest of Mexico. She is seen as a strange feminine-specific mixture of evil and victim, not unlike Eve.

So Many Songs . . .

Some of our favorite songs linking women and the Devil include:

Band	Song	Song line linking women to the Devil or evil
Electric Light Orchestra the (ELO)	"Evil Woman"	Ha ha woman what you gonna do; you destroyed all the virtues that Lord gave you . . .
Eagles	"Witchy Woman"	She's been sleeping in the Devil's bed . . .
The Doors	"Woman is a Devil"	Woman is the Devil . . . she'll take all your money . . .
Marty Robbins	"Devil Woman"	Devil woman, you're evil like the dark coral reef; Like the winds that bring high tides, you bring sorrow and grief
Cliff Richard	"Devil Woman"	She's just a devil woman, with evil on her mind
Black Sabbath (with Ozzy)	"Evil Woman (Don't You Play Your Games with Me)"	Now I know just what you're looking or; you want me to claim this child you bore . . .
Black Sabbath (with Dio)	"Lady Evil"	There's a lady they say who feeds the darkness; It eats right from her hand . . .
Led Zeppelin	"Dazed and Confused"	Soul of a woman was created below . . .
Shorty Long and William "Mickey" Stevenson	"Devil with a Blue Dress On"	She's the devil with the blue dress, blue dress, blue dress, Devil with the blue dress on; Devil with the blue dress, blue dress, blue dress, Devil with the blue dress on . . .
Santana	"Evil Ways"	I'll find somebody, who won't make me feel like a clown; This can't go on . . . Lord knows you got to change . . .

And let's not forget about these songs in the Rock genre generally (some Hip Hop, Rap, and House, too) that are about deceptive, dangerous, devilish, or evil women:

Elton John, "The Bitch Is Back"
Meredith Brooks, "Bitch"
Bowling for Soup, "The Bitch Song"
Eric Cartman, "Kyle's Mom's a Bitch"
Led Zeppelin, "Your Time Is Gonna Come"
Elvis, "Hard-Headed Woman"
Michael Jackson, "Dirty Diana"
Eagles, "Lyin' Eyes"
Shiny Toy Guns, "Le Disko"
The Kinks, "Alcohol"
Matchbox Twenty, "She's So Mean"
Hall and Oates, "Maneater"
Nelly Furtado, "Maneater"
Neon Trees, "Animal"
Bon Jovi, "Bad Medicine" and "You Give Love a Bad Name"
Booty Luv, "Black Widow"
Cage the Elephant, "Black Widow"
Disturbed, "Serpentine"
Foreigner, "Cold as Ice"
Roxette, "Dangerous"
James Blunt, "Dangerous"
Kardinal Offishall, "Dangerous"
Idle Eyes, "Tokyo Rose"
Tommy Roe, "Hooray for Hazel"
The View, "Girl"
Spandau Ballet, "Highly Strung"
Amber Pacific, "The Girl Who Destroys"
KISS, "She" and "Modern Day Delilah"
Bell Biv DeVoe, "Poison"
Alice Cooper, "Poison"
The Coasters, "Poison Ivy"
Jonas Brothers, "Poison Ivy"
Drowning Pool, "Turn So Cold"
The Monkees, "Words" and "She"
Cream, "Strange Brew"
Crash Kings, "You Got Me"
Little Feat, "Dixie Chicken"
Bullet, "White Lies, Blue Eyes"
The Cult, "Fire Woman"
Eric Church, "Hell on the Heart"

The Black Keys, "Money Maker"
Bruno Mars, "Natalie"
Stephen Jerzak, "She Said"
Olly Murs, "Troublemaker"
Example, "Won't Go Quietly"
Fleetwood Mac, "Gold Dust Woman"

. . . and there are tons more.

It's really, really easy to find songs in every generation that either link women to the Devil or pure evil, or just demean women in general. But songs are just entertainment, right? So songs that vilify or demean women aren't problematic, if they are meant to be funny or meant to entertain. Music doesn't really affect people's views, does it? Consider the following contemporary songs. Eminem's song "Kill You" discusses raping and killing his mother. Robin Thicke's recently infamous video for "Blurred Lines" focuses on bestiality, drugs, and the general degradation of women. We aren't arguing that artists should be censored or that their freedom of speech should be abridged, but that the continual and pervasive manner of attributing to women the second-class status of sexual objects is morally problematic, even if meant to entertain.

Othering

Beauvoir claims in *The Second Sex* that Othering is a repeating theme in every culture and allows groups to define themselves in opposition to those that are unlike them in some way. In other words, I define my group of individuals by setting my group (the "us") against other groups (the "Other"). There are useful and productive aspects of Othering, like group cohesion and national identity and, on an individual level, Othering may be important to a person's ability to forge their own identity and develop a strong sense of self. However, Othering has significant harmful aspects as well, especially when it goes unquestioned and when one assumes that the Others so formed are inferior and that the lines drawn by Othering are somehow essential.

Othering can happen because of race, deformity or disability, and gender. But many people in our society argue that we have evolved past the boundaries of race and ethnicity in the

US, given that a person of color has been elected President. Without tackling this claim, we can safely say that the gender divide has yet to be conquered on this level. Even though opportunities for women have increased exponentially in the last hundred years, we shouldn't forget that less than a century ago, women were barred from participation in government—a condition that still exists in many other societies even today. And this secondary feminine Other described in the mid-twentieth century by Beauvoir is expanded and modified by Anzaldua, who reminds us that the line drawing involved in Othering persists in many problematic ways.

Oversimplifying the Lived Experience

Gloria Anzaldúa's most commonly talked about theory is that of the Borderlands, a term by which she means not only the geographical space between Texas and Mexico, but also the psychic, emotional, and metaphorical distance between identities. Anzaldúa questions national identity as well as sexual identity (masculinity and femininity, heterosexuality and homosexuality). For Anzaldúa, defining an identity using binary terms—the attempt to construct identity using a fixed category in terms of its opposite—is an oversimplification of lived experience. Instead, she advocates developing a "mestiza consciousness" that arises out of an awareness of the Borderlands, a way of seeing the world that allows for ambiguity and includes an embracing of contradiction.

Anzaldua herself wrote in a kind of "Spanglish"—a combination of English and Spanish found in border regions—and requested that her words not be translated into either English or Spanish. In her mind, she envisioned a progressive world where borders did not delineate between the good and the bad, men from women, the normalized from the Other.

Just a Conniving Handmaiden

So woman isn't the Devil, but his conniving handmaiden. While it may be the case that Othering is an expected human discrimination, the pervasive historical and contemporary Othering of women, exemplified by comparisons between women and the Devil and demons and witches, contributes to the seemingly insurmountable deficit women face. Women have been and are treated as the "second sex"—continually defined by their relation to men. And according to writers like Gloria Anzaldua, this line drawing, although expected, is nonetheless problematic as it creates a false dichotomy between genders.

We like to think of our society as progressive—one that's beyond racism and sexism. But while the first man of color occupies the White House, the pay gap between men and women of equal background and training is approximately $4,500. The latest data from the US Census Bureau on the gender wage gap has it holding steady: in 2012, women made approximately seventy-seven cents for every dollar made by men in similar positions. We'd like to think our society is beyond these problematic discriminations, but it's difficult to rise above the history of "mankind" as a history of portraying women as the handmaidens of the Devil. But that's okay because maybe the Devil really did make us do it.

IX

How Much
Sympathy?

24

A Sympathetic Look at Lucifer Morningstar

AARON RABINOWITZ

So here's a question: Why should we have sympathy for the Devil? I mean, we're clearly fascinated by the guy, we write a book like this, endlessly pondering his motivations and the morals we ought to take from his story. And with that endless pondering comes a shift in our view of the Devil from a boring old baddie to something far more complex and interesting.

Modern representations of the Devil—who I will refer to by his proper name of Lucifer Morningstar—presented by writers like Neil Gaiman and Mike Carey, give us a deeper picture of the character and further insight into his motivations. I believe it's in Lucifer's prime motivation that our sympathy is centrally located: Lucifer's desire is simply to have free will in a world determined to prevent free will. That desire is so quintessentially human, it engenders sympathy even for the guy who tried to storm Heaven and dethrone God.

Roughly speaking, free will is the capacity to govern oneself and not be restricted by external forces, and autonomy is when one uses that capacity. If someone is being coerced, perhaps with violence or threats, or if someone is enslaved outright, then they clearly lack autonomy. Conversely, when someone chooses to value something without any external pressures, and then is allowed to pursue that thing without hindrance, then that would be a clear-cut case of autonomy. Anyone who values the idea of pursuing life, liberty, and happiness without interference from others clearly understands the desire for autonomy.

Prince of Freedom?

The idea that Lucifer personifies the desire for free will might seem odd. We know the Devil for his rebellion against Heaven, his hubris, and his willingness to do anything to get what he wants, but we're often hazy on the motivations. Why does Lucifer try to overthrow God? Is he just a jealous prick, or are there legitimate reasons for his actions? This is where modern representations of Lucifer in various storytelling mediums have done us a great service, by clarifying something that ancient authors either couldn't quite see or were afraid to write: why Lucifer did what he did. These modern authors have found the consistent line that exists in all of the myths about Lucifer, and that line is the passionate desire to break free from God's overbearing plan and to act from a place of real autonomy—to be a real person, not a puppet in someone else's show.

Consider in the Bible that Satan is mostly only used as a plot device rather than as a character, and so his motivations aren't really discussed. However, if we look at Lucifer's actions in the Bible through the lens of valuing free will above all else his actions appear not only reasonable, but possibly even *commendable*.

As the serpent in the garden, Lucifer contravenes God's authoritarian command and encourages Eve to exert her free will and make her own choices, whether God likes them or not. He facilitates the first act of human free will. He is to free will as Prometheus is to fire, bringing autonomy down to human beings from on high, against the orders of upper management.

Furthermore, he isn't exactly urging Adam and Eve to do some unspeakable evil with their free will. All he does is urge them to eat of the tree of knowledge, which to me seems like a good thing, not something that should get you banned from paradise. It ends up feeling as if God's an overbearing authority figure and Lucifer is the more mature alternative, encouraging humans to think for themselves and not just blindly follow God's commands. If not for Lucifer's influence, humans would still be ignorant automatons, living in Paradise but with no self-awareness. Viewed in this light, I find it difficult to see anything Lucifer does in the Garden as evil.

In the book of *Job*, Lucifer takes a bet with God over whether Job will maintain faith in God's super-secret divine plan even in the face of extreme suffering. I have no idea what God is doing making bets with Lucifer, but it's easy to see why Lucifer would bet the way he does. He really wants to see Job, and all of humanity by extension, reject a God who makes people suffer both for his secret plan and, in this particular case, just to prove a point. It's no wonder that the story of Job doesn't get as much play these days, as The Adversary seems like the only reasonable and humane person in the whole debacle.

A Misunderstood Character

Then there's the temptation of Jesus in the desert. While it might seem easiest in this case to just write Lucifer off as a tempter for temptations sake, this would be a mistake. In every case where Lucifer is accused of temptation, he's really just imploring humans to act freely, rather than submitting always to God's will. Jesus is no different. Lucifer knows that Jesus is just going to end up another brutal casualty in God's scheming, and so he tries to get Jesus to reject God's poisonous cup first, before God refuses to take it away.

Beyond these few minor appearances, and perhaps some role in the fever dream of *Revelation*, Lucifer's largely absent from the Bible. We're mostly left to infer Lucifer's motivations. It's only natural that with such scant source material, most folks simply wrote the Devil off as a two dimensional archenemy, someone who just does evil because it's in his nature to do evil, or because he's just petty and bitter at God. That view served the ends of the Church, who were happy to use him as a boogieman meant to frighten and ostracize people who might disagree with God. Yet even a cursory glance at these stories suggests that Lucifer is a misunderstood character and that dismissing him as plain old boring evil is a huge mistake.

Given the minor role Lucifer plays in the Bible, it's no surprise that our modern image of the Devil is dominated by Milton's Devil in *Paradise Lost*. Milton expands heavily upon the biblical narrative by giving it a prequel. He presents the story of the war between God and the Devil and the fall of the Devil as a parallel for the fall of humanity. It's in this extended mythology, where Lucifer is actually given a voice, that we first start to really hear his own motivations, expressed beautifully in the famous line "Better to reign in Hell than serve in

Heaven." This quote could be misinterpreted as arrogance, but I think what's actually being conveyed is that a life of freedom and struggle is superior to a life of slavery and comfort. By writing about Lucifer as an actual character in a divine melodrama, rather than as just a mindless demon, Milton gives us our first glimpse into Lucifer's motivations. Lucifer just wants to make a choice that God hasn't already decided for him, and then to act in a way that God hasn't already written into some precise little plan. Unfortunately, Milton was still writing in a time when you could get in trouble with the Church for what you wrote, so it was left to later writers to really clarify what drove the Devil to make war with God.

Thank Lucifer for Modern Authors

Luckily for us, modern authors with less to fear from the Inquisition and a broader understanding of mythology have provided us with a much richer characterization of Lucifer, doing justice to the character and to the ideas he personifies. For my money, there's no better portrayal of Lucifer than that of Neil Gaiman and Mike Carey. Gaiman is quite possibly the undisputed champion of mythology-based fiction and his *Sandman* graphic novels are the gold standard of high-concept art in that genre. The fourth book of the series, where Lucifer is featured most prominently, is so outstanding that it won the H.P. Lovecraft award for best short story of the year, a never-before-achieved feat that caused them to change the rules to make sure it would never happen again. The character then passed, with Gaiman's blessing, to Mike Carey, who took Lucifer Morningstar and gave him the leading role he has always deserved. In so doing, Carey provides the most complex and compelling look into the character that I have ever encountered. These guys did what previous authors couldn't, they gave Lucifer a third dimension so deep it almost makes you forget he's fictional.

Like in the Bible, in Gaiman's *Sandman* series Lucifer plays only a supporting role, but it's a choice role to play. The series itself centers on Morpheus, also known as Dream of the Endless, a being who both personifies and rules over all of dreaming. In Book Four of the series, when Dream enters Hell in order to confront and possibly do battle with Lucifer, he finds something no one really thought possible: Lucifer has quit. Think about that for a second, Lucifer quitting Hell, like it's a job and he has given his two weeks notice. What a novel idea! If that were all Gaiman did with the character, it would already be an amazing innovation.

Gaiman goes further though and presents Lucifer as a foil to Morpheus. At this point in the story, Morpheus is so trapped in his own way of thinking about duty and obligation that he repeatedly wonders throughout the book if he ever has any choice at all. Lucifer counters these emo dramatics with a beautiful smile and the cheerful thought that there's always a choice, even Hell is a choice. Lucifer has reached a level of maturity where he sees that the whole game, from the endless accumulation of souls in Hell to the shadow war with God, is just another part of a world full of predetermination and control. All he's ever wanted was just the freedom to act in ways not already determined by God, and yet he suspects that everything he has done up to this point has all been just a part of God's big plan. That's what frustrates Lucifer the most, for how can he truly feel ownership of any of his actions and by extension his selfhood, if God has laid out ahead of time everything he will do? It makes him little more than a mechanical clock, unwinding according to a prewritten program.

So Lucifer quits Hell, choosing to opt out of the whole cosmic struggle rather than play the part written for him. We may ask if God foresaw this action as well, given that he does nothing to prevent Lucifer from leaving Hell, but with God it's always hard to know. At least Lucifer's actions in *Sandman* feel like the actions of a mature character, someone who has thought a lot about what he wants and is still striving to achieve it, rather than the confused actions of a teenage devil rebelling against his overbearing father.

That's where Gaiman leaves Lucifer, until another gifted writer named Mike Carey received Gaiman's blessing to feature Lucifer Morningstar as the protagonist in his own series. Finally, after two thousand years, Lucifer's given a leading role and allowed to pursue his dream of freedom from God's determination. To that end, he sets about building a second creation, connected to our own but theoretically completely free from God's design. He opens his creation up to anyone who wanted to live there instead of in God's universe, and he has only one commandment: Thou shalt not worship anyone. In this way, he tries to create a universe where free will can actually exist, rather then just existing at the discretion of God's divine will and according to his predetermined plan.

I won't spoil the story of how Lucifer's attempts at freedom works out, the important thing to see is that when you look at the character in real depth, as Carey does, what emerges is an unrelenting drive to be free in his thoughts and actions. That is the essence of Lucifer Morningstar. Anything less than genuine autonomy is abhorrent to him.

Giving the Devil his Due

Once you get to this point, I believe it becomes quite clear why we sympathize with the Devil. Like Lucifer, we share in the same plight. Like Lucifer, we have enough self awareness to know about and desire autonomy. Yet we also have enough understanding of the universe to suspect that autonomy is either completely unattainable or extremely rare. It doesn't take a belief in God to question your autonomy. Every day our freedom to choose and act is impinged upon by countless external forces. Obligations towards those around us and social customs demand that we act in ways we might not like. Basic survival needs force us into jobs that we wouldn't choose freely. Every day it seems science is learning more about how we work, making it harder and harder to claim that we are anything more than a complex arrangement of electrical impulses playing out patterns that determine what we think and feel. All these things together can make a person feel like life's all just predetermined.

And so, the fear that free will isn't really possible in this world, is a fear that extends far beyond the determining will of an all-powerful deity, and forces all of us to confront the same dilemma that Lucifer faces: how do I reconcile my desire to be free with a world that seems Hell-bent on preventing it? Many of us will spend our whole lives trying to get a taste of real autonomy, others may feel so overwhelmed by the world that they will give up that desire and just try to not be too miserable as the world pushes them around. Whatever we choose, and however it works out for us, we're striving for the same thing that Lucifer is, and that makes us compatriots in the same struggle.

Much Respect

I feel that Lucifer Morningstar deserves not just our sympathy, but also our respect and admiration. It seems that no one has fought harder or sacrificed more than he has to try to bring freedom to a universe that lacks it. This may sound like a rather bizarre conclusion about the most hated antagonist in all of mythology, but I find it hard to interpret the stories any other way. And I must admit that I don't find these conclusions all that strange, given that, in my experience, Christianity is a system for limiting free will.

If Christianity really is a "neo-Platonic slave cult" as Nietzsche said, or an "opiate for the masses" if you prefer Marx, then it would make sense that the great antagonist of Christianity would personify a passionate desire for free will. The moral they want us to take is that a strong desire for autonomy is the source of sin, and that human will should always be subservient to the greater will of God.

For anyone who sees Christianity this way, or for anyone who just thinks people should be free, I believe that sympathy for the Devil is as justified as it is inevitable.

25
Meaningless Evil

TIM JONES

The Devil is usually a figure either of evil or of fun. We're terrified of him or, alternatively, we laugh at him, perhaps because this is easier than showing that we're scared.

A fascinatingly original picture is painted by the novelist Milan Kundera. In *The Book of Laughter and Forgetting* (1979) Kundera suggests that seeing the Devil as 'evil' and the angels as 'good' is to take the angels' account of things at face value. Instead, Kundera links the Devil with meaninglessness and the angels with too much meaning. The Devil challenges or rejects an overpowering sense of what rules we should follow and what qualities or ideas we should find significant, which the angels seek to impose upon the world around them.

This isn't to say that the Devil is a hero and the angels are villains, for we all need *some* meaning in our lives. Imagine having sex for a moment, if that's not too much like hard work. Angelic sex would be excessively serious and puritanical. Think straightforward missionary with little in the way of noisy enthusiasm. This is one obvious example where transgressing the rules that tell us something should be deeply meaningful can be lots of fun.

But sex that means nothing at all would be completely un-erotic too, because without us feeling that sex *should* be significant there is no taboo around it for us to enjoy breaking. If the Devil's resistance goes too far and all meaning breaks down, we'd probably wind up equally miserable.

Kundera's perspective on the Devil's motivations gives us a chance to take another look at the stuff he gets up to in more familiar stories. Can we reinterpret his actions in light of Kundera's argument and see that what the Devil represents *is* just a meaninglessness that refuses to take as gospel an angelic world of too much meaning where it's not really deserved? Or perhaps Kundera's being far too nice to the guy and he's just pure evil after all.

Origin Story

Since origin stories are all the rage, let's go back to the beginning and look at an account of how the Devil came to be the guy he is today.

The Quran shows the Devil, back when he was an angel who signed his name as Iblis, hanging out with Adam himself in the Garden of Eden. As we see in surah 20 (the twentieth chapter), Allah asks all of his angels to bow down before the man he's moulded from clay. Unlike the others, Iblis says no. For his sins, he's cast out of Paradise and becomes . . . the Devil! Cue dramatic music and a montage where he picks out a fun costume.

Isn't it putting it a bit strongly to call this refusal to follow God's orders an act of *evil*? We could see it more positively as a refusal to accept a pretty dictatorial ordering of the world that places one person at the top—one person to whom everyone else must meekly fall in line, without being given any evidence whatsoever about what actually makes this person so superior. Perhaps it's even a pretty brave act of rebellion. Hasn't history taught us to question the meanings given to us, rather than accept them blindly? At worst Iblis is just an independent thinker, of the sort that philosophers look upon pretty fondly.

Surah 38 looks into this incident a little more deeply. And Iblis's reasons for refusing God's orders might not seem quite so praiseworthy. His problem is not so much with being ordered to bow down before Adam on its own. He hates the fact that as a being made of fire, he is 'better' than the man made of mere clay who is being pushed as his superior.

His ideology suddenly appears rather different from one that loves meaninglessness, since he clearly has his own hierarchy of significances—one where fire trumps clay. That he is made of fire absolutely *means* something positive to him, just as Adam being made of clay means a weakness that puts Iblis ahead of him. Iblis isn't rejecting meaning itself in favor of meaninglessness, but just the single system of meaning that won't recognize his own superiority. Iblis's angry words to Allah suggest that he would have no problem at all with Allah asking Adam to bow to *him*. Knocking against each other here are two clear systems of meaning. One sees Iblis placed beneath Adam, and another, which Iblis has no problem at all with arguing for because it sees Adam placed beneath him. Iblis is actually all *for* meaning, just so long as it puts him at the top.

This matches pretty well the account given in the Old Testament's Book of Isaiah, which says the Devil was expelled from Heaven for wanting to raise himself above God. He's hardly the crusader against the imposition of meaning that Kundera paints him as; he just loves to push his own significance over anyone else's.

Temptations, Temptations, Temptations

Let's turn to what the Devil actually gets up to, once he's been set on this path. The most extended sequence that he's involved in is the temptation of Jesus during his stint in the desert, as described by the Gospels of Matthew and Luke (and much more briefly by Mark) in the New Testament.

The Devil starts with quite a convincing act. Jesus is probably pretty hungry after forty days and nights of fasting and the Devil simply points out that he could help himself out by turning some of the rocks around him into bread. This would lessen Jesus's own suffering without really seeming to give the Devil himself anything at all. And why *should* Jesus suffer when he has the means to help himself? The Devil is just suggesting he use his superpowers to put himself first for a change.

But isn't the Devil also, somewhat craftily, highlighting that Jesus's difficulties are self-inflicted, since he could choose to magic up some food as soon as the hunger pangs get a bit much? A side-effect of this tactic is its bringing into question exactly how meaningful Jesus's difficulties actually are. It's a bit like a rich family member moaning about not having enough spending money when there's tens of thousands in investments that can be cashed in at a moment's notice. Someone who's actually starving might look upon the Devil reminding Jesus he can produce food in abundance at a moment's notice and think he's being somewhat disrespectful towards people who aren't lucky enough to be the son of God—who don't, therefore, have the easy route out of his problems that Jesus does. Is Jesus actually doing something meaningful by going into the desert, or just rather disrespectfully showcasing a ton of privilege?

By raising these questions the Devil maybe misses the point. Consider that the very meaning of Jesus's struggles in the desert comes *from* him having the power to have a much easier time of things. The physical difficulties of fasting are never meant to be what's meaningful; instead it's the mental difficulty of him having an easy get-out that he must constantly deny himself. The Devil's attempts to do down the meaning of Jesus's difficulties might only remind Jesus and his fans where the *genuinely* meaningful nature of his experience really lies.

The same logic applies to the second temptation, which sees the Devil try to persuade Jesus to jump off the top of a temple. Because he's the Son of God, the Angels will carry him safely to the ground and so he has nothing to worry about. Again, is his being in this situation actually all that meaningful when he can supernaturally escape from it without any actual difficulty? Or is it meaningful precisely *because* he could easily do this, but chooses not to?

Whether or not he's successful, both these challenges show a Devil keen to pick apart the actual significance of Jesus's behavior. To suggest that Jesus and his fandom think again about whether or not these supposedly noble actions are really all that meaningful. To make it look as though Jesus is just pissing around, rather than facing any of the actual difficulty that would make a dedication of this time in the wilderness to God genuinely valuable. In each of these cases, he isn't really looking for anything for himself.

But the final temptation shows the Devil's real motivations. Now he comes right out with it and asks Jesus to worship *him* instead of God, in exchange for dominion over the world. Once again, he isn't just furthering a cause of meaninglessness; he actively seeks an alternative hierarchy to the one put forward by God—a hierarchy with him at the top and with the person God would have him bow down to squarely underneath him. In casting doubt on the meaningfulness of the actions through which Jesus is demonstrating his faith in God, the Devil hopes to make it easier to get his own claws in. After all, offering Jesus the world on a plate without requiring that he test himself at all is a pretty canny move, bang after questioning the meaningfulness of the way he'd been painstakingly hoping to prove his faith in God.

So there's an ulterior motive to what the Devil has been up to. Muddying the significance of Jesus's actions is a means to an end for him, rather than an end in itself. Meaninglessness isn't all he's about at all.

Grinning Beelzebub

The story of William Golding's *Lord of the Flies* (1954) is pretty familiar, if not from the novel then from one of the two movies. A planeload of children crash on an island and try to keep some sort of civilization going until they can be rescued, but begin to fight amongst themselves until it all goes to pot and the fat kid with glasses gets crushed by a rock.

One way of looking at this novel sees the Devil himself at work on the island, lurking in the background but manifesting toward the end in the shape of a rotting pig's head covered in flies—a fitting form for him to take, since "Lord of the flies" is a literal translation of the Hebrew word *Beelzebub*, which he's sometimes called in the Old Testament. Under his influence, the society established by Ralph crumbles in favor of Jack's primeval anarchy.

And behind the societal breakdown that the Devil watches over and delights in is an erosion of meaning. This novel reminds us how important meaning is to society by showing the horror that comes from meaning's failure. Look at how Ralph's order was maintained in the first place. The conch that Ralph uses to call assemblies and give each kid permission to speak quickly becomes the glue holding their society together. When the conch sounds, it means you hurry to the meeting area; when you're holding the conch, it means you can talk. But it's really just an inanimate object, right? Nothing more than a glorified seashell. The power it has to keep Ralph's society functioning doesn't come from what it naturally *is*, but from the meaning that the kids collectively choose to give it. By investing this mundane object with a much grander significance, they stop it being just a shell and shape it into a tool powerful enough to bind a society together.

For the role they give the conch to keep on working, the kids need to continue what's really just an act. The moment they stop acting as though it's much more than just a conch, it once again becomes just a conch and so loses all its power to keep civilization from turning to chaos. Obviously the kids don't actually *have* to attend a meeting just because they hear the conch blown and neither do they literally *need* to hold the conch to be able to talk. There's nothing about it that's literally vital to letting you use your tongue or your vocal cords; they'd work perfectly fine regardless. But as long as the kids act as though these made-up meanings are actually binding, their society can function okay. Once Jack and his lot start seeing the conch as just a conch—the moment that they deny that it means anything beyond this—then anything goes and children start killing each other.

This doesn't necessarily just apply to life on the island. Piggy has a pretty positive opinion of grown-up society back on the mainland, arguing to Ralph that at home the problems they're facing would be quickly settled over a cup of tea. But we've already seen Ralph think of 'wild' Dartmoor and the ponies that roam there, evoking a wildness on the fringes of the English mainland that might spill out and threaten the order of the 'tamed' towns and cities. Life there isn't naturally any more orderly on the mainland and the civilization that Piggy looks eagerly back to is also just a veneer. Perhaps what separates us adults from children like Jack is that we've become better practiced at buying into the meanings that we write onto our own conches without being so susceptible to watching helplessly as these meanings fall apart.

Meaning, then, is important. The final chapters when the conch has fallen back into meaninglessness see human lives too begin to mean nothing to Jack and his hunters. By the closing scenes, Simon and Piggy have already been murdered. As Ralph's chased through the forest, the violent flames surrounding him on all sides show an island that has literally transformed from a lush paradise into Hell itself. The Devil's very own domain brought to Earth *by* the erosion of the meanings that held the kids' society together kick-starting the erosion of the meaning of life itself.

And notice how the pig's head that symbolizes the Devil's presence on the island is repeatedly described as grinning. Kundera might try and get him off the hook by suggesting that he'd be shocked by his crusade against meaning causing so much overt horror when this wasn't his intention. But clearly he's bloody loving it.

Final Verdict

So what does all this say about Kundera's perspective on the Devil's motivations and actions? From the moment the Devil stopped being a well-behaved angel, he definitely carries an agenda based around picking apart meanings and significances. Not only of the rules that are placed in front of him, but of those that guide the actions of the people around him. Kundera's got that bit right.

But it's dangerous to think he's just doing this to protest against the idea of overbearing meaning for its own sake, like some sort of freedom fighter against angelic oppression whose only fault might be taking things a little far, rather than being directly evil or malevolent by design. The scenes we looked at from the Bible and the Quran show him with his own system of meaning. One where *he*'s the most significant guy on the block, rather than God or Adam. He's only against systems of meaning that don't put him on top and sees tearing these down as the first step towards installing his own.

Golding's *Lord of the Flies* suggests an even more frightening reason why Kundera might not be coming down on the Devil quite hard enough. What happens on the island, once the conch has lost its meaning as a symbol to keep society together, is truly horrific. Children murdering each other in a fiery environment that's pretty much Hell on Earth. Through watching over the breakdown of the meaning of objects like the conch, he seeks to turn our world into a copy of his own.

I'd be much less inclined to agree with Kundera that the Devil's not really evil, honest, after seeing the consequences of his stripping away of meaning upon a group of children and the delight he takes in it. We've probably all got pissed off at being told to consider things meaningful or significant that we're not sure really are. And it can definitely be a lot of fun to question the meaning of established rituals and practices. But when a society where meaning breaks down can actually become Hell on Earth, then we probably shouldn't push things too far in this direction. Even if Kundera's right about the Devil just being keen to expose the things that we see as significant as not really all that meaningful, the consequences of this are potentially so terrible that it's no better than if he were actually evil. Because we need to invest meaning wherever we can if society isn't to literally go to Hell, a Devil who watches, grinning, as meaning falls apart is equally as scary as a Devil who's only interested in being evil.

If the Devil were actively setting out to be evil, pulling down meaning is exactly what he'd be doing anyway.

26
The Devil You Don't Know

JAMES EDWIN MAHON

The Devil has always been a more attractive character in literature and popular culture than his opposite figure, God. In countless movies like *The Devil's Advocate* or *Angel Heart*, the Devil tends to get all of the best lines—and be played by some great Italian-American actors. People, it seems, have sympathy for the Devil.

However, I wonder if people really do like the Devil. I suspect that they don't. I suspect that they like the qualities possessed by the character of the Devil in these stories, qualities that have nothing, really, to do with being the Devil—such as intelligence, sophistication ("Please allow me to introduce myself, I'm a man of wealth and taste"), a sense of humor, charm, even rebelliousness. In the Christian tradition, the Devil is always the underdog, and everybody loves the underdog ("Better to reign in Hell, than serve in Heav'n"). Yet there is nothing whatsoever *evil* about being an underdog, about being intelligent or funny, or even about wearing Prada.

If, as I suspect, nobody likes the Devil, and instead people like qualities possessed by the character of the Devil in these stories, then I'm left with a question. What *in* the Devil *is* the Devil? Who the Hell is he? Or more accurately, what is evil, really? And why don't people like it?

I'm going to look at three different accounts of the Devil—or rather, three accounts of what it means to be truly, diabolically evil. Call this my evil three-pronged pitchfork.

1. The first account is the most popular account. We can easily see why this is the most popular way to understand the Devil. It is, however, a false account.

2. The second account is less popular but much more interesting. It may be the most fun account of the three. However, this is just the first account in disguise.

3. The third account is much, much less popular. It's the most difficult account of the three to understand. Nevertheless, it's the true account. The Devil really is in the detail of this account.

Machiavellianism

In England, a popular name for the Devil is "Old Nick." According to legend, this name for the Devil is derived from "Nick Machiavel," a character who features in a number of Elizabethan plays, such as Ben Jonson's *Volpone*. Nick Machiavel is obviously named after Niccolò Machiavelli, the notorious author of *The Prince*, a book which advises rulers on how to get their way by being totally devious and brutal. It's one thing to be demonized; it's another thing entirely to be so bad that the Devil is named after you!

It makes a nice story, but "Old Nick" was used as a name for the Devil before the publication of *The Prince* in 1532. It's true, however, that Machiavelli, or "Nick Machiavel," was identified with the Devil. "Machiavellian" has passed into the English language, and it is precisely the kind of thinking that we might expect from the Devil. Even if Old Nick was not named after Machiavelli, it's accurate to call him Machiavellian in his outlook.

Why did people think that *The Prince* was the work of the Devil? Presumably, because this treatise on how to be a ruler advocates behaving in ways that people thought were completely wicked. Most likely, they have in mind the chapter "How Princes Should Honor Their Word," which is actually a chapter *against* honoring your word, and in *favor* of lying whenever it's necessary to maintain your grip on power.

Here Machiavelli says that "a prudent ruler cannot, and must not, honor his word when it places him at a disadvantage," and that he must know how "to be a great liar and deceive." Although he should "appear to be compassionate, faithful to his word, kind, guileless, and devout," nevertheless "his disposition should be such that, if he needs to be the opposite, he knows how." In order "to maintain his state," a ruler "is often forced to act in defiance of good faith, of charity, of kindness, of religion" and "should know how to do evil, if that is necessary." It follows that "If a prince wants to maintain his rule he must learn how not to be virtuous."

There you have it. Machiavelli advocates doing evil, if evil is necessary for your own advantage. He advocates leading a double life, in which you present yourself to other people as kind, compassionate, honest, and religious, because that's what you're supposed to be, but in which you actually are the opposite of all of these things, at least when it's necessary. To quote one of the best lines from an earlier chapter (as if the other lines were not good enough), Machiavelli says that "cruelty is used well (if it is permissible to talk in this way of what is evil) when it is employed once for all, and one's safety depends on it." So, Machiavelli advocates *being cruel*, which he admits is evil, when being cruel will keep you safe.

This, then, is Machiavellianism. Your advantage or self-interest justifies any action whatsoever. Nothing is ruled out. If necessary "the family of the old prince must be destroyed." Torture, beheading, imprisonment—whatever it takes to gain and maintain power is justified. No wonder people though that this was diabolical.

Nevertheless, I do not think that this prince is the Prince of Darkness. If evil were merely a matter of doing whatever is necessary for your advantage, then the Devil would just be *amoral*. The Devil would simply think that moral rules are just for show, and he would be purely, and completely, self-interested. I don't think that pure self-interest—even if that involves committing the most terrible of atrocities—captures what the Devil is about. It's not enough, to be the Devil, to have no regard for morality at all. It's not enough to kill, maim, torture, lie, manipulate, break faith, and in general do whatever's necessary, to order to maximize your own well-being, and to not care about wronging anyone. That's the sort of thing that is considered perfectly rational by the likes of Callicles in the *Gorgias*, and Thrasymachus in the *Republic*, two of Plato's greatest works. This is so common a view that it seems hard to make it the perspective of the Devil. That's just *Realpolitik*. We don't need the Devil for *that*.

If Machiavellianism is not what the Devil is about, then why is it commonly thought to be so? The answer, I think, is that people can grasp Machiavellianism. It's not alien to them. We all experience the motivation of self-interest. And that's a clue to understanding the true account of the Devil. Because the Devil is not like us.

Pleasure in Others' Misery

It might be said that Machiavelli's account of wickedness, as bad as it is, is too tame. Call this the banality of Machiavelli's evil. Perhaps most of the time, when people kill, maim, torture, lie, manipulate, break faith, and so forth, their motivation is self-interest. Indeed, if Machiavelli is right, the prince is always motivated by self-interest. But surely, it will be said, people are sometimes motivated by something worse than self-interest. For example, people are sometimes motivated by *spite*—a feeling the Ancient Greek philosopher Aristotle said was *always* base. Sometimes we can just wish people ill, regardless of our own projects and goals.

Arthur Schopenhauer, the nineteenth-century German philosopher, argued in his book *On the Basis of Morality* (1840) that in addition to being motivated by self-interest—"all human actions, as a rule, have their origins in Egoism, and to it, accordingly, we must always first turn, when we try to find the explanation of any given line of conduct"—people are motivated by "ill-will, or spitefulness." This motivation is quite different from self-interest. As he says, "it is true that Egoism may lead to wickedness and crime of every sort"—witness Machiavelli's prince—"but the resulting injury and pain to others are simply the means, not the end, and are therefore involved only as an accident." By contrast, "malice and cruelty make others' misery the end in itself, the realization of which affords pleasure."

Whereas the guiding rule of egoism is "injure all people, if it brings you any advantage," the guiding rule of spitefulness or malice is "injure all people as far as you can." The vices inspired by self-interest are "greed, gluttony, lust, selfishness, avarice, covetousness, injustice, hardness of heart, pride, arrogance." But the vices that are inspired by spitefulness are "envy, ill-will, malice, malice, pleasure in seeing others suffer, prying curiosity, slander, insolence, petulance, hatred, anger, treachery, fraud, thirst for revenge, cruelty, etc."

This does seem more like it, if it's the Devil that we're after. And indeed, Schopenhauer says about these twin motivations that "The first root is more bestial, the second more devilish." About his account of motives, quite appropriately, he says, "Here I bring to an end my review of these terrible powers of evil; it is an array reminding one of the Princes of Darkness in Milton's Pandemonium." With all due respect to Milton, however, it is from the German language that we have the term *Schadenfreude*, or taking pleasure in the suffering of others. This Schopenhauer singles out for attention: "In a certain sense the opposite of envy is the habit of gloating over the misfortunes of others. At any rate, while the former is human, the latter is diabolical. There is no sign more infallible of an entirely bad heart, and of profound moral worthlessness than open and candid enjoyment of seeing other people suffer."

This "devilish," "diabolical" motivation that Schopenhauer has in mind, whereby one takes pleasure in the suffering of others—is this evil, then? It seems like it, at first glance. What could be worse than to make others suffer, simply for your own enjoyment? Isn't that cruelty? Isn't that sadism? Doesn't this capture the Devil better than self-interest?

Strange as it may seem to say this, my answer is that no, this is not evil. At least, this is not the evil that we're looking for. While it seems true that making people suffer simply for my own pleasure is worse than harming them because they are getting in the way of something that I want, and hence, that *Schadenfreude* is worse than Machiavellianism, nevertheless, we have not yet plumbed the depths of the Devil's depravity. For even in the case of malicious action, I do what I do in order to gain pleasure for myself. It is, in the end, a self-interested motivation. Perhaps the worst of its kind, but still.

What's needed is something purer. Pure evil. That sounds like the Devil.

Diabolism

The eighteenth-century German philosopher Immanuel Kant may not be the first person you think of turning to when you need a proper account of the Devil. Nevertheless, I believe that Kant has the right idea. To get at that idea, however, requires a bit of digging.

In his famous work on ethics, the *Groundwork for the Metaphysics of Morals* (1785), Kant maintains that morality involves treating yourself and others as beings who have "dignity" and who are "infinitely above all price." We are all equal in value, and that value is infinite. All wrongdoing, says Kant, is of essentially the same kind, even though it may take different forms (lying, stealing, murder, and so on).

All wrongdoing involves treating other people, with their various projects and goals, as inferior to myself, with my projects and goals. A wrongdoer treats others as expendable and manipulable, when in fact they are equally as important as him. When I lie to you, for example, I do so in order to get you to believe something that I want you to believe, for my purposes. I treat you as a thing, to be manipulated, for my ends. I would never dream of allowing you to do the same thing to me, since that would frustrate my ends.

However, that means that every time I do something wrong I apply a double standard: it's okay for me to do this to you (lie, steal, murder, whatever), but it's *not* okay for you to do this to me. What applying that double standard reveals is that I consider you to be *inferior* to me. But nobody is inferior to anyone else. We're all equal—equally possessing dignity, equally infinitely valuable. Even, it seems, Bernie Madoff, to whom I may not lie, and from whom I may not steal, and whom I may not murder. (This despite the fact that Mini-Me ModelWorks brought out a Bernie Madoff doll in which he is dressed in a red suit and red shoes, holding a pitchfork. The doll, "Smash Me Bernie," comes with a hammer).

What lies behind all wrongdoing is what Kant calls "the dear self." That is, self-interest is the root of all evil. By 'all evil' here is meant all the evil that men do. What motivates the lying, the stealing, and the murdering is self-interest. That is why you do these things.

Moral behavior, by contrast, is motivated by respect for the equal, infinite value of each person. This is what Kant calls the motive of duty. When I avoid wronging you from the motive of duty, then I avoid wronging you from the motive of respect for you. I have what Kant calls a "good will." Here we have to understand that the same morally right action can be motivated in different ways. In the *Groundwork*, Kant gives the example of the shopkeeper who charges every customer the same price, and does not overcharge inexperienced customers. This is what he morally ought to do, and so, he does what is morally right. Customers are thus "honestly served." But the shopkeeper, Kant imagines, is motivated to do what is right entirely by self-interest. He charges everyone the same price because "his own advantage required it." In other words, honesty is the best policy for his business.

Another possible explanation for the shopkeeper's behavior is that he charges everyone the same price out of a feeling of love. Kant rules this out as a motive for shopkeepers, but it's interesting to think about: "it is out of the question in this case to suppose that he might besides have a direct inclination in favor of buyers, so that, as it were, from love he should give no advantage." Kant doesn't consider the motive of a feeling of love—the motive of affection or sympathy—to be a true moral motivation. It falls short of fully respecting the value of another person. It might be why I help a cat, stuck in a tree, but it is not why I do not steal from you, my customer.

All wrongdoing, says Kant, is motivated by self-interest. If the shopkeeper overcharged inexperienced customers, he would be doing so out of self-interest. It might be said that Kant was being insufficiently imaginative here, and that he did not think of the reverse of loving shopkeepers. Imagine malicious shopkeepers—shopkeepers who overcharge customers just to see them suffer. Kant could presumably reply that even malicious shopkeepers are motivated by self-interest. They desire to gain pleasure for themselves. In that sense, these sadists would not be so different from those crooks.

There is, however, a third possibility. Imagine a shopkeeper having a motive to overcharge customers that was the mirror image of the motive of duty. Such a shopkeeper would not act out of self-interest, or even out of malice, for those motives are mirror images of the motives of altruism, and sympathy, respectively. Such a shopkeeper would think, "This is wrong. This is disrespectful of another person. *That* is why I will do it."

Such a person is not motivated by pleasure—not even sadistic pleasure. Such a person would instead be motivated as Satan is in *Paradise Lost*, when he says "Evil, be thou my good." The Devil, on this account, is *immoral*, and not merely amoral.

Kant did indeed imagine this possibility. He called it the "diabolical will." And he claimed that it is *impossible* for human beings. For a diabolical will, he thought, you needed the Devil. The Devil does not harm innocent people because it is necessary for some end of His (such as to gain wealth or power) or even because it pleases Him. The Devil kills, maims, tortures, lies, manipulates, and so forth, because it is the wrong thing to do. Such a motivation, Kant says, is not possible for us. We are incapable of being moved to act by the thought of something's being wrong, as such. Only the Devil is so moved.

The Devil You Don't Know

If this is what the Devil is, then two things follow.

First, it's very difficult, if not impossible, to conceive of the Devil. The Devil is a kind of pure evil that has nothing in common with our evil acts, and is alien to us. That's why He does not appear in literature and popular culture. As it turns out, the Devil we know is better than the Devil we don't know.

Second, nobody could possibly have sympathy for the Devil.

X

Possible Devils

27
Can the Devil Get You?

GREG LITTMANN

Can the Devil get you? For much of the world's population, not being sent to Hell and into the clutches of Old Nick is quite simply the most important thing to achieve in life.

Their concern is understandable. Hell, according to the reports we have, is at the very least a dismal place and at worst, is a smorgasbord of endless torture. As potential futures go, spending forever being burned, skinned, or otherwise horribly mutilated is as bad as things could get. If the Devil can get you, you had better work hard to make sure that you avoid winding up in Hell.

On the other hand, if the Devil can't get you, you're off the hook, perhaps literally. I'm going to assume that the Devil exists, because what I'm most interested in exploring here is the nature of *you*. Does your nature as a human make it possible for you to have an afterlife in Hell after you die, or does your nature make that impossible? What would it even mean for you to go to Hell?

Can the Devil Get Your Soul?

The most popular conception of damnation is a matter of Hell receiving a human's soul. But what is the soul and why should you care if the Devil gets it? As commonly understood, the soul is something non-physical that becomes separated from the body when you die, and the reason why you should care whether the Devil gets it is that the soul is the *real you*.

According to this widely held view, your physical body stays on Earth to rot after your death, while the real non-physical you travels on to a new existence, perhaps one where you're tormented forever in the pits of Hell. This model of damnation relies on a theory of mind known as "substance dualism," often referred to simply as "dualism." This is the view that there are two kinds of thing in the universe: physical things and non-physical things. Physical things are governed by the laws of physics. They include your body, tables and chairs, and anything else that you can see and touch, or even detect with scientific equipment. Non-physical things are not governed by the laws of physics and include human souls and any other spirits.

The view that people are non-physical souls that are separable from their bodies is relied on by almost every ghost story. For instance, in Shakespeare's *Hamlet*, Hamlet encounters the spirit of his dead father on the castle walls, though Hamlet knows perfectly well that his father's body lies undisturbed in its tomb; while in the *Nightmare on Elm Street* movies (1984–2010), the fact that Freddy Krueger's body was burned to ashes doesn't keep his soul from continuing to bully teenagers.

This view of the soul is also assumed by stories of possession in which one body ends up with two souls, one of them an invader. According to the gospels of Matthew, Mark, and Luke, Jesus and his disciples cast numerous evil spirits out of possessed people, and exorcism is still practiced by most Christian denominations. Such invasion of bodies by spirits is familiar in popular culture. In the film *The Exorcist* (1973), a demon sets up residence in thirteen-year-old Regan MacNeil, taking control of her body and forcing her to do things like twist her head around at unnatural angles and spew green vomit onto priests. In the *Evil Dead* films (1981–2013), demons pass easily from human to human, possessing them at will. Not content with this, they also possess trees, items of furniture, and even individual human body parts, leading to a showdown in *Evil Dead II* (1987) between the hero, Ash, and his own hand.

Welcome to Hell

So what's Hell like when your soul gets there? Perhaps you will remain as a non-physical spirit, subjected to torments that we embodied folk can't even conceive. Alternatively, perhaps your non-physical soul will receive a new physical body in Hell, so that you can be tortured physically. In principle, if you are a non-physical soul, the Devil could even torture your new body so badly that he destroys it, then simply pop your soul into a new, unscathed body to be tortured afresh.

The New Testament consistently represents Hell as being a place where people suffer in fire, which sounds like physical bodies undergoing physical damage. For example, Revelation 21:8 warns "But the fearful, and unbelieving, and the abominable, and murderers, and whoremongers, and sorcerers, and idolaters, and all liars, shall have their part in the lake which burneth with fire and brimstone . . ." Mark 9:44 elaborates that the damned will suffer from painful worms *as well as* endless burning—"their worm dieth not, and the fire is not quenched."

Representations of Hell in art have often depicted it as a physical place containing damned people who have physical bodies. In Italian poet Dante Alighieri's epic, *Inferno*, written around 1314, Dante relates his fictional journey through Hell. He enters by walking through an enormous gate on which is written "Abandon all hope, you who enter here" and afterwards interacts with Hell just as if it were a dangerous physical place that he must find his way through. The damned he meets are as solid as he is and are undergoing hideous physical tortures like being hacked apart by swords, bitten by snakes, submerged in poo, and, of course, burned by never-ending flames. In Christopher Marlowe's play *Doctor Faustus*, written around 1600, Faustus sells his soul to the Devil and pays at the end by being carried off alive to Hell to suffer torments like being boiled in lead, impaled on forks, and—indicating that the Devil has a sense of humor—made to endure Hell's rest area, which consists of a burning chair.

This image of Hell as a physical place with embodied inhabitants persists in modern popular culture. "Your mother sucks cocks in Hell" the possessing demon promises Father Karass in *The Exorcist*. In the *Doom* series of computer games (1993–2012), Hell can be entered physically and the demons there physically shot to bits—as if Dante had had enough and wasn't going to take it anymore. Similarly, in the *Hellboy* movies (2004–2008), Hell is the home of physical demons wanting to come to our world to physically rip *us* to bits. *Drag Me to*

Hell (2009) even follows *Doctor Faustus* in presenting banishment to Hell as something that could happen to a living and embodied individual, ending as it does with the ground opening up under the cursed heroine's feet and demonic arms pulling her into flames below.

Do You Have a Soul to Take?

It all sounds terribly painful! However, the Devil can only get your non-physical soul if you *have* such a soul. Do you? A soul is standardly conceived as something that influences the physical body, controlling it like a puppeteer controlling a puppet—the soul makes the body sit down or stand up, for instance, and determines everything else that the body does and says. But any interaction between the physical and the non-physical would violate the laws of physics, the laws by which physical things operate.

Consider the case, common in horror movies, of disembodied souls moving physical objects. In the *Paranormal Activity* movies (2007–2012), home owners are tormented by an invisible and intangible demon that moves things around at night—opening and closing doors and throwing pots and pans around the kitchen. According to physics, moving objects at rest requires a physical cause. For the non-physical to change the physical would break the rules that, according to science, best describe the way that our physical universe operates.

It might be tempting to believe that the problem of non-physical souls influencing physical things disappears if we allow that the soul is in possession of a body, as your soul is now in possession of yours. King James I of England (he who commissioned the King James Bible) personally wrestled with the issue of how non-physical demons can do things like open doors and windows. His solution, presented in his treatise *Daemonologie* (1597), was that they do it by possessing the dead—"For if they haue assumed a deade bodie, whereinto they lodge themselues, they can easely inough open without dinne anie Doore or Window, and enter in thereat."

However, placing a soul inside a body doesn't solve the problem of non-physical things effecting physical things. After all, bodies are themselves physical things. If your soul is non-physical, how can it influence your physical body at all? How can it, for instance, make your body so much as move a finger? The answer is that it can't, at least, not without breaking the laws of physics as we understand them. Try moving a finger right now. Did you succeed? If you did, then it seems that you are not a non-physical soul.

Does the Devil Want Your Body?

Perhaps then, if non-physical souls don't exist, you are your physical body. If you are your body then in order for Hell to receive you, the Devil has to get his claws on your physical remains after death. Taking you to Hell would require taking your corpse away and resurrecting it. That sounds like pretty good news! After all, corpses generally stay in their graves rather than mysteriously vanishing, so it looks like the Devil isn't getting people.

Some believe that the time for bodily resurrection has not come yet. Rather, we will all be resurrected in our old bodies at the same time at some point in the future. This view is held by orthodox Catholics among others, the Fourth Lateran Council having declared in 1215 that "All of them will rise with their own bodies, which they now wear, so as to receive according to their deserts."

Perhaps the most dramatic problem with such a view is that the matter that makes up our bodies has already been matter in other people's bodies in the past and will be matter in other people's bodies in the future. Dead organic matter doesn't lie undisturbed in the ground. It is consumed by living organisms and recycled again and again in new bodies, including human bodies. A resurrection of all humans in their original bodies would at best yield a single undifferentiated lump of twisted flesh without any functioning brains, a lump that it would be impossible, even in principle, to carve into separate individuals because every individual overlaps with many others. Even if it were taken apart atom by atom for rebuilding, it would remain logically impossible to resurrect everyone in their original bodies.

However, the theory that you are your body has problems of its own. Perhaps the most obvious is that it overlooks the particular importance of the part of your body that does the thinking—your brain. It's your brain that holds your memories and determines your personality and actions. Imagine that you had to choose between having your brain sent to Hell in a new body and having your body sent to Hell with someone else's brain inside it. In seems obvious that the less painful option for yourself is to let your body burn but spare your brain. Certainly, it is the body with your brain in it that will remember being you and who will hold all of your beliefs and attitudes. Your old body with a new brain, on the other hand, only *looks* like you, and not even that after a bath in boiling lead.

Perhaps the answer is to track the physical matter of the brain, while ignoring the matter in the rest of the body. On this model, the Devil has you if he has your brain, and not otherwise. One problem with this is that it seems arbitrary to place such special emphasis on the brain's matter rather than the way the brain functions. We place particular importance on brains over other organs because it's the brain that determines how we think and act; but if it's the way that we think and act that is really important, why are we tracking matter at all? After all, your brain matter could be re-arranged in such a way that your personality is wiped and replaced. Conversely, your old personality could be replicated on an entirely new brain, like software on a new computer. As long as the new brain is a perfect copy of yours, it would cause its body to speak and act exactly like you do.

Can the Devil Recreate You in Hell?

What if the Devil *did* construct a physical copy of you in Hell? Would *that* person count as the real *you*, now helpless in the Devil's cruel embrace? Some philosophers believe that you are neither a soul nor a body but a particular program, like a computer program, running on your brain. If we view you as a program, then presumably you don't need to be run on your old body in order for you to survive after death. Rather, the program that is you could stop running on its old hardware—the body you are using now—and start running on new hardware somewhere else, perhaps a body writhing in the flames of Hell. Indeed, as on the dualist model, the Devil can torture you until your body is completely destroyed and then just build a new body for you and start again.

Worse yet, the Devil can build as many of you as he wants and each of these people really will be you. After all, since you are just a program, and the same program can be run on multiple systems at once, the Devil can torment as many of you at once as he likes. Over there, you are being hurled by pitchfork into a lake of boiling lead, over there, you are being impaled on swords, over there, you're going to the dentist. If there is infinite matter available in Hell, the Devil could torture an infinite number of you at once, an act that makes ordinary eternal torture look like an act of mercy.

In fact, if the Devil is allowed to do as he likes in his own realm, he can raise you from the dead for torture even if you went to Heaven after death. After all, if you're just a program, going to Heaven after death would be a matter of having your program run on a new body in Heaven. Nothing about that rules out also having your program run on a different new body by the Devil in Hell. You could, in principle, wind up in both Heaven *and* Hell, both eternally saved and eternally damned, playing a harp over here, having your intestines pulled out over there.

Is That Burning Person Really You?

If it makes no sense to you that more than one future person could be you, you aren't alone. The account seems to leave out something vital to personal identity—about what it is for you to be *you*—that prevents that sort of duplication. Since the future of *you* is exactly what we are concerned with here, that's a serious worry. We want to know whether *you* might burn for eternity in the flames of Hell, not just whether someone programmed to *act* like you burns forever. If the view that the mind is a program can't give appropriate answers to identity questions in theoretical situations like that involving multiple copies of you after death, then it isn't really capturing personal identity, and if it doesn't capture personal identity, it can't tell you about *your* possible future.

Philosophers who hold the program view of mind can and do offer more-complex accounts than the simple one I have drawn above and for many of them, it wouldn't follow that both the persons in Heaven and Hell are you. One way out is to add a requirement for personal identity that your original body be present, in which case, an afterlife is impossible and the Devil can never get you. The only other option is to insist that when there is more than one copy of an individual, none of them are really that individual. On this model, neither of the copies of you, in Heaven or Hell, is really you, just because it isn't a *unique* copy.

But this solution is arbitrary. If the copy of you suffering in Hell would really be you if it were the only copy to exist, how does the creation of another copy make it not you? If all that pain would be *your* pain if only one copy of your program were running on a body, how does creating a new copy somewhere else make it not your pain at all? Can you imagine being terrified to know that a copy of you will burn in Hell when you die but then relieved to find out that there will be *ten* copies of you burning in Hell, on the grounds that as long as more than one copy of you is being tortured, none of the copies count as the real you? It seems arbitrary that the creation of multiple copies should reassign agony from one person to another. It seems more likely that the program account isn't really tracking what makes you *you* at all, and so can't answer the question of whether the Devil can get you.

Are You Fit to Pit?

So can the Devil get you or not? Can he imprison your soul in body after body, dropping you again and again into boiling lead while he laughingly explains the laws governing interaction between the physical and non-physical? Can he build a vast pit filled with millions of burning people, all of them *you,* or pave the road to Hell, not with good intentions, but with living faces, all of them yours? We won't settle the question in one short chapter. Other philosophers believe that there are replies to all of the arguments I've offered and there were many arguments that I have no space to explore. At most, I can provide you with food for thought and leave it up to you to hunt for the answer.

What is clear, though, is that we can't consider the likelihood and nature of life after death without addressing fundamental philosophical questions about personal identity—about what it is that makes a person themself rather than someone else. To understand what sort of futures are open to you, you first need to understand who you are.

28

Is Mara Satan?

JOHN M. THOMPSON

As a college professor of Eastern religions and philosophies, I face many challenges in the classroom. While some of these are shared by all instructors (how to cover the requisite material in the limited time we have, what's the best way to ignore that hot student in the front row, what to do about habitual "net surfers," why won't the university install coffee dispensers in classrooms, and so on) others are unique to my specific field.

Chief among these challenges is the tendency for students to interpret new material in terms of their own tradition—usually Christianity. Students will tend to view Siddhartha Gautama, the historical Buddha, more or less as Jesus, or identify *nirvana*, the awakened state of peace beyond the travails of ordinary life, with "Heaven" or "salvation from sin."

A common example (one even encouraged by some textbooks) is the tendency to categorize Mara, a mythic Indian being associated with death and the sensual delights of this world who figures prominently in the Buddha's life story, as "the Buddhist Satan." While this can be helpful at first, it really is highly misleading, as it imposes a simplistic moral-cosmic dualism that runs counter to Buddhist teachings. In fact, there's more to Mara than being devilish, and if we can understand Mara we can arrive at a more nuanced understanding of human life and spirituality than superficial Satanic comparisons promote.

Death and the Earth

Mara is an incredibly storied character. His roots go back to the *Vedas*, the oldest surviving Indian texts, in which he is a deity (*deva*) associated with death and the Earth. Etymologically speaking, the word "Mara" derives from ancient Indo-European terms having to do with dying that may also be connected to Mother Earth and hence, actually have a *positive* connotation.

Mara generally means "death" or "maker of death," and as such, he is often associated with Yama, the god of death. Over the centuries before Buddhism, Mara rises in stature, becoming a chief deity of the *kamadhatu* (realm of desire or pleasure) who, as the result of his vast merit, dwells in the sixth heaven, from whence he presides over *samsara* and all sentient beings. As a divine ruler, Mara exerts authority over all his subjects and opposes any who seek to escape from his realm. Among his various titles are Vasavartin ("Controller") and Papiyams ("Evil One").

It's really only with the rise of Buddhism that Mara becomes a major figure in Indian mythology. Early Buddhist texts suggest that he was more of a nuisance or distraction from the spiritual path rather than Evil incarnate. He is particularly famous for various encounters with Siddhartha when Siddhartha was a *bodhisattva* ("Buddha-to-be").

Accounts in *Sutta Nipata*, an early text, have Mara trying to convince Siddhartha to opt for a traditional brahmanical life of Vedic study and sacrificial ritual rather than renouncing home and hearth for the life of a religious wanderer (*sannyasin*). Later stories in texts such as the *Mahavastu* ("Great Chronicle") and the *Buddhacaritas* ("Life of the Buddha") expand on such episodes, having Mara variously trying to block Siddhartha's departure from his father's palace or to convince him to pass promptly into *parinirvana* ("final demise," fully passing beyond our world, or dying).

The most famous episode involving Mara is his confrontation with Siddhartha under the *bodhi* tree, a scene often called *Maravijaya* ("The Defeat of Mara"). In its most fully elaborated versions, the demon is incensed at Siddhartha's determination to overcome *samsara* after his many previous trials, and so unleashes his vast armies to overcome Siddhartha with fear. Failing that, Mara then sends his three (or five) daughters (sometimes equated with sloth, lust, and other failings) to seduce the young monk and thus foil his quest for awakening. When they also fail, Mara himself appears to challenge this young upstart, calling into question Siddhartha's right to challenge his reign.

In response, the Buddha-to-Be breaks from his meditative posture, reaching out his right hand to touch the ground. This gesture, the "Earth touching *mudra*," is one of the most popular artistic depictions of the Buddha and remains one of the most powerful symbols in all of Buddhism. At this point, the Earth Goddess herself emerges to testify on Siddhartha's behalf and Mara, like a naughty schoolboy caught bullying his classmates for their lunch money, slinks off in shame.

Grasping

Mara's role in Buddhism, however, is not finished. In various versions of the Buddha's life story, he continues to shadow the Buddha, tempting Ananda, the Buddha's faithful attendant, to request Buddha to remain in the world until the end of the current *kalpa* ("cosmic epoch"), even appearing to the Buddha as his earthly life nears its end. The Buddha, however, firmly puts the demon off until the full completion of the Buddha's earthly ministry. All in all, as Buddhist tradition develops over time, so does Mara's role, until he becomes a seemingly ubiquitous presence haunting all who venture along the Buddhist path (*marga*); he is the very personification of *trsna*, the "grasping" that enmeshes us in *samsara* (the system of the world) and thus consigns us to continual death-and-rebirth.

While Mara does resemble Satan in certain respects, these two troublers of humanity also differ significantly. While, like Satan, Mara is a god-like being who does play an adversarial role for those seeking full Awakening, he is not truly "evil" in an absolute sense; *samsara* is *not* "bad" (it is the vast world system in which we all reside, including the various *devas*) and Mara as its overlord is only managing his turf, *not* seeking to overturn the cosmos. Mara has not "fallen" (he has a decidedly elevated status), nor is he locked in some sort of eternal battle against the One True God; he is one of many deities inhabiting the Indian cosmos.

Mara also has a much larger role in Indian scripture, particular in Buddhism, than the Devil has in the Bible. For

instance, the *Samyutta Nikaya* ("Collected Discourses," one of
the five authoritative scriptures of Theravada Buddhism)
includes two collections of stories in which Mara tries to tempt,
frighten, trick, and disrupt the lives of various monks and
nuns. By contrast, Satan makes very few appearances in the
Bible itself. Of course Satan, too, is a more complex figure in
the Bible (and Christian tradition as a whole) than is often
reckoned in popular culture.

Devilish Depictions

This brief synopsis of Indian portrayals helps us to see how
students can get the wrong idea about Mara by following some
contemporary Western textbooks.

- For instance, Robert S. Ellwood and Barbara A. McGraw's
  Many Peoples, Many Faiths (a fairly widely used textbook, now in its ninth edition), merely speaks of Mara as
  "an old Vedic nature god or demon."

- Huston Smith, author of *The World's Religions,* perhaps
  the most widely-read introductory textbook at both the
  high school and college level, gives a more detailed
  account, speaking of Mara variously as "The Evil One,"
  "Kama, the God of Desire," "the Tempter," and "Mara, the
  Lord of Death." Moreover, he goes on to relate that Mara's
  final effort was his trying to convince the Buddha that no
  one else would understand the truth of Awakening and,
  failing to dissuade the Blessed One, "was banished from
  his life forever."

- While Stephen Prothero, whose recent best-selling book
  God Is Not One is in many respects intended as a correc-
  tive to such texts as Smith's, confines his account of
  Mara's encounter with the Buddha to one sentence:
  "Sensing trouble, Mara, the demon of sense pleasures,
  sent a Bangkok of distractions his [Siddhartha's] way, but
  the Buddha-to-be would not be stirred by such triviali-
  ties." Perhaps more seriously, Smith (and Prothero) both
  explicitly liken Buddha to Christ in their discussions of
  his encounter with Mara, and thus implicitly liken Mara
  to Satan.

I'm *not* saying that these authors are "wrong" and should therefore be vilified for willfully misrepresenting the "Truth" about Mara and his role in Buddhism. It's just that their presentations all too easily lend themselves to making such easy equivalences and thus hinder our students' (and readers') education. In that sense, these writers are unwittingly behaving like Mara (or maybe Satan?) in subtly dissuading us from facing what is actually true and doing what we are called to do. Mara is *not* Satan, and part of our job is to help students see that Buddhism really entails a very different cosmic view than does Christianity.

Still, as I have mentioned, there *are* some Western authors who avoid the simple "Mara = the Buddhist Satan" equation.

- Best-selling author Karen Armstrong in her elegant book *Buddha* discusses Mara's place in the Buddha's life rather insightfully. Drawing on Jungian psychology, she presents Mara as the Buddha's "shadow self," the veritable embodiment of the dark forces of self-conceit and violent rage the come from childish insistence on living only in terms of one's egocentric concerns.

- Similarly, in his classic *The Hero with a Thousand Faces*, Joseph Campbell, the somewhat controversial but much beloved *doyen* of world mythology, calls Mara "Kama-Mara, . . . "Love and Death," essentially depicting him as the personification of *eros* and *thanatos*, the twin forces that Freud identifies as the unconscious drivers of much human action and source of much misery.

- Stephen Batchelor, scholar and former monk, in *Living with the Devil: A Meditation on Good and Evil* reads the literature on Mara (and Satan for that matter) as narratives of our fundamental struggles to live wisely in the midst of the seemingly perpetual contradictions of "good" versus "evil."

Again, I'm not arguing that Armstrong, Campbell, and Batchelor always get Mara "right," only that they resist the temptation of depicting Mara in simplistic devilish guise. In part, of course, this is due to Armstrong, Batchelor, and Campbell taking the time to explore and elaborate upon the vast lore surrounding Mara. But there's more to it than this. These authors' depictions of Mara are also more faithful to the traditional Indian accounts, and more explicitly reveal the deeper *psychological* dimensions of Indian mythologies.

Indian traditions refuse to divide "being" (reality) from "thinking" (experience) in a clear and distinct fashion, and like many bodies of traditional lore, have a far more sophisticated (if implicit) understanding of "mind" than much of Modern Western philosophy. So there *are* some readily available books that provide more sophisticated views of Mara in his His Not-Quite-Satanic Majesty. But we can also learn something about Mara from a surprising source: Keanu Reeves and *Little Buddha*.

Kudos to Keanu!

While Bernardo Bertolucci's 1993 movie *Little Buddha* focuses on an American family dealing with the fall-out from a Tibetan lama identifying their son as the reincarnation of his late master, the movie also depicts the early life of Siddhartha Gautama, the historical Buddha, up through his awakening. Siddhartha is portrayed by Keanu Reeves, in a series of flashbacks based on traditional Indian accounts.

The specific scenes in which Mara confronts the Buddha-to-be, while replete with all manner of "movie magic," are fascinating and actually resonate more with Buddhist tradition than most Western books. Moreover, I'm convinced that this richer portrayal of Mara opens us up to better understandings of (and appreciation for) the figure of Satan himself.

Little Buddha, while somewhat controversial (as all movies dealing with explicitly religious subjects are) provides a fascinating and provocative portrayal of Mara. Although the scenes depicting the life of Siddhartha (portrayed in rather stilted fashion by Keanu Reeves, himself a Buddhist) smack of Sunday-school literalism, Mara comes off as rather nuanced, particularly after his full-blown "assaults" with demon armies and seductive succubae. At this point in the movie it seems that Siddhartha has withstood the attacks but we quickly find out that this not the case.

With the camera focused on *bodhisattva* Keanu still sitting serenely under the Bodhi tree, the narrator breaks in to say that Mara is not finished. At once we see a clear mirror-like pool on the ground directly in front of Siddhartha, and Mara emerges from its still depths, gripping (or being gripped by?) the *bodhisattva's* arm. And Mara is Siddhartha's perfect twin, his mirror-image.

The back-and-forth between the two Siddharthas, while short and simple, is surprisingly subtle. Mara praises Siddhartha for his (apparent) victory and asks him to be his god. Siddhartha calmly refuses, referring to Mara as "architect," the skilled designer of the dwelling in which he lives. Mara replies that the house is Siddhartha himself. After several more exchanges, Siddhartha declares "Oh Lord of my own Ego, you are pure illusion. You do not exist. The Earth is my witness," at which point he reaches out to touch the ground, performing the famous "earth touching *mudra*."

Almost immediately Mara reverts back to his "true" form (he is played in this scene by Anupam Shyam, an Indian TV and movie actor famous for depicting villains) and then fades away. For the next minute or so, Siddhartha in close-up remains silent, smiling, while off to the side, the three children who in the movie's main story are candidates for the alleged reincarnation of the dead Tibetan lama, appear as if they have been watching the entire scene. The camera then pulls back as Siddhartha achieves full Awakening, a cartoonish nimbus of light surrounds him, and then he, too, fades away while we return to the main story of the movie.

Little Buddha is by no means a cinematic masterpiece, although it is better than many other movies that deal with explicitly religious subjects (such as *The Ten Commandments* or *The Passion of the Christ*). Yet its portrayal of Mara is uncannily insightful. Mara is, in the end, not some separate spiritual force of evil so much as the sly and subtle twin of the self, the idealized image we have of ourselves. And it is this objectified yet false self, the "Lord of my own Ego," that truly holds us back from True Awakening, Buddhahood itself. Like Keanu-Siddhartha, we cling to ourselves and thus remain stuck. The key Buddhist insight that Bertolucci depicts so well is that, like Siddhartha, we can recognize Mara and call him out, piercing through his illusory guise: "Get thee behind me, Satan!" (Mara?) Once Mara is unmasked, we can see that he is *not* who we truly are and his grip (our grip on our selves) no longer holds us.

So What? Sew Buttons?

To use a decidedly non-Buddhist image from the gospels, new wine should not be poured into old wineskins, as they will burst and the wine will be lost. Rather, we need new wineskins (see Matthew 9:17). Real learning requires new concepts that, while like the old, are more flexible and can take in the new as well.

Mara and Satan are *not* "the same" in any truly meaningful sense. The *mythoi* of ancient India and the Mid-East differ enormously in tone, setting, and basic assumptions concerning humanity and the ultimate purpose of life. Still, the playful dialogical comparison between them can be instructive, as it can open up new insights and, I would argue, reveal certain dimensions of our shared humanity that we would do well to note. Comparing and contrasting depictions of Mara and Satan reveals a multiplicity to each of these figures, particularly when we include some non-canonical popular sources.

In truth, both Mara and Satan are "Legion," like the demonic spirits who, in Mark's gospel, possess the poor outcast consigned to dwell among the tombs in the Gerasene country-side (Mark 5). Mara is a shape-shifter, a trickster like Loki and Coyote, by turns cruel, humorous, even somewhat heroic in certain ways. Mara is attractive and repellant, much like Milton's portrayal of Satan as Lucifer ("Light-bringer") or even Blake's deceptively simple drawings of Biblical scenes. Whatever else they may be, they all are so many guises of the dark, shadow side of our own psyches.

We are Mara/Satan

When it comes right down to it, *we* are Mara/Satan, or, rather, they both personify aspects of ourselves that can be troubling if not downright scary. It's better to know this than to remain ignorant of these aspects of our selves. Cleopatra was a queen, but she made a lot of poor choices, and ended up dying at her own hand. It would be best if we did not emulate this particular "Queen of De Nile" (and yes, that's a somewhat devilish pun).

"Getting" Mara means respecting his power and seeing clearly how he and we are bound together. If Mara is our enemy, he's an enemy deserving our deepest empathy. Realizing *that* means developing genuine sympathy for this Devil—something Keanu Reeves and Mick Jagger (to say nothing of the rest of us non-celebrity schlubs) should really appreciate.

29
If the Devil Didn't Exist We'd Have to Invent Him

ROBERT ARP

François-Marie Arouet, a.k.a. Voltaire (1694–1778), was a French Enlightenment writer, historian, and philosopher famous for his witty attacks on the Catholic Church, his advocacy of religious freedom and separation of church and state, and his critique of Leibniz's (1646–1716) optimistic philosophy (this world is the best of all possible worlds God could have created) in a book that most of us had to read in high school or college, *Candide: or, The Optimist* (1762).

He's also famous for having said, "Si Dieu n'existait pas, il faudrait l'inventer"—"If God did not exist, then it would be necessary to invent Him"—in a poem-like work called *Epistle to the Author of The Three Impostors* (1768). There's some debate about what Voltaire meant by this claim; however, most scholars think that Voltaire was a deist who believed that some kind of powerful God created an ordered universe, then "wound it up" and let it do its thing unimpeded, much like a clockmaker does with a clock. Voltaire likely also thought that this God was moral and just, that Heaven and Hell exist, that we have immortal souls, and that God would have no problem sending your soul to Hell as a righteous and just punishment if you were a jerk in this life. The fear of eternal damnation is a great way to keep people acting fairly civil toward one another in this life—thus, even if God did not exist, then it would be necessary to invent Him to scare people straight (so to speak) for the sake of social order. The claim makes more sense now, doesn't it?

Claim the Claim You're Claiming

We'll get to the Devil in a moment, but first I'd like to consider whether Voltaire's claim—"If God did not exist, then it would be necessary to invent Him"—is true or not.

As critical thinkers, one of the essential things we must do is check to see if a claim made by anyone is true or false, by providing evidence. If a claim is false, or lacking in evidence to support it, then we should reject it. We don't *really* want to believe false things, do we? And it seems to me that Voltaire's claim about a god has been pretty important, and influential, in the history of Western thought and civilization.

Our thoughts, beliefs, opinions, perceptions, and ways of looking at things are made known through claims, in mental, spoken, or written form. A *claim* is a statement, assertion, proposition, judgment, declarative sentence, or part of a declarative sentence that communicates that something is or is not the case concerning the world, self, states of affairs, or some aspect of reality as we view it.

Frank has the belief that some god exists, so he makes the claim, "God exists" in a philosophy class, or Jane is of the opinion that abortion is moral so she makes the concluding claim in her term paper, "Abortion is moral." A young-Earth creationist takes what is said in the Bible literally and claims, "God created the universe between 5,700 and 10,000 years ago," while a particle physicist claims, "Fermions exist and can be contrasted with bosons, which also exist." A member of the Flat Earth Society claims, well, "The Earth is flat," while a Moon-landing Denier claims that . . . you guessed it. I hear a cuckoo clock chiming somewhere in the distance.

The Claim Is True as Is Evidenced by . . . Well . . . the Evidence

But claims also are true or false—and they have to be one or the other. For example, the claims "This chapter is being typed on a laptop computer," "There are bacteria living on human skin not visible to the naked eye," and "Voltaire was French" are true, whereas the claims "Rob Arp was president of the United States in 2000," "A vixen is a female cow," "The Sun revolves around Venus," "Noah was able to get two of every species of living thing on an ark that he and his family constructed," and "I am standing and sitting at the same time" are false. So how do we know that?

Well, a claim is shown to be true or false as a result of *evidence*, of which there are many different forms. For example, there's evidence in the form of:

- Your own *direct* sense data, as when you see, hear, touch, taste, or smell something first-hand—this book in your hands (or the e-reader in your hands) is a good example.

- Your own *indirect* sense data achieved through correctly calibrated instruments such as microscopes, telescopes, meters, and other such devices—remember seeing algae under a microscope for the first time in biology class with some amazement?

- The testimony of others you trust whose direct or indirect sense data are reliable—as when your retired parents claim that the Eiffel Tower exists because they went to France on a tour and actually saw it, even though you yourself never have; or when it's claimed in a scholarly journal that some field biologist discovered a new species of beetle (which happens quite often, actually).

- Simple, powerful explanations, as one finds in any of the mathematical or life sciences—it's not the cold weather *itself*, for example, that is the reason why more people get the flu in the wintertime; it's a combination of (a) our bodily defenses are lower in colder weather (because our bodies are focusing energies on staying warm) and (b) the flu virus is transmitted through the air and on surfaces and more folks are staying together indoors during the wintertime (thus, there's more chance of getting the flu).

- Simple, powerful definitions, as one finds in any reliable dictionary or encyclopedia—the *Oxford English Dictionary* and *Encyclopedia Britannica* are standards for the English language.

- Appeal to well-established theories—for example, gravity, the second law of thermodynamics, cell theory, evolution, and the Big Bang theory.

- Appeal to appropriate authority—as when the degreed, licensed, board-certified, and insured doctor says your abdominal pain is caused by an appendicitis, or respected astrophysicists at Oxford tell us that the universe is expanding, or theoretical mathematicians at Harvard tell us that it's impossible to square the circle.

- Good arguments, where it can be demonstrated that a concluding claim must be true or likely is true by virtue of true premises and the fact that the concluding claims follows from the premises.

In fact, when someone asks for proof of the truth of a claim or says, "Oh yeah, prove it. Show it to me. Justify it." what they're really asking for is evidence, and when a claim has been proven true, this means that evidence for its truth has in fact been provided.

Rob Arp Was President of the United States in 2000 . . . NOT!

So, the claim, "This chapter is being typed on a laptop computer" is shown to be true by the fact that people sitting in this Starbucks right now (myself included) can see me typing, the claim, "There are bacteria living on human skin not visible to the naked eye" is shown to be true because anyone can see them with a microscope, and the claim, "Voltaire was French" is true because not only do we have appropriate and reliable historical records that indicate he was French, but also scholarly historians tell us this is the case, too. On the other hand, the claim:

- "Rob Arp was president of the United States in 2000" is false because the direct sense data of a whole heck of a lot of people indicate that George W. Bush was President of the US back then.

- "A vixen is a female cow" is false by definition (since a vixen is actually a female fox).

- "The Sun revolves around Venus" is false because of direct sensory evidence provided by nightly observations over a period of time, indirect sensory evidence provided by numerous telescopes, and the well-established helio-centric theory showing that Venus actually revolves around the Sun.

- "Noah was able to get two of every species of living thing on an ark that he and his family constructed" is false because the ark would needed to have been the F-ing size of the continent of Africa!

- "I am standing and sitting at the same time" can be shown to be false with the evidence of a simple argument (which is a kind of "reduction to absurdity" argument):

    FIRST PREMISE: If it's true that "I am standing and sitting at the same time," then I would be in two places at once, which violates all known physical laws of the universe, and would be completely absurd.

    SECOND PREMISE: Absurd things—such as violating all known physical laws of the universe—simply can't be tolerated by a rational mind.

    CONCLUSION: Therefore, it's *not* true (it's false) that "I am standing and sitting at the same time."

Some claims are easy to show as true or false with evidence, like the claim that "The Sun is a squared-shaped star," "Al Gore was the forty-third President of the US," "The Earth is flat," or "The Moon landing was staged on a Hollywood set." Some claims are a little harder to show as true or false with evidence, like the claim that, "Fermions exist and can be contrasted with bosons, which also exist," "There was more than one shooter involved in JFK's assassination," "The universe is between 5,700 and 10,000 years old," or "A man actually rose from the dead some two thousand years ago."

Some claims seem to defy definitive judgments about truth or falsity and lend themselves to continual debate, dialogue, and discussion. Claims like "God exists," "Abortion is always immoral," "I have an immortal soul," "A constitutional republic is the best form of government," and "The only thing I can be completely sure about is that I must be existing in order to be thinking" would fall into this category. That's probably why ideas, issues, and arguments surrounding these claims can be found discussed and debated in philosophy classes, books, journals, and conferences all over the world.

That's a Big If

Now, "If God did not exist, then it would be necessary to invent Him" is actually an example of a *hypothetical* or *conditional claim*, which is a complex claim made up of two atomic claims taking the "IF (some claim), THEN (some other claim)" form. The claim that comes after the *if* in a conditional claim is also called the *antecedent* (as in "God did not exist") and the claim that comes after the *then* in a conditional claim is called the *consequent* (as in "It would be necessary to invent Him (God)"). We make conditional claims all of the time, like:

Antecedent	Consequent
"If it's raining . . ."	". . . then my car is wet"
"If I want to get downtown . . ."	". . . then I have to take the expressway"
"If you abort . . ."	". . . you're murdering a person"
"If she's going to the party . . ."	". . . then I'm sure as Hell not going."
"If the Fido you're referring to is a dog . . ."	". . . then it's definitely a mammal."
"If he committed the crime . . ."	". . . then the door would've been left open"
"If people are all self-centered jerks to one another . . ."	". . . then people *should be* self-centered jerks to one another"
"If I get A's in all of my classes this year . . ."	". . . my parents take me to Disney World in the summer of 2014"

Notice that, since a conditional claim is actually made up of two smaller atomic claims, there are four possible combinations for the truth and falsity of each claim—True-True, False-True, False-False, True-False—as in:

	Antecedent	Consequent
	"If I get A's in all of my classes this year . . ."	". . . my parents take me to Disney World in the summer of 2014"
1st possible combination	The claim, "I get A's in all of my classes this year" could be **True**	The claim, "My parents take me to Disney World in the summer of 2014" could be **True**
2nd possible combination	The claim, "I get A's in all of my classes this year" could be **False**	The claim, "My parents take me to Disney World in the summer of 2014" could be **True**
3rd possible combination	The claim, "I get A's in all of my classes this year" could be **False**	The claim, "My parents take me to Disney World in the summer of 2014" could be **False**
4th possible combination	The claim, "I get A's in all of my classes this year" could be **True**	The claim, "My parents take me to Disney World in the summer of 2014" could be **False**

The only way to show that a conditional claim is false is by showing that the antecedent is true while the consequent is false at the same time. So, of the four possible combinations—True-True, False-True, False-False, True-False—only the *True-False* (a true antecedent and a false consequent) combination makes the entire conditional claim be false. In fact, a good critical thinker always tries to see if they can *make* the antecedent be true and the consequent be false at the same time in a conditional claim; if it can't be done, then the conditional claim is true. You may be wondering why it is that the False-True and False-False combinations are still true, but because of space limitations, I'll have to leave aside any discussion of that (. . . shameless plug here, see my *Critical Thinking: An Introduction to Reasoning Well* textbook for those explanations).

Frank, Sally, and John the Prick

It makes complete sense that a conditional claim is false if the antecedent is true while the consequent is false. Let's say that Frank is new in the metro area of a big city and he thinks, "If I want to get downtown, then I have to take the expressway" but it's false that he "has to take the expressway" because there are plenty of other bigger streets and many side streets that someone can take to get downtown. In that case, his conditional claim, "If I want to get downtown, then I have to take the expressway" is false and you might even point that out to him because he needs to get downtown for an appointment in a half hour, but there's a big accident on the expressway.

So too, if your parents promised that if you get A's in all of your classes this year, then they would take you to Disney World in the summer of 2014, and you *do get all A's* (so, the antecedent part is true) but instead *they take you out to Olive Garden for dinner* (so, the consequent part is false), then you rightly can say to them, "Mom and Dad, It's true that I got all A's, but false that you took me to Disney World, so your conditional claim, 'If Sally get A's in all of her classes this year, then Sally's parents will take her to Disney World' is completely false. You *lied* to me! Not fair! And to top it all off, my spaghetti is cold! Waa waaa waaaa!" (As a postscript: later that night after Sally stomped up to her room, Sally's parents called her into the living room and surprised her with a trip to France.)

Taking another example of a conditional claim from above, let's say John is a bitter, cynical, self-centered jerk who's had a rough life. You're in a conversation with him and he decides to wax philosophically (and psychologically and sociologically) about the human condition, making the following claim in an attempt to justify why he's such a self-centered jerk: "If people are all self-centered jerks to one another, then they people *should be* self-centered jerks to one another." He then follows this up by saying, "It's a dog-eat-dog world out there, man, and I'm always gonna be the bigger dog." As a critical thinker, after challenging the claim that all people are self-centered jerks by pointing to examples of Mother Teresa types, heroes who sacrifice themselves for others, and people who died trying to help folks in the World Trade Center on 9/11, you can point out to him that, even if it was *true* that people are self-centered jerks, it's *false* that they *should be* self-centered jerks because this would lead to a miserable, Hobbesian, *Lord of the Flies*–like, *Sopranos*-type of existence. Thus, you could say to John that his entire conditional claim, "If people are all self-centered jerks to one another, then they people *should be* self-centered jerks to one another" is false and should be rejected. People *should not be* self-centered jerks, even if they in fact are.

How to Be Good Without God

We're almost to the Devil part, so hang on. Now we can apply what we know about evidence and the truth or falsity of claims (including conditional claims) to Voltaire's claim, "If God did not exist, then it would be necessary to invent Him." Is that claim true? I think that the claim can be considered false because, even if it were true that there's no just and moral God (which, to tell you the truth, is most likely the case), it's false that it would be necessary to invent such a being to keep folks scared straight. In other words, in the absence of a God—and a Hell and immortal souls, too—we *wouldn't* need Him for the sake of social order.

Now here's my evidence showing that the claim, "It would be necessary to invent Him (God)" is false: In fact, there are plenty of moral systems in existence that assist in maintaining social order, but make no mention of a god whatsoever. And many have been around long before anyone even conceived of the Judeo-Islamic-Christian God that Voltaire envisions. I'll mention only two here which have been influential especially in the past two hundred years.

First, there is the view inspired by Immanuel Kant (1724–1804) and his followers that persons, by virtue of their conscious rational capacities, are free and autonomous beings having an innate worth or dignity. Kant articulates a set of wholly reasonable and rational moral principles by which people can live harmoniously in three forms of what is known as the *categorical imperative*. I'll mention only the first form of the categorical imperative here: Whenever you act, make sure that your action is something that can be universalized without contradiction. In other words, ask yourself the question: "What if everyone did what I'm about to do?" and if it undermines or negates what you want to do, then it's immoral and you should not do it!

For example, let's say you wanted to borrow money from someone knowing that you will not pay it back. Now, think what would happen logically if all people *universally* did this: the very idea of "borrowing" would completely go away since no one would ever trust another person to borrow because Person A would know that s/he would never get the money back from Person B. And, you yourself, then, could never borrow any money with *or without* the intent of paying back! So, you would be contradicting or undermining your own action, which is irrational and unreasonable to do; hence, it's immoral. When you universalize in this Kantian way, so too:

- **Lying is immoral because it contradicts truth telling, and when you lie you depend upon the very idea of truth telling so that people will believe your lies!**

- **Suicide is immoral because it contradicts self-preservation of one's life, and if everyone committed suicide there would be no life to kill, including your own!**

- **Giving discounts to friends at your store is immoral because it contradicts fair prices for all, effectively negating any possibility of giving discounts in the first place!**

It's a rationally based moral theory through and through with no mention of a god whatsoever, and any kind of "performative contradiction"—like the ones mentioned above—is immoral. Kant is able to use this universalizability method to show that truth-telling, justice, and every other kind of right and good thing you can think of *really is* rational and, hence, moral; while lying, injustice, and every other kind of wrong and bad thing you can think of *really is* irrational and, hence, immoral. And these moral laws form the basis for social laws, and hence, order in a society.

A second moral theory is called *utilitarianism* and has been advocated by numerous communities for millennia, although John Stuart Mill (1806–1873) was the first to offer the most robust version of it. Utilitarians argue that an action is morally good insofar as its consequences promote the most benefit, payoff, or pleasure for the most persons affected by the decision. The way in which the utilitarian determines the good consequences to all affected in a situation is through a pro-vs.-con kind of calculation, a sort of cost-benefit analysis whereby one adds up all of the goods / benefits / pleasures on one side and compares them with all of the bads / detriments / pains on the other side.

The moral decision, then, is the one where the most goods / benefits / pleasures will result, and that's the one the utilitarian chooses. "Always go for the greatest good for the greatest amount" is the mantra here, where *good* can mean benefits, pleasures, happiness, and every other kind of perceived positive thing in some social setting (group, institution, town, city, society, culture, country). Actually, it's a very rational procedure—and again, there's no god mentioned whatsoever. In conjunction with Kant's ideas, utilitarian principles can act as a basis for social laws, and hence, order in a society.

Finally . . . the Devil

So it seems false that, "If God did not exist, then it would be necessary to invent Him." Now, what about adding a twist here: is it true that, "If *the Devil* did not exist, then it would be necessary to invent *Him*"? Actually, God and the Devil kind of go hand-in-hand from Voltaire's perspective. You need to have a Hell and the Devil, obviously, if you want to scare people straight. After all, the moral and just God exercises his morality and justice precisely by allowing you to choose Hell and eternal life with the Devil. (I have said that God *sends you* to Hell, but actually He doesn't really do that—He just allows you to choose Hell based upon your having led a jerky life and justly metes out the sentence.) So, from Voltaire's perspective, it would be necessary to invent the Devil along with God, if both did not exist.

The moral systems of Kant and Mill work best for rational adults who choose to do what's right and good, rather than fearing punishment for not doing so. One thing that leaves a bad taste in my mouth is how childish the whole God/Heaven and Devil/Hell ideas seem to be. "God's watching you," "The Devil sees you," "You don't want to burn in Hell, do you?"— these are the kinds of claims we hear from, or are implied by, Christians and their doctrine. Guilt, guilt, guilt! It just seems selfish and wrong to do what's right and good out of guilt or fear. And this is somewhat contradictory and ironic, given Jesus's message of self-sacrifice, goodness, peace, and love.

Further, although they appeal to the rational part of our humanity, the moral systems of Kant and Mill have a kind of built-in guilt and fear anyway. So, if you need the guilt or fear factor to motivate you to stay on the straight and narrow, you can find those elements in these wholly secular theories. Yet another reason *not* to need God or the Devil.

Maybe It Is Necessary to Invent Him

Having said this, most people aren't rational at all. Plus there are plenty of psychopaths, sociopaths, and others who fall on a similar spectrum, causing all kinds of pain and suffering in this world—consider any standard serial killer or dictator throughout history. And we're naturally self-seeking, self-centered bastards who have to rise above this animal part of our nature. Most of us respond very well to guilt and fear, and we're as much emotional, sensitive, feeling beings as we are rational. So maybe it really is necessary to invent God and the Devil to scare people straight for the sake of social order.

I've heard many Christians say that they need God and the Devil, too, because they "can't do it alone." They can't live a righteous life doing what's right and good without what they see as inspiration from God and the Devil. God motivates and assists through grace. The Devil motivates, too, but in a way that people don't want what He's offering.

I guess so long as a god or a devilish being acts as a motivator to do what is right and good, but doesn't conflict with other standard moral intuitions, then I'm okay with someone believing in these beings. God and the Devil, just like any spiritual being or realm, can act as useful fictions to help maintain order. The fact of the matter is that the best ethical parts of the World's religions can be made consistent with a secular morality, and there are plenty of religious folk who use rational consistency, scientific investigation, historical precedent, fairness, justice, respect for persons, and other moral principles that are common to moral decision making. So, in the end, it may be that it's necessary for certain people to invent the Devil, as an archetype of evil to be avoided at all costs.

XI

The Devilish Debate

30
Satan—A Good Guy?

OLLI PITKÄNEN

For most people, Satanism brings to mind black cloaks and candles, ritual sacrifices, pentagrams, and black magic in the way presented, for example, in Dario Argento's 2007 movie *The Mother of Tears*. This stuff could be considered Devil worship, not Satanism, and Devil worship is seen largely as a construction of the media and entertainment industry—no sane grown-up would practice it in reality.

Satanism actually is an atheistic, Nietzschean-based philosophy of life given this name by Anton LaVey (1930–1997), who founded the Church of Satan in 1966. Believe it or not, Satanists don't actually believe in Satan! A Satanist doesn't consider Satan a real entity, being, or thing, but a symbol of the human carnal nature repressed by the Christian tradition.

Although the metaphysical beliefs of Christianity are continually fading, Christian values are still culturally dominant in our Western society. As a symbol, Satan represents a radical rebellion against Christian (or post-Christian) morality and elevation of sensuality, individuality, and positive pride over conventionality and the illusory idea of agape love. Satanist followers of LaVey would like to reserve the term 'Satanism' exclusively for this kind of thinking.

It's often claimed that no one before LaVey used the particular term 'Satanism', and so he's justified in defining its content as he wishes. This is simply false, however. The term has been used as a synonym for Devil worship and in other contexts at least since the sixteenth century. The Polish decadent dramatist Stanislaw Przybyszewski was already a self-proclaimed

'Satanist' at the turn of the twentieth century! Even if this were not so, the term is currently used in very diverse ways by many different people. There are numerous self-proclaimed Satanist movements whose doctrines vary anywhere between the image of traditional Devil worship and the atheistic form of Satanism practiced by LaVey's Church of Satan.

Atheistic and Theistic Satanism

So, considering Satanism only within the framework of the Church of Satan is obviously too narrow. What then is Satanism exactly? I suggest that we shouldn't take any definition as the final one. Defining Satanism is like defining religion in general: it requires relatively little work to reach a somewhat stable intuitive grasp of the matter, but an exact and final definition is a completely different matter. The essential characteristics of *any* form of Satanism include:

- **A symbolic or metaphysical endorsement of a Devil figure—not necessarily the Judeo-Christian Satan— that represents a rebellion against the existing moral, societal, or even cosmic order**

- **The idea of a higher kind of knowledge compared to the ordinary knowledge found in average thinking**

- **A view that sees most people as conventional, average, and mundane**

- **A radically individualistic view of humanity**

Perhaps the clearest division between different conceptions of Satanism is the division between atheistic and theistic Satanism. An atheistic Satanist—like Anton LaVey and today's members of the Church of Satan—understands Satan merely as a symbol for the way man should conceive himself, not as an actual entity. Satanism is seen as a way to finally break with the repressing Christian tradition. The masses find comfort and safety in dogmas, but a Satanist values more the (often brutal) truth, and strives to realize the authentic self beyond conventional morality. Although there are many different variants of atheistic Satanism, atheistic Satanism generally endorses moral subjectivism—the view that there are no eternal, transcendent, or context-independent values, but that morality is in practice just your own choice, and metaphysically just a natural result of evolution.

A *theistic* Satanist, on the other hand, believes that Satan is an actual entity of some sort—interestingly enough, usually not the personified Devil of Christianity. If atheistic Satanism is morally subjectivistic, theistic Satanism is often nihilistic. For example, the Order of Nine Angles combines a radical interpretation of Friedrich Nietzsche's idea of the *Übermensch* (overhuman, superhuman, above-human) with certain neo-pagan metaphysical doctrines.

The *Übermensch* is someone who is enlightened, rises above other humans, and has to create a whole new set of values and worldview. The aim of the Order of Nine Angles—a loose umbrella organization consisting of several independent groups—is to create a new, "more sinister" (completely unethical) human being, as Nicholas Goodrick-Clarke notes in his book, *Black Sun: Aryan Cults, Esoteric Nazism, and the Politics of Identity*.

If the Church of Satan emphasizes moral subjectivism for purifying humanity from sick and life-denying values of Christianity, the Order of Nine Angles sees humanity in general as an obstacle for limitless self-overcoming. Initiations in this extreme form of Satanism are taken by forcing oneself and others beyond one's physical and mental limits. The use of violence is not only allowed, but also encouraged as it will weed out the weak and harden the competent.

The Black Light

Similar ideas are found in the doctrine of the Temple of the Black Light. Their anti-cosmic Satanism (also known as 'chaos-gnosticism') conceives the whole cosmic order ordained by God to be an illusion.

Behind the ordered cosmos there's actually a timeless and formless Chaos, which is the true essence of being. An ordinary human clings to the cosmic illusion, but a Satanist attempts to be consciously one with Chaos, which nevertheless reigns at the bottom of existence. While a human individual or even a Satanic organization as a whole is categorically unable to bring down the existing causal order directly, it's thought that by resigning from the moral order we can transcend the physical order and gradually leave the boundaries of humanity behind. As with the Order of Nine Angles, violence is encouraged for creating shocks that lead either to individual's destruction or evolution.

Theistic Satanism is generally marked by underlined scorn against everything "mundane," especially ordinary morality and conventional humanism. There are some similarities in this ethos to classical religious radicalism—the founder of the Order of Nine Angles, David Myatt, actually converted to Islam—but in theistic Satanism's case the illumination is sought from darkness and chaos instead of traditional religious values. The Joker in the Batman movie *The Dark Knight* and other Batman stories represents the ideal of a theistic Satanist, for he despises the "mundane" criminal motives such as money or power, and aims only at general chaos, not caring too much about his own earthly existence.

Theosophically Speaking

There is, however, at least one group of theistic Satanists who, instead of moral nihilism endorse *moral realism*, a view that there are objective, universal, and mind-independent truths about good and evil, and good is something everyone must pursue. Moreover, this group states that Satan doesn't ultimately represent evil, but good!

The Brotherhood of the Star of Azazel is an international society of theistic Satanism, founded in Finland in 2006. *Azazel* is a term that has Hebrew and Arabic roots, and it can mean either a scapegoat or the name of a fallen angel or demon. The teachings of this group consist mainly in the texts available on their website and published books written mainly by an author behind the pseudonym Johannes Nefastos. The basic philosophy behind the group's beliefs can be found in the theosophical movement of the nineteenth century, especially in the works of Helena Blavatsky (1831–1891).

With roots in medieval mysticism and later in sixteenth- and seventeenth-century thinkers such as Jakob Boehme (1575–1624), theosophy—literally, "god-like wisdom" (from the Greek *theos*, god, and *sophos*, wisdom)—is an esoteric philosophy that bases knowledge of the natural world on the knowledge of the divine. According to theosophical thought, there is some truth in all religions, but no particular religious doctrine alone is the only and final truth. Further, scientific thinking and even mainstream Western philosophy are seen as limited and limiting to knowledge; they rely too much on empirical and rational proofs, since there may be truths that can't be verified or even understood unambiguously.

Every member in the Star of Azazel is required to agree with the Three Theosophical Articles, which are:

> To form a nucleus of the universal brotherhood of humanity without distinction of race, creed, sex, caste, or color; To encourage the study of comparative religion, philosophy, and science; To investigate the unexplained laws of nature and the powers latent in man.

Reduced to a single idea, it's the "philosophy of oneness" in theosophical thought that is important for the Star of Azazel. According to this way of thought, everything is ultimately "one in the Absolute." All things seek unity with the Absolute, but this unity is never perfectly actual; there is always more or less latency in it. World history is seen as a process where everything evolves teleologically (in a goal-directed manner) towards the actual absolute unity. Human beings as the most brightly conscious beings have a special quest to take this process as their determined task, and by doing this to help the whole process. In practice, this striving for unity indicates first and foremost prohibition of any kind of unnecessary violence (for example self-defense may be allowed). On the philosophical level, it obligates to seek syntheses between conflicting ways of thinking.

The Satanic Connection

At this point you're probably saying, "Okay, this is interesting metaphysical stuff, but what on Earth has this to do with Satanism and the Star of Azazel?"

The answer can be found in the proto-Satanist elements of Blavatsky's writings. First, she notes that whenever there's a dogmatic religion, it certainly won't last forever. According to theosophical thought, the evolution of religions—atheism included—is teleological; religions will inevitably develop towards greater unity the more people give up their particular dogmatic belief systems. But this evolution can only happen through opposition to older dogmas that will then blend into newer less-separatist ones. The majority of people will always cling in the old dogmas, and therefore they find this process painful. Satan represents this painful but ultimately beneficent element in evolution. From this point of view, even Jesus can be seen as a *satanic* figure, for he aimed at a radical transformation of the Jewish doctrine dominant in his time. In our time, a Satanist will transform the doctrines dominating our time: scientism, atheism, superficial humanism, and (already diminishing) Christianity.

Another Satanic element in theosophical thought is derived from the following problem, which every religious thinker must face: if the world is teleological, why is there so much seemingly unnecessary evil in the world? Either the origin of evil is in Satan, in which case God is not omnipotent, for Satan works against his will, or Satan just fulfills the will of God, in which case God is the origin of evil. Neither option seems acceptable.

Theosophists have attempted to solve this problem by understanding God in two different senses. According to them, the traditional monotheistic conception of God, who is *both* infinite *and* morally good, contradicts itself. Moral goodness is an attribute of a finite being (however powerful), because only a finite being makes choices. Even if there's a God as described in the Judeo-Islam-Christian Bible, he isn't the Absolute God beyond all dualistic attributes (such as good and evil). A personal God may be the creator of the world and be infinitely powerful compared to humans, but there's still the possibility—and a duty, as we'll see!—for moral rebellion against God.

Satan Doesn't Will Evil

Although it's true that humans cause much of the pain, suffering, destruction, disorder, and other evils in the world, there's much cruelty and evil that the natural world is responsible for. Further, if humans freely choose evil, where does the preceding temptation to choose evil *originally* come from, if not from God? The final scapegoat must be either God or humanity itself.

According to the tenets of the Star of Azazel, Satan doesn't will evils to happen. He only presents all the difficult aspects in life to humans, most importantly the moral badness of God's universe. Satan's bright face, his true essence, can be properly seen only when humanity has evolved so high that all strains have been synthesized into unity. Until then, Satan appears with his dark mask, more or less terrifying depending on the level of inner strains of humanity.

According to the Star of Azazel there is a certain kind of unity in chaos, but the primal chaos is the starting point, not the end or *telos* of existence. If it's not assumed that the world once ascended from chaos by chance, it must be thought that there is still the Absolute behind the primal chaos. The primal chaos is then seen already as latent order. The emergence of the world order from chaos isn't a singular anomalous event in time but a continuous and teleological process where chaos remains at the ground of existence making possible the necessary element of randomness in life.

Therefore, a violent return to the primal chaos—as would be advocated by the Temple of the Black Light, for example—is considered by the Star of Azazel not progressive, but regressive. Without any ethical considerations, order would nevertheless rise again from the primal chaos even if all order could be entirely destroyed. One can of course still psychologically rebel against the Absolute itself, but the Absolute isn't a separate being who *decides* to create the world but simply the highest unity of being. Therefore the rebel's furious thoughts remain *within* the Absolute like everything else in general. Rebelling against some particular God, like the God of Christians, is a completely different matter, and that's what Satanism is about, according to the Star of Azazel.

We know that the Church of Satan is a form of atheistic Satanism with moral subjectivist and nihilist tendencies, while members of Star of Azazel are theistic Satanists who advocate moral realism and teleological purposiveness in the universe. But there are some common standpoints between the two. For example, both groups view the existing religious and ethical dogmas as something we must question in order to find our true self. The Star of Azazel would only add that, although no dogma must be taken as final, all dogmas reflect more or less the real ethical and religious truths, which in their entirety are

always partly beyond our current understanding and especially beyond verbal expression.

A Strange Satanism?

This kind of positive view of Satan may seem strange, but
traces of it are actually quite common in popular culture. This
indicates that there is something (often unconsciously) appealing in conceiving Satan in a positive way. The famous
Romantics William Blake (1757–1827) and Lord Byron
(1788–1824) appraised Lucifer as a symbol for illumination
and justified rebellion.

In Mikhail Bulgakov s *The Master and Margarita* (1967)
Satan arrives in Moscow causing mayhem all around. Except
that it only superficially appears so. Satan neither engages in
any destructive act, nor does he encourage anyone to do so. He
merely gives people what they want. And what they want leads
to public chaos, so Satan becomes the *azazel*, the scapegoat.

In the most popular fantasies of our time, *Star Wars* and
The Lord of the Rings, there is a clear devil figure, who represents absolute evil. However, the forces of evil in these fantasies immediately vanish as soon as the protagonist does the
best he is able. It's not a long way from this to an interpretation that the absolute evil of Sauron or Emperor Palpatine
represents a projection of humanity's own inner evil. When
Luke Skywalker refuses to kill the defeated Darth Vader
(although he still seems irrevocably evil), and is then tormented by the Emperor, Vader surprisingly rises and kills the
Emperor. The dark mask—an essential symbol for the Star of
Azazel—covering Vader's human face is removed, and evil has
vanished.

Similarly, in *The Lord of the Rings* Sauron perishes immediately when the One Ring is destroyed—a task which is
clearly within human resources, although very demanding. The
ring has a will of its own and longs to return to its master, but
the ring cannot *force* its bearer to evil; it only appeals to the
wearer's pre-existing desires. The interpretation by the Star of
Azazel is that there is no actual evil will beyond what humans
will and beget. Humans actually project their own evil on to
Satan, and Satan merely presents the inevitable choices
between good and evil to them.

Not Your Father's Satanism

All in all, the Star of Azazel represents, as far as I know, a unique conception of *morally realistic theistic Satanism*. This kind of worldview can be considered highly controversial. It will, of course, be objected to by Christians—but also by atheists, as well as moral subjectivists and nihilists. Even an observer with a completely neutral attitude may claim that the doctrine of the Star of Azazel is simply confused or eclectic to the point of incoherence.

However, if the philosophy of the Star of Azazel can be regarded as coherent, it offers a view that combines the Faustian ethos of Satanism with genuine moral realism. At least anyone seriously concerned with the problem of the nature and origins of evil shouldn't overlook the theosophical conception of God accompanied by a Satanic twist.

31
Hedonism and Unholy Writ

CLINT JONES

One of the hallmarks of Anton Szandor LaVey's *Satanic Bible*, which he describes as a diabolical book and the basis of Satanist philosophy, is its recurring references to hedonism grounded in Epicurus's understanding of the typical self-indulgent lifestyle.

The English word *hedonism* is derived from the Greek words ἡδονισμός (*hēdonismos*) meaning "delight" and ἡδονή (hēdonē) meaning "pleasure." For LaVey, hedonism is the surest way to achieve both bodily and spiritual happiness and fulfillment. By following the tenets of Satanism, LaVey and his followers develop not only a rejection of evangelical Christianity, but also a core ethos of self-restraint.

Yet LaVey's understanding of Epicurean thought is flawed. This isn't to say that the Satanic faith of LaVey and his followers fails to provide a moral framework, but rather that the context of that moral point of view is tainted by a misinterpretation of the hedonism developed by Epicurus and his followers. LaVey's brand of symbolic Satanism, if it is truly meant to be Epicurean, fails to achieve its goal of reclaiming the life God intended for us—the life that Satanism aspires to help us rediscover and achieve.

Virtues and Vices

Virtue, for Epicurus and his followers, is the only thing that is inseparable from pleasure. The real cultural purchase of pleasure as virtue has never really faded, and it has had its share of champions throughout the ages. Perhaps the oldest associated notion of this resides in popular culture as a serpent delicately coaxing an unwitting Eve into consuming forbidden fruit—especially if Milton has his way.

And, while we might haggle over the accuracy or the interpretation of such motifs, the important thing to pluck from the tangled mess of socio-religious history is that pleasure is usually cast as transgression and, thus, must be a vice. Most religions, and more than a few philosophies, have built their foundations around such a notion with few notable exceptions.

Symbolic (LaVeyan) Satanism versus Theistic Satanism

LaVey's *Satanic Bible* is widely considered the foundational text of organized, public, Satanic worship; it has never gone out of print since its first edition in 1969 and continues to function as one of the main, if not primary, sources for the contemporary Satanic movement. However, while *The Satanic Bible* is recognized by most followers of Satanism, it isn't taken as central to the beliefs of all sects of Satanism. LaVey's followers comprise The Church of Satan and claim to be the first and oldest church dedicated to the worship of Satan.

LaVey's brand of Satanism is *symbolic* which results in it being categorized as an atheistic approach to Satanism. It's more of a philosophical approach to living a life devoted to the ideals attributed to Satan. *Theistic* Satanism, on the other hand, takes Satan to be a real being, the Devil, capable of governing the lives of his followers in much the same way that God, as a deity, is believed to be a real being capable of causal influence in both the world and the lives of His followers. Satanic theists have similar beliefs about the worship of Satan and the lifestyle that accompanies such commitments, but the distinction is important for this investigation because in a theistic interpretation of Satanism it's common to believe that Satan is responsible for laying down the ground rules for proper worship—in much the same manner as God does in the early books of the Old Testament. Satanic theists don't promote violence, hate, evil, or anything of the sort; rather, they uphold the values that Satan embodies: freedom, sexuality, creativity, hedonism, strength, and success.

Satan isn't an actual being for LaVey, but rather exists as a "powerful force which permeates and balances the universe" and "is far too impersonal to care about the happiness or misery of flesh-and-blood creatures on this ball of dirt." Given this interpretation of Satan, many of LaVey's philosophical influences are anti-theistic, allowing him greater flexibility of interpretation, but also requiring that his systematic approach to incorporating Satanistic beliefs into our life is grounded in arguments rather than faith. Still, LaVey does hold that Satanism "represents all of the so-called sins, as they all lead to physical, mental, or emotional gratification!" This is especially important for LaVeyians because *The Satanic Bible* is an attempt to promote the same core values as his theistic counterparts, but *without* the impetus of faith-based motivations. As LaVey argues, "there is nothing inherently sacred about moral codes . . . they are the work of human hands."

LaVey utilizes historical, cultural, and philosophical evidence to lay the foundation for the system of beliefs his Satanism promotes as well as to provide the protocols necessary to prevent the whole system from devolving into chaos as each person is encouraged to explore the permissive nature of Satanism. The problem with LaVey's permissiveness is that he relies on a misunderstanding of hedonism in the classical, Epicurean, philosophical sense—which isn't to cast aspersions at LaVey. His misinterpretation is the misconception most common in the status quo, the real failing is in his endorsement of the common misinterpretation as though it were the truth.

LaVey's Synthesis of Satanism

LaVey's struggle to create an identity that was uniquely Satanic—as opposed to merely atheistic—stemmed directly from his perception that the dominant spiritual belief systems, and Christianity in particular, were largely hypocritical. However, his synthesis of the cultural components upon which he relied is not meant to be taken piecemeal—as he says, "it is an integrated whole, not a smorgasbord from which one can pick and choose." And the philosophical approach he advocates "is meant only for a select few who are epicurean, pragmatic, worldly, atheistic, fiercely individualistic, materialistic, rational, and darkly poetic."

As LaVey understood his project, the integrated whole of his philosophical system would provide followers with all the components necessary for a fulfilled life while simultaneously avoiding the pitfalls of hypocrisy central to Christianity and similar faith-based systems. "Satanism moves into the realm of religion," LaVey notes, "by having an aesthetic component, a system of symbolism, metaphor, and ritual in which Satan is embraced not as some Devil to be worshipped, but as a symbolic external projection of the highest potential of each individual Satanist."

LaVey's Brand of Hedonism

For LaVey hedonism is a means not only for rejecting the dominant cultural values embodied by spiritual belief systems, but it is also a means for establishing the grounds for a truly virtuous life in contradistinction to those systems. What LaVey means by the *virtuous life* is hyper-individualistic in its orientation and is an attempt to produce the framework for a set of values that doesn't merely invert the dominant views, but actually replaces them with the permissive ideology of hedonism.

Hedonism is generally thought of as being indulgence without limit, a lifestyle that allows for the fullest and most complete satisfaction of desires. In its popular interpretation this usually means that you don't need to order your desires or show concern for how those desires are fulfilled with the exception of a few, a very few, principles that set boundaries for harm toward others. LaVey, for instance, allows for sexual gratification without concern for taboos or social conventions generally, but his Satanism still finds rape to be an illegitimate means for doing so: "Satanism encourages any form of sexual expression you may desire, *so long as it hurts no one else*." However, this type of hedonism finds few philosophical underpinnings since pleasure as a virtue requires, in most philosophical systems, a considered and measured approach to pleasure as virtue—that is, pleasure as a Good.

In his synthesis of Satanism into a symbolic belief system, LaVey cobbled together the thoughts of a wide range of thinkers from largely divergent cultural fields—philosophy, literature, music, and art to name only a few—in his consideration of hedonism. The hedonism of Epicurus specifically figures prominently in *The Satanic Bible*. LaVey's use of Epicurean thought is flawed, however, not because Epicurus doesn't consider pleasure a virtue, but because LaVey's considerations are supported by a misinterpretation of the larger project of Epicurus.

Tetra-Whatchamacallit

So, what does Epicurus mean by *hedonism*? Epicurean hedonism is best approached through two focal points in his philosophy—the *Tetrapharmakon* and his partitioning of desire for things into three types. The *Tetrapharmakon* is Epicurus's 'four medicines' for a good life, that is, a life of virtue.

- First, Epicurus admonishes us not to fear god or the gods because gods don't have time for us in their own existences. The gods are too busy maintaining order and doing what gods do to worry about our petitionary prayers, trials, travails, needs, or wants. So, if we accept the fact that the gods aren't concerned with us, then we need not concern ourselves with the gods. This should free us of the guilt we feel in relation to the demands we've been led to believe the gods have of us. This is quite similar to LaVey's position that Satan is a balancing force too impersonal to care about us.

- Second, we shouldn't fear death. Death is an absence of feeling and since we can't suffer once we're dead, we shouldn't worry about when or how we're going to die. Again, accepting this fact should free us from the fear which plagues our minds and makes us too cautious to enjoy all that life has to offer. LaVey describes death as the "great abstinence" in direct opposition to life "the great indulgence" and Satanism encourages us, based on this principle, to "make the most out of life—here and now" which is, again, quite similar to the Epicurean position.

- The third facet of the *Tetrapharmakon* is that what is good is easy to obtain. This means that living simply is easy and best, but this isn't asceticism. Rather, for Epicurus, indulgence begins in learning to desire simple things in abundance so that we can truly indulge in other things and appreciate them more without having to have them in our lives all the time.

- Finally, what's painful is easy to endure. Pain is short lived—it's temporary and fleeting, which means that no matter how bad something is, we'll generally be able to suffer it without too much to complain about.

These four concepts are necessary to understanding Epicurean hedonism because they help direct our understanding of the order of desires necessary to a properly philosophical hedonistic life.

Three Types of Desire

All desires are, for Epicurus, one of three types: natural and necessary, natural and unnecessary, and unnatural and unnecessary. Those things that fall into the category of natural and necessary are things like water, food, shelter, friendship, and clothing. Things that you need to survive and live a comfortable, happy, and pleasurable life.

Natural and unnecessary things are those things that we naturally desire, but could, if necessary, go without, like sex.

The last category is for everything else. So, while food is necessary chocolate cake isn't, though that doesn't mean that you shouldn't have chocolate cake, it merely means that you shouldn't have it with every meal every day. This is contrary to the hedonism LaVey emphasizes because a Satanist ought not to care if someone's a glutton, especially since behaving that way harms no one else. Yet, if we focus on increasing our access to the natural and necessary things, then we can achieve a fulfilled and happy life supplemented and punctuated by the truly indulgent things. The caveat here comes from the third rung of the *Tetrapharmakon*—what's good is easy to get. Plucking an apple from a tree or a carrot from the ground in the garden is easy, making apple pie, while delicious, requires a bit more effort and not just in the baking but in the ingredients necessary to make the pie. So, every once in a while, we should have pie, but for the most part we should just be happy with the apple.

Why LaVey Gets It LaWrong

This is the key to understanding Epicurus and it's also the key to understanding why LaVey gets hedonism wrong in his Satanic synthesis. Epicurus does allow for the sating of all of our desires, but he *doesn't* allow for us to satisfy every whim all the time with reckless abandon. Epicurus doesn't encourage gluttony or having sex all the time precisely because these activities done in excess are *contrary* to the good life—the person being hurt is *yourself.*

Epicurus divides desire into the three categories, and he does so precisely because indulgence as *moderation* is what allows for the fullest gratification of our desires, while promoting the good life based on pleasure as the highest virtue. Satanism, as LaVey presents it, is unhindered by such concerns of the good life and his Satanism fails to be hedonistic in a sense that would lead one to a good life. LaVeyan Satanism is certainly a hedonistic rejection of values and—ironically enough—it ultimately fails to provide a virtuous framework with which to regain the virtues LaVey believes were lost to us long ago when spiritual belief systems began to dominate our worldviews.

A Satanism Devoid of Virtue

The Epicurean philosophy LaVey relies upon is a distortion built upon a deep and grave misunderstanding of Epicurus's teachings and the hedonistic tradition that developed as a result of those teachings. No doubt LaVey is equally guilty with regard to other philosophical influences, but when popular philosophers get caught up in popular culture sometimes they often produce sound bites and not sound philosophical understanding. As such, but especially where Epicurus is concerned, LaVey's brand of Satanism has no philosophical anchor points to support his core Satanic theology. The result is a Satanism devoid of genuine virtues grounded in pleasure and a value system that doesn't adequately promote the values embedded in the core hedonistic tenets espoused by LaVey as central to the successful practice of Satanism.

When all's said and done, Satanism's claims to spiritual superiority fail because adhering to the hedonism of LaVey's Satanism won't allow us to reclaim a lost utopian paradise embodied, say, in the narrative of Eden prior to the expulsion of Adam and Eve. Rather LaVey's Satanism will likely result in a deep sense of dissatisfaction, or worse, leave us living a life that is merely base and vulgar, relying on seeking out pleasures of the most immediate and, therefore, unfulfilling types.

You might say that such an existence is, well, Hellish.

32

Our Satan: Or, Are You Loco for Loki?

MAGUS PETER H. GILMORE

Now is the age of the anti-hero, as the admiration of arch-villains has spread from being the purview of an intellectual minority of iconoclasts to having been embraced whole-heartedly by pop culture.

The cinema, where myths become tangible for us, celebrates the "bad guys," which is why Loki gets far more attention than Thor or any of the other Avengers—save perhaps the self-indulgent carnal genius, Tony Stark. Superman in his most recent incarnation has moved away from the polite Boy Scout so ably embodied by Christopher Reeve to Cavill's troubled alien who allows mass slaughter of urban dwellers during his fisticuffs with fellow Kryptonians and resorts to murder to resolve their conflict. Heath Ledger's psychotically demonic Joker usurped the attention usually due Batman in Nolan's movie, being even more disturbed than the Dark Knight. But Burton also got the tango of duo-lunatics right with Keaton and Nicholson atop that gothic cathedral, since both are equivocal characters when one considers their psychological underpinnings. We've seen Del Toro's take on Hellboy twice in the cinema, a conflicted hero who strives to follow one fork in the road of his destiny while his infernal nature calls out for him to follow instead the Left-Hand Path. The heroes are now "dark" and their enemies darker still. The tradition of "the opposition" usually being far more fascinating than the "do-gooders" who counter them has been part of human mythology since the dawn of our species' creation of mythic fiction, yet our current dominant art form is blurring those lines and the masses are embracing this "evilution." There is a rising sympathy for the Devil.

Satan is the primordial supervillain, a compelling subject for exploration in fiction. Portrayals range from an easily vanquished comedic foe to the deadly serious collector of damned souls. Yet certain creators not comfortable with the supremacy of the dictatorial Jehovah approached the Prince of Darkness as an inspirational figure. He has been cast as a rebellious hero, a skeptical interrogator revealing truths, and the champion of carnality.

As the High Priest of the Church of Satan, successor to Anton Szandor LaVey, who founded the organization in 1966, my interest in this mythological character is self-evident. My biases should be obvious to anyone conversant with the atheist philosophy of Satanism, which offers a pragmatic perspective espousing skepticism, materialism, personal liberty, and responsibility. We Satanists are thus ahead of this curve, for we have been extolling Satan, which means "adversary" or "accuser" in Hebrew, as a stimulating symbol of our potential for self-direction, creative achievement and the celebration of joy in living. For us, he's been how we externalize the best within us. Now that you regular folks are hankering after our kind of hero, we have to wonder, "What took you so long?"

Invocation to Satan

Satan is often depicted in literature and mythology as interacting with mankind, offering satisfaction for unfulfilled desires— but at a price. When Anton LaVey founded the Church of Satan in 1966, he offered Satan as an empathetic and inspirational symbol for carnally oriented humans, far more emotionally resonant for us than some celestial deity. Unlike that distant, patriarchal "sky daddy," LaVey embraced that earthy characterization and so refers to him as "brother and friend" in his "Invocation to Satan." He then presented ritual as a means for emotional catharsis rather than worship. In essence, Satanists externalize their own highest potential and commune with that image as part of ritual. But such fantasy is meant only for the theatrics of the ritual chamber. Outside of that, Satanists are expected to work towards their goals using conventional means, now freed of hindering emotional baggage.

Thus, the Devil's "price" for the Satanist is loss of both faith and naiveté, but the reward is an accurate grasp of reality *and* oneself, enabling one to more effectively move the world according to one's will. In LaVey's thinking, Satan is an icon for satisfaction in the here and now, rejecting spiritual moralists' claim that the cost for happiness and material success in the tangible world will be torture in the speculative "afterlife." Secular thinkers, including LaVey, understand that those holy hucksters have never had any proof of such *post mortem* existence, but our species has not lacked gullibility so con games both spiritual and material have always played major roles in human culture. Comprehension of human beings and their society allows the Satanist to achieve vital existence in a world where most seek spiritual pipe dreams. To LaVey and his adherents, the world is a carnival and the Satanist is the carny, not the flash-dazzled mark.

Olli Pitkänen and Clint Jones in their observations about Satanism address the thinking of Anton LaVey. Pitkänen works towards a scholar's definition of Satanism designed to reconcile varied philosophies that, while they hold some similarities, seem to me to be separated by gulfs that should require separate classifications. Jones misrepresents LaVey as his goal is to dismiss Satanism as having any value.

Theosophist Ramblings

Olli Pitkänen generally grasps and accurately presents LaVey's thinking, though I've not seen the "many different variants of atheistic Satanism" he claims exist. He is enamored of an obscure sect calling itself "The Star of Azazel" which sees itself as descended from Blavatsky's Theosophist ramblings. Pitkänen proposes his own broad definition of Satanism, currently an evolving topic in academia, so that mysticism might be lumped-in with LaVey's skeptical, pragmatic, materialist views.

Amongst the four characteristics he sets out as essential for any form of Satanism, the first works when considering the Church of Satan since it is part of our literature that Satan symbolizes "a rebellion against the existing moral order," though LaVey had no qualms about either societal or cosmic order which Pitkänen includes.

His second calls for claims to a "higher kind of knowledge compared to the ordinary knowledge found in average thinking." For LaVey, spiritual doctrines denied the animal nature of mankind, marking his normal behavior to be sinful thus binding people to those religions in search of forgiveness for their inborn impulses. An impossible ideal of being sinless is offered and you must punish yourself for failing to reach it. This is found in Eastern doctrines as well as Christianity. To eliminate a guilt-ridden existence, LaVey advocated embracing man as he is, warts and all, rejecting religion-imposed guilt. But he did not consider that this required any sort of "higher knowledge." It is a state that, in theory, any self-aware individual who is not compelled towards spiritual beliefs could achieve. "Undefiled wisdom" is meant as awareness unclouded by spiritual values. It is not meant to be seen as either higher or lower, but as simply an acknowledgment of the undistorted facts of existence. While this is not common, LaVey felt that it could become so once doctrines like Christianity had less influence on societal values. So I suggest to Pitkänen that he might alter this to "deeper knowledge," meaning more perceptive rather than "higher" which has spiritual implications of accessing higher planes of existence or information.

His third characteristic, with Satanists seeing most people as "conventional, average, and mundane," seems pointless. Conventions are by definition what most people have embraced. An average is by definition the middle point of the extremes and in bell curve graphs it is always the most populated center. Thus these two are not particularly Satanic in perspective. "Mundane" can mean dull, and certainly I think few would argue that most people are scintillating. However, mundane also means earthly, rather than heavenly or spiritual, and that is a positive to LaVey, something to be embraced after realizing the spiritual is simply a fiction. Thus I think this third characteristic needs retooling.

Finally, the fourth is "a radically individualistic view of humanity." This seems rather nebulous. I suspect that Pitkänen might mean that Satanism radically champions the individual, as I've often stated, as opposed to the more collectivist approach usually taken by spiritual paths.

There Are Satanists and There Are Nuts

We Satanists who embrace LaVey find the combining of theist and atheist elements under the umbrella of Satanism untenable. Sure, it makes it easy for scholars, but how often is such absolute opposition reconciled in one term? Are there enough shared elements to make that work? LaVey initially allowed people who believed in Satan to join his organization to help it grow, but the gulf separating their behavior and psychology from the associates he wished to attract moved him to decide that they were no longer acceptable. When Michael Aquino (a theist believing he speaks for the existing deity Set) formed a schism in 1975, LaVey in response affirmed:

> The Church of Satan is an organization dedicated to rational self-interest, indulgence, and a glorification of material and carnal elements. I held these beliefs in the beginning as I do now. If others re-interpret my organization and philosophy into a fundamental kind of supernaturalism, it stems from their needs to do so.

LaVey referred to the Setians as devil worshippers. Later, during the Satanic Panic of the 1980s–1990s when journalists and evangelical Christians claimed "satanic cults" were sacrificing animals and children as well as promoting pedophilia and drug use, LaVey would say that "there are Satanists and there are nuts."

Sacrifices of humans and animals only fit a framework when there is belief that such killing satisfies some sort of supernatural entity as a means of gaining some favor. Such slaughter has no place in an atheist philosophy that enjoins its members that success comes from self-discipline and hard work. Law enforcement investigating murders with occult symbols or ritualistically mutilated animals used to define these as "Satanic crimes." More recently, because of the growing understanding of LaVey's doctrines, informed law enforcement officials are not applying the word "Satanism" or "Satanic" automatically. If scholars promote the idea that theists who at times advocate sacrifice, violence and murder as being Satanists, they do a disservice to what we've worked for as well as again muddying the waters when it comes to practical perceptions. Not all scholars wish to make this conflation, and I support efforts towards establishing a more drastic separation in terminology. Perhaps "devil worship" seems too unwieldy— perhaps "demonolatry" might be more suitable, since Satan is not universally revered amongst these believers.

Hymns to Satan

The representatives of the Church of Satan are well aware that "satanism" has long been employed as an insulting condemnation of what was judged to be heretical thinking and behavior by dominant Christian sects. LaVey himself sought out writings sympathetic to Satan as a positive figure, and he was pleased to point to Milton, Shelley, Byron, and Twain as predecessors. If he'd known of Carducci's "Hymn to Satan" he would have likely included him on the dedication page. Przybyszewski is a fascinating individual, but his works are only now coming to light in English translations. He saw himself as a Satanist, but LaVey would not have embraced his idea of life as suffering.

No predecessor of LaVey created a coherent philosophy that resulted in a worldwide movement that had staying power. Indeed, these rare past writers are currently being uncovered by researchers primarily because of their efforts to combat LaVey's practical hegemony of Satanism. LaVey's popularization of this term has led to a growing number of people applying it to themselves, often with little understanding of LaVey's principles. This may be a new phenomenon in religious growth. Have those who've studied early Christian sects seen something similar?

Some scholars comb the Internet for recent instances where "Satanism" has been appropriated, frequently by those seeking attention though association with LaVey's nearly half-century-long position in the center ring. Yet if it were not for the ease of access allowed by the World Wide Web, such examples would likely remain as obscure and ephemeral as have LaVey's few precursors. For those who study Satanism in the future, it will be interesting to note if any of these imitators have spawned perspectives that are actively embraced by individuals to serve as their means for engaging the world, or if they are merely fossils preserved in the amber of academic papers.

Reckless Abandon?

Clint Jones attempts to pull the Epicurean rug out from under LaVey, but this fails as he has misinterpreted LaVey's texts. Jones explains that the Epicurean form of hedonism is one which requires moderation and encourages all forms of pleasure, not solely those that might be deemed "base and vulgar"— a valuation of certain indulgences I've usually encountered from those with repressed libidos. Jones seems to think that LaVey promoted unbridled hedonism, trying to "satisfy every whim all the time with reckless abandon." An unbiased reading of LaVey's texts shows quite the contrary.

As a realist who endorsed the idea of a social contract for structuring civilization, LaVey would hardly have supported such a point of view that would promote chaos and criminality. Utilizing self-controlled indulgence towards a wide range of pleasurable activity is precisely what LaVey promotes throughout his entire body of work. In the chapter of his first book, *The Satanic Bible*, titled "INDULGENCE . . . *NOT* COMPULSION" LaVey frames his model for the pursuit of satisfaction stating:

> The true Satanist is not mastered by sex any more than he is mastered by any of his other desires. As with all other pleasurable things, the Satanist is master of, rather than mastered by sex.

For the Satanist, all forms of sexuality are acceptable so long as they are experienced by consenting adults in a safe and responsible fashion. LaVey has some fun playing with the idea of moderation of pleasures when dealing with the so-called Christian "seven deadly sins." He posits that gluttony would be reigned in by vanity-fueled pride so that efforts at weight loss and muscle toning would ameliorate possible gustatory over-indulgence. Envy and greed are possible motivators, but sloth can temper overly driven "Type-A" personalities. Anger can serve as a cure for passivity, especially when confronted with injustice.

LaVey Was an Atheist

Jones also seems to neglect the fact that LaVey was an atheist who considered spirituality to be a religion-fostered illusion. Or perhaps Jones is mired in terms that presuppose spiritual values, even when referencing an anti-faith that rejects the spiritual as non-existent. LaVey has no claims to "spiritual superiority," instead he offers a perspective meant for those who by nature are carnally inclined. The superiority of Satanism, for those it suits, is in valuing being realistic about the human animal, rather than idealistic and delusional—our view of most spiritually oriented folk.

Another Jones misprision is of LaVey's characterization of Satan as well as his thoughts about God. LaVey explains that a Satanist might view God as an impersonal balancing factor in nature, far too removed and utterly indifferent to "the happiness or misery of flesh-and-blood creatures on this ball of dirt upon which we live." LaVey asks:

> Is it not more sensible to worship a god that he, himself, has created, in accordance with his own emotional needs—one that best represents the very carnal and physical being that has the idea-power to invent a god *in the first place*?

LaVey states that all Gods are fiction and worshipping them is worship by proxy of the God's creator. So in embracing Satan, whom you create in your own image, you then cut out the "middle man." Self-deification, not devil worship, is thus achieved. In my works I have termed this position—a subset of atheism—as being "I-theist."

In his paragraph dealing with "LaVey's Synthesis of Satanism," Jones quotes my words from the introduction to *The Satanic Bible*, yet attributes them to LaVey. However, he at least has presented our point of view in that passage. While *The Satanic Bible* was his first work presenting Satanism to the world at large, LaVey later expanded on his concepts in subsequent books and interviews. He clarified some aspects as his own thinking broadened.

If Jones had perused those later works, or even my writings, he might have achieved a better grasp of the subject. Or not, as certain paradigms can be prisons which prevent the clear viewing of alien perspectives. Ultimately, LaVey plundered earlier philosophies as building blocks for Satanism, but he did not try to legitimize his efforts by claiming that he was a successor to or disciple of earlier free-thought advocates such as Nietzsche, Stirner, Epicurus, and Rand, among others. He did not court the approval of academics or philosophers, rather he felt that he was offering his own synthesis to stand on its own. Measuring his congruence with earlier thinkers erroneously assumes that LaVey felt he was attempting to gain credibility via association with them.

Living a Fulfilling Life

The Satanism of Anton LaVey is intended for carnal individuals who find that Satan well serves as a resonant symbol for living a fulfilling life. It's a life that embraces the reality of an indifferent universe wherein we inhabit a small planet that seems governed by Darwinian struggles for survival. We Satanists find that to be bracing, challenging, and exciting. We're not trying to "reclaim a lost utopian paradise embodied ... in the narrative of Eden prior to the expulsion of Adam and Eve," as Clint Jones supposes. Hell, no! We Satanists find that fairy tale to be ludicrous, and the idea of being ignorant pets caged by Yaweh-daddy is truly revolting to us.

We seek freedom and knowledge, accepting the task of being self-supporting as pampered thralldom is not for us. Since Satanism is not for everyone, those who are born with a spiritual orientation might find, if forced to employ Jones's misapprehension of our philosophy, that it might produce in them "a deep sense of dissatisfaction" leaving them "living a life that is merely base and vulgar, relying on seeking out pleasures of the most immediate and, therefore, unfulfilling types." Likely Jones never met any Satanists, for we partake of all forms of pleasure from the delightfully primal joys of sex, fine food, and beverages, to the more advanced achievements of our species in literature, music, art, cinema, architecture, as well as all the other extraordinary creations of fine minds that we can access, encounter, embrace, and deeply enjoy. To the Satanist, the sole life we have is enjoyed to the fullest—on all possible levels—in a balanced and controlled manner, and that is the very definition of satisfaction.

Welcome to Our Party

It's clear from popular culture that we Satanists are not the only ones pondering the panoply of depictions of the Great Adversary. Many of you now finding admirable traits in diabolical characters could see the Prince of Darkness in a new light. If so, then welcome to our party! Since our Satan is an externalized projection of ourselves, and we are our own highest value, Satan has thus always been a positive for us in the Church of Satan. No theological conundrums are required—for Satan *is* us.

Your personal definition of Satan, and other equivalent attractive villains, will determine whether you are in vogue as one of the Devil's own, or find yourself on the side of the angels, however besmirched they have become of late. You might be surprised to find aspects of our perspective to suit you, fellow Loki aficionados. Then you might also come to realize that Satanists are not so outré as you may have previously assumed.

33

A Response to Magus Gilmore

OLLI PITKÄNEN

Magus Gilmore offers a twofold critique of my chapter. First, he thinks my definition of Satanism doesn't apply properly to the Church of Satan. Second, he denies that it's meaningful to attribute the label "Satanism" to any religious thinking.

I'll start with the second critique. Definitions are never entirely stable. If we talk, for example, about materialism, is it the materialism of Democritus, materialism in Newtonian terms, materialism based on modern quantum physics, or perhaps materialism in the Marxist sense? Some common denominator no doubt exists, but I doubt that any final definition can be given.

There are various self-proclaimed Satanist groups besides the Church of Satan, each including dozens to hundreds of members. Why should the Church of Satan alone be justified in using the term 'Satanism'? Gilmore's argument is that "No predecessor of LaVey created a coherent philosophy which resulted in a worldwide movement that had staying power." With some reservations I might agree with this. The Church of Satan made the term 'Satanism' popular and no doubt contributed a lot to the rise of later Satanist movements. However, Gilmore also seems to claim that these later movements assert themselves only in relation to the Church of Satan. This claim seems arrogant to me.

As Anton LaVey isn't considered a prophet from Heaven outside our culturally formed human world, I think the following must be admitted. Had not the Church of Satan come to the frame in 1960s, very probably some other Satanist movement, quite possibly more religious in tone, would have been born. This movement would then have defined 'Satanism' according to its preferences. Moreover, as Gilmore is probably aware, many of the newer Satanist groups find "Satanism without the belief in Satan" absurd. Although this argument against naming LaVey's philosophy Satanism is clearly invalid (because it already assumes that there must be some entity which humans try to reach by their conceptualizations), I think it demonstrates well the difficulty in Gilmore's argument. The sympathy for adversary figures, which I acknowledge with Gilmore as a typical characteristic of our present culture, can be emphasized both in secular and in religious framework. Therefore, later religious forms of Satanism could quite well have been born without the impact of the Church of Satan.

Definition, Definitions, Definitions

This takes us to the first critique, the definition of Satanism. I readily admit that my definition is imperfect as I'm skeptical of any conclusive definition in general. Still, I think my definition somewhat captures the essential elements in any form of Satanism I m familiar with.

Gilmore accepts my first criterion that Satanism includes "a rebellion against the existing moral order" (while he stresses that "LaVey had no qualms with either societal or cosmic order"). However, he is not fond of my expression that a Satanist aims at "higher kind of knowledge compared to the ordinary knowledge of average people." Gilmore suggests the word "deeper" instead of "higher," because the word "higher" has a religious undertone. This seems to be a correct elaboration; the word "deeper" is perhaps more neutral than "higher" regarding a/theism.

Gilmore finds somewhat dubious my second criterion that Satanism includes "a radically individualistic view of humanity; a rebellion or higher [= deeper] knowledge makes sense only if most of the people are seen as conventional, average and mundane." Gilmore is right that "mundane" can also mean "earthly," which has a positive echo for the Church of Satan. Perhaps I should use the word "dull," which is also Gilmore s own choice of words for the less lofty sense of "mundane." The precise terms "average" and "conventional" can be debated but my point is the following. Something like eighty-five percent of all people are traditionally religious. A similar percent of the remaining secular people take without questioning the current norms of their culture. Isn't a Satanist a person who questions (if not necessarily abandons) these conventions, and consequently considers himself being in this sense "above the average"?

Concerning Gilmore's suggestion that Satanism more likely "champions the individual" than is "radically individualistic" (as I put it), I stand pat because theistic forms of Satanism don't that much "champion the individual" as he currently is, but focus on evolution which according to them has an objective end that can yet be realized only *through* individualism.

A Vision of Superhumanity

Lastly I'll criticize Gilmore's view of spirituality that supposedly represents the official stance of the Church of Satan. Gilmore writes:

> For LaVey, spiritual doctrines denied the animal nature of mankind, marking his normal behavior to be sinful thus binding people to those religions in search for forgiveness for their in-born impulses. An impossible ideal of being sinless is offered and one must punish oneself for failing to reach it. This is found in Eastern doctrines as well as in Christianity.

Gilmore's formulation applies without qualification only to Semitic religions. Certain mainstream Hindu doctrines for example emphasize the full acceptance of human life with its carnality, not even to mention marginal groups such as Aghoris who deliberately break all possible taboos. When it comes to Satanism, abandoning moralistic dogmas and accepting the "darker" sides of humanity is in my view the common starting point in all forms of Satanism. Even moral realists of the Star of Azazel consider the Christian idea of sin a repressive obstacle for the realization of self. As a denominational atheistic Satanist, Gilmore can argue for the *truth* of LaVey's atheistic philosophy, but he should provide some further argument, why spiritual doctrines must always indicate the repression of humanity, and consequently be never *defined* as Satanism. A vision of superhumanity does not in my view entail the denial of the current state of humanity.

34
Another Response to Magus Gilmore

CLINT JONES

Let's grant that it's true that we're in the midst of an "evilution" and we see immediately the need to clarify the ideology of LaVey's Satanism—I have not rendered judgment against the Church of Satan on holistic grounds regarding this point, but to the extent that this "rising sympathy for the Devil" is emboldened by the hedonism permeating the ideology of the Church of Satan it's a fair criticism to say that LaVey's interpretation of Epicurus is flawed.

While I suspect that other ideas have been maladapted to the systematic thought of LaVey, I do not attribute this necessarily to his deliberate intention. Epicurus and his adherents have suffered centuries of misunderstanding which is why a place like Las Vegas can describe itself as an Epicurean paradise even though Vegas is the farthest thing from it—and this is why, I suspect, Epicurean descriptors wind up in *The Satanic Bible* even though they are used to describe anything but an Epicurean understanding of hedonism.

However, Magus Gilmore alleges that my goal is to pull the metaphorical Epicurean rug out from under Satanism in order to "dismiss Satanism as having any value," and I categorically deny such a challenge is derivable from my criticisms of LaVey. I have put forward in my criticism of LaVey that his use of Epicurean thought fails to support his programmatic proposals for achieving a particular kind of life—presumably a life of some value—and that if LaVey's account of indulgence is to support that life it ought not to be described as Epicurean. To the extent that Satanists want to describe their lives/lifestyles as Epicurean, then they need to adjust their understanding of that particular philosophical position—an undertaking that will, to be sure, undermine the satanic understanding of hedonism as it is endorsed by LaVey.

This, however, raises an important question regarding LaVey's use of Epicurean thought to construct his system of belief. Magus Gilmore accuses me of failing to grasp LaVey's most robust understanding of the positions he advances in *The Satanic Bible* because I have failed to peruse additional texts and writings. This is true, I have avoided engaging those texts because my project was to demonstrate the need for a clarified and better understood notion of Epicurus at the root level in LaVey's Satanism. If *The Satanic Bible* is the most widely referenced resource on Satanism for the non-Satanist or budding Satanist then it seems like the logical place to start a critique of the hedonism embedded in the satanic belief system. If, as Magus Gilmore alleges, LaVey's understanding broadened and developed over time we are immediately, I think, justified in questioning the validity of such developments if 1. they are grounded in a misunderstanding of the source material they are based upon and 2. LaVey never retracts his understanding of Epicurean hedonism as he has included it in his *Bible*.

More to the point, rather than me being locked into some sort of paradigmatic prison, the problem seems to be more easily traced to what Magus Gilmore describes as LaVey's plundering of earlier philosophies—I think this is certainly apt and we might term LaVey's mining as "cherry-picking." Working with the choicest morsels, and especially those that jived with his desire to express a particular kind of life, LaVey was able to cobble together a quite impressive symbolic approach to life actively countering the various hypocritical theisms he lambasts in his biblical writings. Nevertheless, Magus Gilmore contends that LaVey "did not try to legitimize his efforts by claiming that he was a successor to or disciple of" his many influences and further that LaVey "did not court the approval of academics or philosophers." This seems true enough, but I make no such charge against LaVey. Rather, and given the defensiveness of this claim, my criticism would be better characterized as claiming that LaVey—through his plundering—actually laid a shaky foundation at best, especially where his use of Epicurus is concerned, because he pulled out pretty gemstones rather than the weightier keystones of understanding necessary to build a system of belief upon.

Further defending LaVey's amalgamation of previous thinkers Magus Gilmore claims LaVey "was offering his own synthesis to stand on its own. Measuring his congruence with earlier thinkers erroneously assumes that LaVey felt he was attempting to gain credibility via association with them." While it's tempting to allow such a conclusion, the glaring problem here is that any time we utilize the thoughts of others we are—directly or indirectly—seeking to associate with or distance our beliefs from those individuals depending on how we use their ideas. Since LaVey goes out of his way to name his system Epicurean, at least in certain aspects, it is a safe assumption he was *in fact* trying to gain some credibility through the alignment of his thoughts with those of Epicurus as an intellectual forebear. So, while LaVey may have been attempting to offer "his own synthesis to stand on its own" the very act of synthesis suggests, in part, recognizing an intellectual inheritance. For better or worse, LaVey's use and synthesis of ideas from his intellectual forebears entails—whether his adherents like it or not—that his ideas can be judged and measured by his demonstrable understanding of those ideas via how he has employed them. Toward that end LaVey does not understand Epicurean philosophy; hence, the foundation of Satanism, as it is expressed in *The Satanic Bible*, is shaky at best.

Briefly I'll address two additional minor criticisms offered by Magus Gilmore. First, as LaVey presents the indulgent lifestyle there is no reason to assume that a follower of his teachings couldn't interpret them as encouragement to "satisfy every whim all the time with reckless abandon." Magus Gilmore insists that an unbiased reading of LaVey's work reveals a man committed to social contractarianism and who promotes self-controlled indulgence not a hedonism that would lend itself to "chaos and criminality." I whole-heartedly agree that LaVey decries chaos and criminality, which I clearly articulate in my chapter, so, perhaps, all that is required here is an unbiased reading of my chapter. Second, far from eschewing the Eden-esque lifestyle of the Bible, I would argue that LaVey's systematic approach to a worldly, indulgent life—supported by Magus Gilmore—supports just such a picture. Freed from their Judeo-Christian trappings Adam and Eve were magnificently situated to live lives that were remarkably Epicurean—garden and all. If LaVey wants just such a life for his followers—that is, an Epicurean life—then I fail to understand Magus Gilmore's rejection of the point I make.

However, if Magus Gilmore's rejection of this claim is salient based upon LaVey's desires for an indulgent life, then that is a point to me that LaVey did not, and his numerous adherents that derive their knowledge of Epicureanism from LaVey do not, understand the philosophical hedonism espoused by Epicurus.

35
Satan Gets the Last Word

MAGUS PETER H. GILMORE

Pitkänen finds some agreements with my criticisms, but considers arrogant my position that most folks currently claiming the title of Satanist are doing this in reaction to LaVey's work.

I consider my statement to be a factual observation. These self-proclaimed Satanists don't exist in a vacuum devoid of LaVey. Their works are almost exclusively found on the Internet where LaVey's Satanism is clearly dominant. I would be amazed (and skeptical) to hear that any of these "neo-satanists" had not dealt with LaVey's works, whether they stand pro or contra. Pitkänen posits that religious forms of Satanism might have evolved if LaVey and the Church of Satan had not existed, but that is speculative fantasy. LaVey had the initiative to take an insult and used it to name a coherent philosophy that has maintained unflagging global interest. In that, he is unique, and that fact cements his primacy.

I still find Pitkänen's use of the term "radically individualistic" to be inherently vague, since almost any new religion could be defined in that manner in comparison with the existing dogmas that are being supplanted. He has used it since he intends to make room for devil worshippers who actually do not champion the individual. Based on his own expansion of the idea, it seems he might mean "radically unconventional," but when dealing with differing self-proclaimed forms of Satanism one has to consider how many conventions (and of what kind) are being overturned.

LaVey promoted a lifestyle of material success and self-fulfillment through moderated indulgence in all manner of pleasures. While most of Western society claims to be concerned with spiritual issues—including possible consequences of one's actions in a world other than the one they currently occupy, in practice they pursue their own immediate fulfillment in a very material way. That also goes for non-Western cultures that now have ever-growing access to the products of Western capitalism. So LaVey presented a philosophy that accepted what many people *really* seek in life, rather than what they *claim* to be their concerns. He felt Satanism was thus more honest about what it means to be human, and thus it might be graspable by people who might be able to see themselves and their motivations more clearly. Is that "radically individualistic"? Instead, LaVey felt that overtly enshrining selfishness and the sovereign individual was truly radical, and he shared that with Ayn Rand. I find this point in Pitkänen's evolving definition to require more efforts at clarification if he wants to establish a criterion that is unique to what he wants to call Satanism.

Finally, Pitkänen criticizes my statement that spiritual doctrines involve a denial of the animal nature of mankind. I might have been clearer by using "rejection" rather than "denial." This denial is most obvious in Semitic religions, but the negative judgment of the material world is commonplace in Eastern religions as well. I did not state that *all* Eastern doctrines have this stance, since the variations on the major schools of thought are numerous and I am not familiar with every permutation, but enough of them fundamentally hold that commonplace human existence is either illusory or tainted in some manner and that it must be superseded in search of a higher spiritual condition. Those accepting aspects of carnality also include belief in a primary deity and other-worldy realms superior to mundane existence.

Hinduism propounds cycles of earthly reincarnation to be escaped by self-dissolution in joining with the godhead, a *de facto* denigration of the ultimately rejected earthly life. Various forms of Hinduism offer modes for living a "good life" towards eliminating "karmic debt," yet the material world is perceived as a necessary, transitory, and lesser experience. The Aghoris believe that Shiva is a supreme being responsible for everything in existence. Their taboo breaking is not concerned with accepting human nature. Instead, it functions to demonstrate that everything (even acts commonly considered to be revolting) are acceptable because they are all part of Shiva, with whom they seek union. So here an Eastern spiritual path promotes behaviors contrary to natural impulses as is common in Abrahamic belief systems. A Satanist might find some value in aspects of Theravada Buddhism's essential atheism and support of critical analysis of the world, yet ultimately its denial of the self and negative evaluation of desire again put it, like other Eastern disciplines, in a realm of beliefs that find fault with carnal man's natural impulses.

Satanism's Satisfactions

In his response, Jones says about LaVey that, "there is no reason to assume that a follower of his teachings couldn't interpret them as encouragement to 'satisfy every whim all the time with reckless abandon'." I offered passages from *The Satanic Bible* demonstrating why that mode of thinking would be a misinterpretation, yet he did not counter them. Further, Jones denies that he intends to dismiss Satanism as having any value, yet says that his critique is meant to point out that LaVey's use of aspects of Epicurean thought fails to support a "life—presumably of some value." That seems to me rather dismissive, as does the conclusion of his original essay claiming that Satanism will leave one with a unsatisfactory search for immediate pleasures, providing a base, vulgar, and "Hellish" existence. However, we Satanists consider human values to be subjective, thus the worth of a person's life is up to the individual living it, just as is one's own evaluation of the position of one's pleasures on the "vulgar to exalted" scale.

In my experience Satanists encompass a broad range of pursuits, many of them exercising their creative abilities. Personally, I spent eighteen years in Manhattan's art world as operations director of a major gallery exhibiting works ranging from emerging and recognized contemporary masters to historical masterpieces. I found great pleasure in contemplating them at close hand. My undergraduate and graduate degrees are in music composition so I've spent decades studying my favorite art form—the symphony—and have long exchanged ideas on this subject with some of the world's leading musicologists, the works of Mahler and Bruckner being a primary focus. I also spent a number of years on the board of directors of the Gustav Mahler Society of New York. While both of these composers may have been accused of being "base and vulgar" at times, their work has attained recognition as being some of the finest efforts in symphonic literature.

Having identified as a Satanist at age thirteen, I've found that Satanism has given me a firm foundation for my absorption of significant creative works in all forms. Having dealt with thousands of Satanists, I've noted that satisfaction in life is commonplace amongst us. It is what our philosophy offers as its primary goal. Milton's Lucifer mused on how the mind could transform Heaven to Hell and vice versa, so I leave it up to the reader to determine which realm our lives might embody.

Congruencies with LaVey

LaVey certainly embraces a popular mode when viewing Epicurean thought, that of being a connoisseur of all that we choose in which to indulge. Epicurus's philosophy has historically often been viewed in this manner, perhaps demonstrating flaws in his own presentation of his goals. In his letter to Menoeceus, when dealing with death, he states:

> The wise man neither rejects life nor fears not living. Life is not objectionable to him, nor is not living regarded as an evil. Just as he assuredly chooses not the greatest quantity of food but the most tasty, so does he enjoy the fruits not of the lengthiest period of time but of the most pleasant.

Later we encounter this: "For we recognize pleasure as the first good and as inborn; it is from this that we begin every choice and every avoidance. It is to pleasure that we have recourse, using the feeling as our standard for judging every good." When speaking of sexual encounters, which Epicurus considers as possibly harmful and not doing any real "good," he still states: "If you do not break the laws, disturb well-established customs, upset any of your neighbors, do bodily harm to yourself, or waste your resources, give in to your inclinations as you please." Epicurus may have framed a less-than-sensual mode for what he considered to be the most appropriate pleasures, yet many thinkers have used his concepts as fundamental for their advocacy of pursuing a wider range of indulgences.

Further examination of Epicurus's own dictums provides congruencies with LaVey. Epicurus speaks of justice in a pragmatic manner, endorsing a balanced society—as does LaVey. Epicurus rejects superstition and believing in interventionist deities. He also promotes science and reason as tools for understanding the universe that serves as a means towards personal fulfillment. He calls for dealing with death, something not to be feared, by reflecting on those who have passed rather than lamenting them. Ditto LaVey on all of these counts. It's known that Epicurus's contemporaries painted him as a sensualist. LaVey would gladly accept that label, though he pointed out that he is one with refined tastes and self-control, something he also expected from fellow Satanists. Epicurus shared with LaVey a sense of elitism in stating: "I never desired to please the rabble. What pleased them, I did not learn; and what I knew was far removed from their understanding."

While Epicurus advocated a narrower realm of pleasures than LaVey, seeking the absence of pain and palliation of fear, he had this to say:

> If the things that beget pleasure in dissolute individuals could dispel their mind's fears about the heavens, death, and pain, and could still teach them the limits of desires, we would have no grounds for finding fault with the dissolute, since they would be filling themselves with pleasures from every source and in no way suffering from pain or grief, which are evil.

LaVey, who said it was quite fine if spiritual folk defined his approach as "evil," would then likely have said: "Then call me dissolute!" His approach would thus find a place in Epicurean thinking, even if it were not the ideal.

Ignorant, Nude, and Unaware?

Those who found religions and philosophies adapt ideas from earlier thinkers. Jones thinks that pulling out "pretty gemstones" rather than "weightier keystones" from the works of others leads to a shaky foundation. Yet it is up to the original thinker to select what works best for a new synthesis. If that fresh amalgam is one providing an ongoing means leading people to experience satisfying, meaningful lives, then the foundation is sound. Certainly the Hebraic/Hellenic mash-up wrought by Saul of Tarsus was roughly cobbled together, but that did not impede the success of Christianity as being workable for many people over millennia.

Jones returns to his concept of The Garden of Eden as being relevant to both Epicurus and LaVey, wanting to strip it of its Judeo-Christian trappings. That myth posits, aside from talking snakes and other primitive fantasies, an existence that is naive, with Adam and Eve as fish in a tank kept by an omnipotent overlord. Being ignorant, nude, and unaware that such was their condition is something I propose that both Epicurus and LaVey would find absurd. Epicurus advocated understanding existence through reason and the science available in his time saying: "It is impossible for anyone to dispel his fear over the most important matters, if he does not know what is the nature of the universe but instead suspects something that happens in myth. Therefore, it is impossible to obtain unmitigated pleasure without natural science." Adam and Eve are placid empty-heads, like the Eloi depicted by Wells in *The Time Machine* whose Morlock masters understood science and the resulting technology. Epicurus told Menoeceus that the study of philosophy should be a lifelong pursuit, not that life should be an unquestioning passivity, concluding: "We must, therefore, pursue the things that make for happiness, seeing that when happiness is present, we have everything; but when it is absent, we do everything to possess it." We might make a case that maintaining ignorance could lead to bliss, but I imagine that Epicurus would consider that a misinterpretation of his intentions and I know LaVey considered awareness and understanding to be essential.

So, in perusing the surviving writings of Epicurus we can find many areas of congruence with LaVey's views. LaVey pointed out that he was inspired by Epicurus and other thinkers who also took cues from Epicurus such as Thomas Hobbes, John Locke, and John Stuart Mill. LaVey employed aspects of his predecessors's ideas as threads for his new tapestry, achieving his goal of formulating a rational, coherent philosophy that serves his target audience as a tool for leading lives that are fear-free, pleasure-filled, highly motivated, and quite satisfying.

Raising Hell

Satanism thus rejects the particular moral dogmas (both Eastern and Western) that frown on man the animal as he is. While in Eastern doctrines forgiveness for one's nature is not explicitly sought, escaping from the taint of worldly existence is a primary goal. Contrary to most Eastern perspectives, Satanism glorifies the unique self and disbelieves in supernatural deities of any sort. We celebrate our carnality and find repulsive all Eastern and Western forms of spirituality concerned with attainment of union with a deity or achievement of a personal state that is beyond the impulses found in carnal existence. Thus, we consider all spiritual doctrines—including those of neo-satanists—to be incompatible with Satanism as we have defined it, which was intended by our founder to be *solely* for the celebration of the carnal and material.

Satanism's glorification of man as an animal, a condition that Semitic spiritual religions consider sinful and most Eastern religions find to be a prison that must be escaped, makes for a fairly unique perspective. Spiritual doctrines view the world we inhabit as being an inferior region to be transcended. They deem it to be lesser, imperfect, or in some manner corrupt. We Satanists elevate their "Hells" through our self-deification, extolling our earthly existence as a precious treasure to be enjoyed to its fullest extent. We are proudly "Hell-raisers," and suspect that others, who have no need for the strictures of idealism directed towards fictional "superior realms," might acknowledge our approach to offer a deeply satisfying life that welcomes moderated self-chosen pleasures, ranging from the vulgar to the sublime. Take your pick!

FROM THE VILE FILE
The Devil Made Them Do It?

ROBERT ARP

ZZZZZzzzzz ... ZZZZZzzzzz ... ZZZZZzzzzz ... John was snoring, so now was the time. Lorena got quietly out of bed and went to the kitchen. She found the sharpest knife she could and, well, the rest is history—at least for her husband John's penis.

The infamous story of John and Lorena Bobbitt makes every man squirm just a bit, no doubt. During the evening of June 23rd 1993 Lorena Bobbitt claimed that—because John had raped her earlier in the evening—she was temporarily insane when she severed her husband John's penis with a kitchen knife while he slept. Shortly after the amateur surgery, she tossed his wee-wee out the window of her car in a field, and it was later found, put on ice, and reattached to John. John then made a couple of porno flicks, so apparently it still works. (Apparently there was a guy standing on the side of the road when Lorena threw the penis out the window. The guy got hit in the temple with it, and now he's cockeyed. Get it? He's *cock-eyed*! That's a joke I heard once—that didn't really happen.) A Virginia jury agreed that Lorena was temporarily insane, by the way, and she was released after a few months of psychiatric evaluation.

Now Lorena never claimed that the Prince of Darkness was forcing her to chop off John's junk, but there are plenty of cases throughout human history of people who were supposedly possessed by the Devil, a demon, or some kind of maleficent force. "The Devil made me do it" was made a household saying in the US by comedian Flip Wilson (1933–1998) who hosted *The Flip*

Wilson Show from 1970 to 1974. Flip used this line in a variety of funny skits, usually just after his character had done something that was obviously inappropriate, like touch someone's rear end. Here's a snapshot of actual court cases from 1977 to 1986 in the US where someone went to trial and claimed, "The Head Honcho of Hell is the one *really* responsible for my actions!"

- *Christian v. State*, 351 So.2d 623 (Ala. 1977)— the defendant was supposedly "possessed by the Devil"

- *Stevens v. State*, 256 Ga. 440, 350 S.E.2d 21 (1986)— accused "possessed by the Devil and his minions"

- *State v. Baker*, 67 Haw. 471, 691 P.2d 1166 (1984)— defendant was "compelled by Satan"

- *State v. Jackson*, 480 So.2d 481 (La. Ct. App. 1985)— defendant claims, "Devil made me do it"

- *Commonwealth v. Schnopps*, 390 Mass. 722, 459 N.E.2d 98 (1984)—accused screams "the Devil made me do it" in court, muzzled the rest of the trial

- *State v. Watson*, 211 Mont. 401, 686 P.2d 879 (1984)— defendant claims he was "possessed by a dirty demon spirit"

- *Van White v. State*, 752 State, 725 S.W.2d 494 (Tex. Ct. App. 1987)—defendant claims she was "under the Devil's influence"

- *McBride v. State*, 706 S.W.2d 723 (Tex. Ct. App. 1986)—accused "was possessed by Beelzebub"

- *Plough v. State*, P.2d 814 (Okla. Crim. App. 1988)— defendant claims he was a "victim of the Devil's will"

Below is a collection of real-life situations where someone was supposedly possessed by the Devil, or did something immoral, illegal, or simply inappropriate and then claimed, "The Devil made me do it."

Dorothy Talbye

"She was so possessed with Satan, that he persuaded her (by his delusions, which she listened to as revelations from God) to break the neck of her own child, that she might free it from future misery." This is part of what Puritan Governor John Winthrop wrote in his journal after Dorothy Talbye was found guilty of murder and hanged on an October morning in 1638. Winthrop, Talbye, and some twenty thousand other English settlers were part of the Massachusetts Bay Colony that existed from the 1630s until around 1700 and was located just north of present-day Boston.

Dorothy's daughter was named Difficult, believe it or not. Apparently, Talbye was quite unwilling to be freed from future misery herself, since Winthrop also noted in his journal that as she was dangling from the rope—apparently without her hands tied—Talbye took the scarf from the top of her head and tried to place it between the rope and her neck and, "after a swing or two, she catched at the ladder." Some researchers wonder whether this was one of the first examples of executing someone State side with a mental disability or handicap.

George Lukins

In 1778, an English tailor from the village of Yatton (in Somerset, England) named George Lukins claimed to be possessed by the Devil. He would often sing in a voice and language that was not his own, which frightened his neighbors. Lukins was sent to a hospital for over twenty months, but doctors could not help him. While institutionalized, a violent Lukins reportedly claimed that he was the Devil. He also barked like a dog and sang hymns backward.

One of the doctors, Samuel Norman, thought that Lukins was a fraud, insanity was a "physical" phenomenon, and exorcisms were for religious "enthusiasts." His caregivers discharged Lukins, nonetheless, with the majority convinced that his affliction was demonic in nature and required religious intervention. Seven ministers from the Methodist and Anglican faiths were called in to perform an exorcism on Lukins at Temple Church in Redcliffe (in Bristol, England). When the rite was over, the ministers claimed that "the man had been delivered from the demons who possessed him," and Lukins exclaimed, "Blessed Jesus!"

Lukins was then described as calm and happy for the rest of his life.

Daniel M'Naghten

In 1843, Daniel M'Naghten shot and killed British Prime Minister Robert Peel's secretary in a botched assassination attempt on Peel's life. In court

M'Naughten's lawyer argued that he was "not guilty by reason of insanity" since M'Naghten believed that the Prime Minister and the Pope were conspiring to kill him.

The jury bought it, and M'Naghten was found not guilty, but was sent to a mental asylum. The public howled in outrage and, within a year, a panel of British judges set forth the legal standard that has been used in numerous countries around the World since then, the M'Naghten Rule. According to the House of Lords who delivered the Rule in 1843: "to establish a defence on the ground of insanity, it must be clearly proved that, at the time of the committing of the act, the party accused was labouring under such a defect of reason, from disease of the mind, as not to know the nature and quality of the act he was doing; or, if he did know it, that he did not know he was doing what was wrong."

In the past 150 years, various legal systems have amended their laws to include standards of "diminished capacity" or "guilty, but mentally ill." In almost all cases, however, a verdict of not guilty by reason of insanity prompts a judge to commit defendants to treatment centers until mental health officials determine that they don't pose a danger to anyone. For some, this could be life. M'Naghten, for instance, died after twenty years in a mental asylum.

In 1964 a jury rejected Jack Ruby's claim of insanity (even though his own mother had been committed years before) and sent him to prison for shooting Lee Harvey Oswald, JFK's assassin.

In 1981, John Hinckley Jr. shot President Ronald Reagan but was declared not guilty by reason of insanity in 1982 and sent to St. Elizabeths (no apostrophe) Hospital in DC, where he still resides today.

A Pennsylvania jury found millionaire John DuPont—of the US chemical company by the same name—guilty, but still mentally ill, in the murder of a wrestling coach back in 1987.

Jeffrey Dahmer dismembered and ate parts of his seventeen victims between 1978 and 1991, but his plea of insanity was rejected and he was sentenced to the Columbia Correctional Institution in Portage, Wisconsin, where he was then beaten to death by a fellow inmate in 1994.

In 1998, Lawyers for Unabomber Theodore Kaczynski argued that he was insane, but Kaczynski himself resisted such a defense and pled guilty. And, I already told you how the story ended for John and Lorena Bobbitt.

Roland Doe

Roland Doe is the pseudonym given by the Catholic Church to probably the most influential exorcized boy in recent history. The books and movies *The Exorcist* (William Peter Blatty) and *Possessed* (Thomas B. Allen) are based on his story. Roland was born into a Lutheran family near Washington DC in 1936, and strange phenomena—such as sounds of people walking, screaming, scratching, as well as objects supposedly shaking and flying across the room—began occurring in Roland's presence sometime in 1949. Roland also suffered from what appeared to be epileptic seizures and had fits of rage and foul language.

The family eventually went to St. Louis where, over the course of several weeks, some thirty exorcisms were performed on him by a group of Catholic priests. One priest claimed to have his nose broken by Roland, another required stitches from a wound inflicted. All of the priests claimed to see various objects in Roland's room shake or move, and two of the priests say they saw the words "evil" and "Hell" (and other marks) appear on Roland's body.

Apparently the exorcism worked, thank goodness, since Roland supposedly went on to become a successful, happily married father and then grandfather.

Clara Germana Cele

A Catholic magazine called *The Catholic Digest* gave an account of this girl in a 1947 article. It was noted there that we can't understand demonic possession by the use of reason but must rely on the faith of the Church to comprehend "such wickedness and evil." The author also claimed that, "Christ gave his Church the power to drive out devils in his name"—thus, the whole "The power of Christ compels you" line from the movie *The Exorcist* that the priest uses while he's splashing holy water on Linda Blair's character.

In 1906, Clara Germana Cele was a sixteen-year-old student at St. Michael's Mission in Natal, South Africa. She apparently prayed to the Devil, making some sort of pact, and was overtaken by strange impulses, had fits of rage and foul language (they all seem to have that problem!), was repulsed by religious artifacts like crucifixes, could speak and understand several languages of which she had no previous knowledge, and became clairvoyant regarding the nasty thoughts and wicked histories of the people around her. During one of her exorcisms, a couple hundred people supposedly witnessed her levitating as priests read scripture.

The article ends by noting that Cele was apparently "cured" after the exorcisms and was mortified to learn of her actions, "acting humbly and asking for forgiveness."

Anneliese Michel

The subject of three movies, including *The Exorcism of Emily Rose*, Anneliese Michel was diagnosed with epilepsy in her teenage years during the 1960s, fell into a depression, then became violent and intolerant of priests, bibles, crucifixes, and other artifacts related to her Catholic faith.

Her parents felt that psychiatry and medications weren't working, so they called in two priests to perform an exorcism instead. Poor Anneliese died on July 1st 1976 as a direct result of malnourishment and dehydration. In fact, there are plenty of pictures of Anneliese looking very frail and out of it that can be found online.

Her parents and the two priests were tried and found guilty of negligence, but they were all given a mere three years of probation and a fine. The case is famous as an example of misidentifying mental illness, as well as negligence and religious hysteria.

Gerald Mayo

"Plaintiff alleges that Satan has on numerous occasions caused the plaintiff misery and unwarranted threats, against the will of plaintiff, that Satan has placed deliberate obstacles in his path and has caused plaintiff's downfall. Plaintiff alleges that by reason of these acts Satan has deprived him of his constitutional rights." Rather than a situation where "the Devil made the man do it," this is a case of the Devil doing it to the man!

In 1971 Gerald Mayo filed a claim before the United States District Court for the Western District of Pennsylvania where he alleged that Satan was responsible for many a misery in his life. The court case called *United States ex rel. Gerald Mayo v. Satan and His Staff*, 54 F.R.D. 282 (W.D.Pa. 1971) never actually made it to court with the judge ruling that it was impossible to serve Satan "papers" or official notice that the Prince of Darkness was being sued in the first place.

Ronald DeFeo, Jr.

"He claimed something demonic made him do it; then he claimed God made him do it." On November 13th 1974 around 3:00 A.M., Ronald DeFeo Jr. shot and killed his father, mother, two sisters, and two brothers in their beds. This mass murder would be the inspiration for the book and movie versions of *The Amityville Horror*. As part of his insanity defense, DeFeo claimed that he'd heard voices telling him to kill, and that something outside of his control made him do it. He also stated that a "figure with black hands" handed him the murder weapon—a .35-caliber, lever-action Marlin 336C rifle—and followed him throughout the house from room to room as he shot his family members one by one. The jury didn't buy the "devilish black hands" insanity defense, and DeFeo was found guilty on six counts of second-degree murder. He's currently serving six life sentences in a New York prison, one for each family member.

Apparently, over the years DeFeo has given numerous inconsistent stories about what happened that night in 1974, and there are accounts that he has admitted that he lied to shore up his insanity plea.

David Berkowitz

Rather than the Devil, this guy claimed that a Devil Dog made him do it! From 1976 to 1977 David Berkowitz stalked the streets of New York City taunting law enforcement and the media with claims that he was, among other things, Beelzebub, Mr. Monster, and the Son of Sam.

When police finally caught him, six women were dead and seven others had been wounded. Berkowitz claimed that he was acting under the orders of Harvey, a neighbor's black Labrador retriever that Berkowitz believed was possessed by an ancient evil and cried out for "blood and death." Even after Berkowitz shot him and threw a Molotov cocktail at him, Harvey survived, only to further Berkowitz's belief that the dog was a channel for the Father of All Lies. "I am utterly convinced that something Satanic had entered into my mind and that, looking back at all that happened, I realize that I had been slowly deceived," was one of Berkowitz's claims.

At his trial, psychiatrists for Berkowitz's defense diagnosed him as a paranoid schizophrenic, but he was found guilty and sentenced to 365 years in prison. While in prison, Berkowitz converted from Judaism to Christianity and, according to *New York Magazine* writer Steve Fishman (who interviewed Berkowitz in 2006), he now "works as a pastor, walking the prison halls with a Gideon's Bible and a calling from God. He's battling Satan, he says, his old friend. And David is sure Satan's afraid of him, because David knows all his tricks."

Arne Cheyenne Johnson

"If the killing was shocking, so is Johnson's planned defense," notes Lynn Baranski in her 1981 *People* magazine article about the "Demon Murder Trial," the case of Arne Cheyenne Johnson. This is a famous case in the US where the defense attempted to prove that the defendant was not guilty by reason of possession. Johnson committed the first known homicide in the town of Brookfield, Connecticut, at that time, when he repeatedly stabbed his landlord in the chest while Johnson's fiancé looked on in shock and disbelief.

At the trial, it was noted that Johnson's family consulted with "demo-nologists" Ed and Lorraine Warren, saying that Johnson had been taunted and harassed by unknown entities for most of his life. The Warrens also claimed Johnson's actions resulted from demonic posses-sion and a psychological disorder.

The judge rejected attempts by Johnson's lawyer to present evidence that he said would show his client had been possessed by a "demon," and Johnson eventually served five years of a ten-to-twenty-year sentence after having married, received his GED, and "showing no signs of being possessed" while in prison.

Anthony A. Hall

In July of 1987 Anthony A. Hall, his sister, Elizabeth Towne, and two accomplices, Dan Bowen and Bunny Dixon, decided to go from Orlando to Virginia so they could work with a carnival. Because they had no car or money, they planned to stop a random car on the road, rob that per-son, and steal the vehicle. They ended up stopping some poor guy, tap-ing him up, throwing him in the trunk of his own car, and then driving to a wooded area where Bunny—an alleged Satanist—carved an inverted cross on the victim's chest and abdomen. Then Bowen shot the guy with a .36-caliber revolver, while Hall shot him seven times using a .22-caliber automatic pistol. Eventually they were all caught and tried for kidnapping and murder. The jury found Hall guilty of both premeditated murder and felony murder and recommended the death penalty.

Hall's defense was that he "acted under the influence of Satan and/or Bunny Dixon and therefore was robbed of his free will and did not know right from wrong under the McNaghten Rule at the time of the offense." The judge addressed Hall and the court after the verdict noting that "there's no defense in Florida—and I hope no other place in the coun-try—that says, 'the Devil made me do it.'"

Eventually Hall was granted an appeal based upon a psychiatrist's testimony that Hall suffers from a number of "schizophrenic disorders and that, on the day of the shooting, Hall was operating with a state of altered consciousness brought on by extreme stress, namely fear for his own life and that of his sister because of Bowen and Dixon." What do you expect from a bunch of carnies?

Julia

"Amid widespread confusion and skepticism about the subject, the chief goal of this article is to document a contemporary and clear-cut case of demonic possession." This is the first line of an article by Dr. Richard E, Gallagher—a board-certified psychiatrist and associate professor of clinical psychiatry at New York Medical College—in the Catholic periodical, *New Oxford Review*, from 2008. It's obviously a rare thing that a scientist and psychiatrist would acknowledge demonic possession, but this guy seriously considers this possibility for his patient, pseudo-named Julia.

While treating her, Gallagher reportedly witnessed Julia levitating off the bed, speaking in tongues, and knowing things about people around her that she could not possibly have known. "As an example, she knew the personality and precise manner of death (i.e., the exact type of cancer) of a relative of a team member that no one could conceivably have guessed." He also reported he saw objects flying around the room.

An Exorcized Catholic Boy

"The exorcists who have seen the images have no doubt: this was a liberation prayer from evil, or a real act of exorcism," claimed a journalist from TV2000, a channel owned by the Italian Episcopal Conference.

In May of 2013, after celebrating Mass in St. Peter's Square, the newly elected Pope allegedly performed a brief exorcism live on camera. As he was moving down the line of disabled people, offering blessings, the Pontiff paused before a boy in a wheelchair. After chatting to a few priests behind him, the Pope grasped the boy by the head, and the boy shuddered and gasped before going limp.

The Catholic Church apparently performs many exorcisms each year, and Pope Francis has said that he believes that Satan is real, and that the battle against evil is one that he must fight every day.

Those Infernal Illustrations

BILL CABLE is a .net developer for UPMC in Pittsburgh. He's also a freelance starving artist. His passion for collecting vintage *Star Wars* toys is only eclipsed by his die-hard love of the Pittsburgh Steelers. He owes his artistic skill to an ill-advised trading of hands with Beelzebot.

> Bill Cable's illustrations are: *Gluttony*, page xviii; *Greed*, page 30; *Envy*, page 68; *Pride*, page 80; *Sloth*, page 160; *Lust*, page 250; *Wrath*, page 292.

HEAVEN MENDOZA was born in Mexico City and raised in Texas. She has a BFA in Media Arts and Animation from the Art Institute of Houston and an MFA in Art from the University of Texas–Pan American and is currently head of the marketing department of the Campus Violence Prevention Project at the University of Texas–Pan American, where she controls all her slaving minions.

> Heaven Mendoza's illustrations are: *Devil 1: Gluttony*, page viii; *Devil 2: Envy*, page 20; *Devil 3: Wrath*, page 48; *Devil 4: Lust*, page 110; *Devil 5: Sloth*, page 224; *Devil 6: Greed*, page 282; *Devil 7: Pride*, page 326.

TRAVIS TRAPP is a student at the University of Texas–Pan American. He'd have a devil of a time trying to be a professional artist, and no one has yet offered a decent price for his soul, so he's going to get a college degree.

> Travis Trapp's illustrations are: *Devil at Work 1*, page 78; *Devil at Work 2*, page 138; *Devil at Work 3*, page 204; *Devil at Work 4*, page 300; *Devil at Work 5*, page 314.

The Original Sinners

ROBERT ARP, PHD works as a researcher and analyst for the US Army, when he's not editing or authoring works in philosophy and other areas. Living much of his life in Bible Belt–ish areas, whenever someone would say to him, "Have a blessed day" (usually at the cash register of some store) he'd respond, "Thanks so much—you have a damned day." The look on the person's face was priceless.

JENNIFER BAKER, PHD does research in virtue ethics and looks to ancient ethical theories as positive examples of how ethics ought to be done today. She finds the Devil's Facebook posts tedious and is considering unfriending Him.

ADAM BARKMAN, PHD is Associate Professor of Philosophy and Chair of the philosophy department at Redeemer University College in Canada. He's the author and editor of more than half a dozen books, most of which have to do with the intersection between religion, mythology, philosophy, and popular culture. Being a Christian philosopher, Adam's least favorite proverb is "the Devil's in the details."

When he's not runnin' with the Devil, hanging out with friends of the Devil, or working them angels, JIM BERTI can be found in Room B208 of Shaker Junior High School in Latham, New York, teaching social studies. He co-edited *Rush and Philosophy: Heart and Mind United* (2011).

GREGORY L. BOCK, PHD is Associate Professor of Philosophy at Walters State Community College in Morristown, Tennessee. His interests include David Hume and philosophy of religion, and he has contributed with his brother Jeff, to *Psych and Philosophy: Some Dark Juju-Magumbo* (2013). One of his favorite quotations from C.S. Lewis is about there being two equally dangerous errors in thinking about devils: "to disbelieve in their existence. The other is to believe, and to feel an excessive unhealthy interest in them."

JEFFREY BOCK has a master of arts in history and helps manage a small web design firm in East Texas. If possession is nine-tenths of the law, he's probably owned by his wife, his kids, and a nice pint of beer.

RAY BOSSERT, PHD teaches in the English Department at Notre Dame of Maryland University. His research and teaching interests include early modern literature and contemporary popular culture; he spends a good deal of time lecturing undergrads on the proper use of the ***demon***-strative pronouns.

ELIZABETH BUTTERFIELD, PHD is Associate Professor of Philosophy at Georgia Southern University where she regularly teaches courses on existentialism, ethics, and philosophy of religion. Following Camus's lead, she agrees that when things start to feel Hellish, we must imagine Sisyphus laughing.

GEORGE A. DUNN, PHD lectures in philosophy and religion at the University of Indianapolis and the Ningbo Institute of Technology (in Zhejiang Province, China). He's a man of neither wealth nor taste, though he is on occasion in need of some restraint.

JEFF EWING is a graduate student in sociology at the University of Oregon, and after this book he has been inspired to start a human soul-market business. Current market value for an average human soul next holiday season will be only five—count them, five—easy payments of $29.99 (plus shipping and handling), or a four-soul package for $550.00. If you buy within the next thirty days, we'll send you a Portable Soul Tote Bag ab-so-lutely FREE, for those on-the-go, need-a-soul days.

MAGUS PETER H. GILMORE, who holds BS and MA degrees in music composition from New York University, spent eighteen years in the art world as Operations Director of the Manhattan gallery, The Drawing Center, before succeeding Church of Satan founder Anton LaVey in 2001 to be the World's primary Devil's advocate. In his parallel devotion to Kaijudaism, Gilmore's esteem for fantastic giant reptiles has had him singing hymns for Kaneko's visionary *Gamer-*

adämmerung as well as for the darkest aspects of his personal totem—the beast of the apocalypse: Godzilla.

SANDRA HANSMANN, PhD is Associate Professor in Rehabilitation at the University of Texas-Pan American and has special interest in Security Studies. She enjoys long drives on the road to perdition, and she looks damned good in a blue dress.

A.G. HOLDIER took an MA in philosophy of religion before being whisked away to the wilderness to teach high school theology courses in Dante's first level of Hell: southern Idaho. When he's not philosophizing about devils (or actually teaching them), his hands are never idle—his research in metaphysics, mythopoesis, and the ontology of fiction is very probably more than just a devilish excuse to read comic books.

ROGER HUNT, MA works for a renewable energy company, is in training as a psychoanalyst, and studied philosophy at Montana State, The University of Canterbury, and Boston University. Undermining the Devil using his own playbook, he focuses on the youth—teaching ethics and moral reasoning to high school students preparing for the National High School Ethics Bowl.

CLINT JONES, PhD earned his doctorate at the University of Kentucky in social and political philosophy with an emphasis in critical social theory. He teaches philosophy at UK and coaches the debate team at Transylvania University. When he isn't actively engaged in corrupting the youth, he likes to unwind with poetry and his favorite bourbon, Devil's Cut, which inspired him to embrace his devilish ways—in moderation, of course.

CYNTHIA M. JONES, PhD is Associate Professor of Philosophy and Director of the Ethics Center at the University of Texas-Pan American. She publishes in bioethics, pop culture, feminism, and ethics and technology. She feels a close kinship with Baba Yaga, Lilith, La Malinche, and all the demonized women of history.

NICK JONES, PhD teaches at the Scholomance, where he lectures on famous long-dead Irish philosophers and controlling the weather. He's also lead singer in the death metal band Slayer, and a congenital liar.

TIM JONES is an Associate Tutor in Literature at the University of East Anglia and definitely hopes to finish his PhD sometime very soon, even if he has to ask the Devil himself for assistance. By the way, if you're reading this, that's actually not a joke.

JOHN V. KARAVITIS, CPA, MBA has had a lifelong love of learning. The story of Faust and how he sold his soul to the Devil in exchange for unlimited knowledge has always intrigued him. Curiously, that story now plays itself out on a grand scale—just replace "Faust" with "college grads" and "his soul" with "student loans."

SHARON M. KAYE, PHD is Professor of Philosophy at John Carroll University in Cleveland, Ohio. She edited *What Philosophy Can Tell You about Your Lover* (2012). Don't read her chapter backwards.

GREG LITTMANN, PHD is Associate Professor of Philosophy at Southern Illinois University Edwardsville, an institution not affiliated with Hell in any way. He publishes on metaphysics, metaphilosophy, and philosophy of logic, and has written over twenty chapters for volumes relating philosophy to popular culture. None of his writings can be used to summon anything—so don't try. If you do happen to call something up, it probably won't be the Devil, but you probably don't want the ghost of Plato roaming around your house either.

JAMES MORSE MCLACHLAN sold his soul in 1989 for a PhD at the University of Toronto in hopes of finding a job in academia. He found one at Western Carolina University where he teaches the dark arts of philosophy and religion to your unsuspecting children and friends. He explores esoteric texts in Romanticism, Idealism, and Existentialism to further his knowledge of these dark arts. His chapter in this book is the foul manifestation of his sins.

JAMES EDWIN MAHON, PHD is Professor of Philosophy and Adjunct Professor of Law at Washington and Lee University. He works on normative ethics and the history of moral philosophy. He agrees with fellow Irish writer Flann O'Brien that if the Devil actually did defeat God, He would be the first person to put out the story that He didn't.

NICOLAS MICHAUD teaches philosophy in Jacksonville Florida. Like all philosophers, he likes to believe that he's helping save his students from damnation by freeing their minds from ignorance and apathy. After writing for this book, he's not so sure salvation is what's in store for them, or you.

STEVE NEUMANN moonlights as a contributor to Massimo Pigliucci's blog, *Rationally Speaking,* while giving the Devil his due earning a living as a Guide Dog Mobility Instructor during the day. The dogs he trains for his clients truly are little angels. But he's not afraid to unleash the Hounds of Hell on a whim from time to time.

JONATHON O'DONNELL, MPHIL is finishing his Ph.D. at the University of London's School of Oriental and African Studies and has interests in continental philosophy of religion and the history of ideas. He spends too much time wondering what the hell "What the hell?" really means.

OLLI PITKÄNEN, MSS works as an awarded doctoral student at the University of Jyväskylä on the subject of the possibility of a metaphysical conception of evil in contemporary philosophy based on F.W.J. Schelling's *Freedom Essay*. Writing for this book gave him the possibility to act out his closeted obsession with occultism and Satanism.

NICOLE R. PRAMIK is a published novelist, adjunct English Instructor, and legal secretary. Her most recent book is *The Guardian*, the first novel in a fantasy trilogy, and she's also charted familiar philosophical seas as a chapter author in *SpongeBob SquarePants and Philosophy: Soaking Up Secrets under the Sea!* (2011). Though she firmly believes the Prince of Darkness is a gentleman, he's still a bloke she wouldn't want to meet.

AARON RABINOWITZ, MA works as an adjunct ethics professor and tai chi instructor in Fort Collins, Colorado. As a lifelong lover of mythology, he delights in discussion of all fictional beings, great and small. He is currently engaged in a twenty-eight-year staring contest with the abyss, but can't say yet who's winning.

DANNY SMITH is a PhD student in philosophy at Penn State University, where he works predominantly on nineteenth- and twentieth-century continental philosophy. He did manage to submit his manuscript before the deadline, but he had a Devil of a job getting it finished in time.

ANNE MARIE STACHURA, PHD is Assistant Professor of Spanish at the University of Texas–Pan American. She enjoys knitting and Hello Kitty. If you believed that last sentence, you probably did not read her co-authored chapter on the devious women of history.

ERIC SWAN, MED is a counselor at Mercyhurst University in Erie, Pennsylvania. His interests include organizational leadership, eastern philosophy, and transpersonal psychology. He hates to admit that there are no good Devil songs by Bob Dylan or Neil Young.

LIZ STILLWAGGON SWAN, PHD teaches philosophy and writes for a living. Her current research concerns several philosophical issues in forensic science including how it is represented (and misrepresented) in TV crime dramas—many of which she became very familiar with during her two years as an unemployed philosopher. While it's true in all sciences that the Devil is in the details, Swan sees forensic science as being unique among the sciences in revealing such a detailed picture of the Devil in humanity.

JOHN M. THOMPSON, PHD is a marginally successful Associate Professor of Philosophy and Religious Studies at Christopher Newport University, as well as a failed comedian. His teaching and research interests are Buddhism and East Asian traditions, and fighting his own demons. While he needs your sympathy, he is *not* a man of wealth and taste.

MICHAEL VERSTEEG is an independent scholar currently living in Ancaster, Ontario. His areas of interest include philosophical ethics, philosophy of religion, and philosophy of history. For the most part, he's usually convinced that the World around him is actually real, though Descartes's Evil Demon sometimes gets the best of him. Some people just think too much.

THOMAS WARD, PHD is Assistant Professor of Philosophy at Loyola Marymount University in Los Angeles. His interests include the history of philosophy, philosophy of religion, and metaphysics—the real kind of metaphysics, not the kind you find at shops where you can buy dream catchers and tarot cards. He's got the joy, joy, joy, joy down in his heart, and if the Devil doesn't like it he can sit on a tack.

Index